PHOTOGRAPHIC SCREEN PRINTING

BY

ALBERT KOSLOFF, M.A.

Director of Technical Information Center and Member of the
Academy of Screen Printing Technology, Screen Printing Association,
International

FIFTH EDITION

Illustrations by the Author

Published by
The Signs of the Times Publishing Company
Cincinnati, Ohio, U. S. A.

International Standard Book Number: 0-911380-42-6

To Esther, David, Nina and Sandy

PREFACE TO FIFTH EDITION

This writer has always believed that the principles of screen printing or mitography are interesting, unique, and limitless. Screen printing has emerged as a phase of graphic communications by which man communicates ideas, motifs, emotions, detail, and color. In this sense screen printing, more than any other graphic arts process, produces visual communication — the transmitting of understanding from one person to another by means of sight and touch; touch, because it can also print three dimensional effects. It encourages creation. In our complex culture, such positive contributions must not be lost. They must be recognized, analyzed, evaluated, and standardized.

The industrial potential of screen printing is of many dimensions because it is the most versatile of graphic communications processes. It is constantly changing and growing and new evolving processes and techniques must be presented to disseminate information and to prevent obsolescence. Since the presentation of the fourth edition of PHOTOGRAPHIC SCREEN PRINTING varied practical developments have taken place industrially and universally which should be communicated. The aim of this edition is to supplement the last edition of the book with related information and practical products and processes which answer developmental needs of the industry. Varied products are explained and treated because they represent acceptable standarized procedures and learning principles. What is being offered industrially today is not necessarily a product but also a process. While there are similarities between the various photographic processes and printing screens, there also differences. This and the desire for presenting each product and process completely are the reasons for repetition of some procedures in explaining each of the varied products and processes. Many illustrations have been used in the book to present photographic screen printing or photomitography.

While screen printing is in definite need of hand processes and manual printing, it has been forced by its own needs and by the impact of other industries to develop mechanical and automated methods of reproduction and printing. Photographic screen printing is a phase of the mechanical methods of producing printing screens in the industry.

The problems of the screen printer are complex and often elusive because of the many variables of this printing industry. Screen printers learned their craft for the most part, from individual experiences, experimentation, individual introspection, and thus developed a pride that is peculiar to the industry. The growth and development, especially since the early 1940's, was just another part of the movement of the world into a scientific technology — a second industrial revolution.

It has been a challenge and a privilege for this writer to have been associated with individuals and groups in varied fields of the industry and in the development and interpretation of the varied facets of the industry. The book was written because there is a definite need to interpret objectively *photographic screen printing*. It is intended for the screen printer, the prospective worker in field, the general printer, the photographer, the advertiser, the educator, student, hobbyist, or anyone else interested in this fascinating vocational or avocational medium of reproduction.

The author wishes to express his sincere appreciation to the following who have aided in varied fashion: *Screen Printing Magazine* and *SIGNS of the Times Magazine* for their permission to use material and illustrations which the writer contributed to past issues of these publications; to Mr. D. R. Swormstedt, Sr., publisher of the above journals; to Mr. Arnold Z. Brav, Editor and Mr. Robert O. Fossett former Editor of *Screen Printing Magazine* and to Mr. David M. Souder, Editor of SIGNS of the Times for their aid; and especially to this author's wife for her aid and encouragement in this undertaking.

To the following organizations and individuals is tendered the grateful thanks of the author for their permission to use photographs and similar aids: Active Process Supply Company, New York, N. Y.; Advance Process Supply Company, Chicago, Illinois; Affiliated Manufacturers, Inc., Whitehouse, New Jersey; American Screen Printing Equipment Co., Chicago, Illinois; Atlas Silk Screen Supply Co., Chicago, Illinois; Autotype Company London, England; Aristo Grid Lamp Products, Inc., Port Washington, L.I., New York; Azoplate Corp., Murray Hill, N. J.; Bond Adhesives Company, Jersey City, N. J.; R. W. Borrowdale Company, Inc., Chicago, Illinois; Bowler Industries, Inc., Greenville, South Carolina; Buckingham Graphics, Inc., Evanston, Illinois; William L. Butler, Elmira, N. Y.; Caprock Developments, New York, N. Y.; Chicago Silk Screen Supply Co., Inc., Chicago, Illinois; Cincinnati Printing and Drying Systems, Inc., Cincinnati, Ohio; Colonial Printing Ink Co., Inc., East Rutherford, N.J.; Chroma-Glo Duluth, Minnesota; Control Process Co., Elk Grove Village, Illinois; L. F. Deardorff & Sons, Inc., Chicago, Illinois; Drakenfeld Division, Imperial Color and Chemical Dept., Hercules, Inc., Washington, Pennsylvania; E. I. Du Pont de Nemours and Co., Inc., Wilmington, Delaware; Eastman Kodak Company, Rochester, N.Y.; Familex Products Ltd., Montreal, Quebec, Canada; Fostoria-Fannon, Inc., Fostoria, Ohio; General Research, Inc., Sparta, Michigan; M. P. Goodkin Co., Irvington, New Jersey; Melvin E. Green and Sheldon Green, Chicago, Illinois; Charles M. Jessup Co., Kenilworth, New Jersey; F. D. Kees Mfg. Co., Beatrice, Nebraska; Kenro Corporation, Cedar Knolls, N.J.; Lacey-Lucy Products, Inc., Manasquan, New Jersey; Lawson Printing Machine Co., St. Louis, Missouri; M & M Research Engineering Co., Butler, Wisconsin; McGraw Colorgraph, Burbank, California; Naz-Dar Company, Chicago, Illinois; nuArc Company, Inc., Chicago, Ill.; the late Howard W. Parmele, Sr.; Jos. E. Podgor & Co., Inc., Pennsauken, N.J.; John Pottage, Wilmette, Illinois; Poster Products, Inc., Chicago, Illinois; Printing Aids, Butler, Wisconsin; Precision Screen Machines, Inc., Hawthorne, N.J.; Redi-Screen Co., Chicago, Illinois; the late Seymour Rieger; Robertson Photo-Mechanix, Inc., Des Plaines, Illinois; San Miguel Brewery, Philippine Islands; Sericol Group, Ltd., London, England; Silk Screen Process, Inc., Cleveland, Ohio; Superior Silk Screen Industries, Inc., Chicago, Illinois; Tetko, Inc., Elmsford, N.Y.; Ulano Products Co., Inc., New York, New York; Vastex Machine Company, Roselle, New Jersey; and Viola Studio, Chicago, Illinois.

Albert Kosloff

CONTENTS

SCREEN PRINTING

Screen printing, screen process printing, or mitography is the most versatile method of printing. Its versatility has made the screen printing industry very conscious of its potential. It is employed to print on any surface, any material, any size or thickness, and on almost any shape. The same excellent results may be obtained by using hand, semi-automatic, or mechanical methods of printing. In this process the printing is done *through* a plate as compared with most methods which print *from* a printing plate.

Specifically, screen printing is that phase of graphic communication which deals with the processes and arts employed in the production of printed matter, applied onto surfaces of varied materials by depositing the ink through a printing plate consisting of a fabric mesh that is partly blocked-out, masked, or impregnated. Photographic screen printing deals with processes employed in the production of photographic printing plates or printing screens and the use of the printing screens for reproduction.

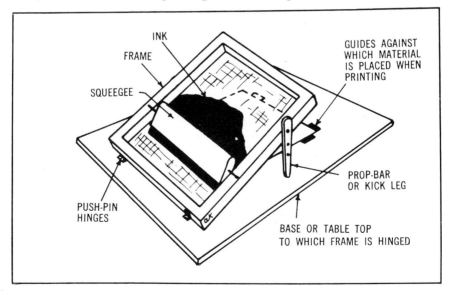

Figure 1. A basic hand printing unit.

1

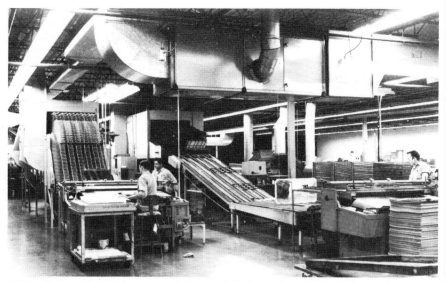

Figure 2. A mechanized screen printing and drying unit consisting of two screen printing presses and two wicket type dryers. (Courtesy of "Lawson Aladdin Cylinder Presses," Lawson Printing Machine Company, St. Louis, Mo.)

The photographic printing screen or hand prepared printing screen consists of a blocked-out or impregnated fabric such as nylon, silk, polyester, or a metal cloth such as stainless steel, phosphor bronze, or copper. The fabric or screen fabric is stretched very tightly and fastened securely, either by hand or with a jig device, generally to a flat frame made of wood or metal or a combination of materials. The open parts in the screen are the design parts or areas to be printed; the rest of the screen or screen fabric is closed up or blocked-out with a special filler or block-out medium.

The object or material upon which the printing is to be done is placed under the screen. The required amount of screen printing ink is poured into the screen on the inside on top of the fabric and the ink is applied onto the material by pulling a device known as a squeegee over the whole printing area of the screen or printing plate. Although the ink may be pushed through pneumatically or with rollers, the usual method is to employ a squeegee. Wood or light-weight metal squeegees are used for forcing the ink through the open parts of the screen. The squeegee ordinarily employed consists of a wooden handle and an insoluble synthetic rubber or plastic blade.

Figure 1 presents a basic screen printing unit which may be employed for printing on varied surfaces with hand-prepared or photographic printing screens. Figure 2 illustrates a more advanced printing unit.

The advantages of screen printing* are many and the techniques and effects obtainable with this are limitless. Brilliant, sparkling, solid and

---

*Other terms that are and have been used for this process are *silk screen printing, mitography, screen printing, serigraph, diagraph,* and *silk gravure.* The term *mitography* (mi-tog′ra fi) was coined by the author in 1942 with the intent of offering a term that is comprehensive, technically correct, and concise. The word was taken from the Greek *mitos* meaning "threads or fibers" and the suffix *graphein* meaning "to write or print." *Photomitography* has reference to the photographic processes of screen printing.

varied colored effects may be applied to almost any surface, shape, material, size, or thickness. It may be used to print on paper, cardboard, wood, metal, textiles, plastics, cork, leather, fur, ceramic surfaces, glass, special surfaces such as decalcomania paper, and combinations of materials. An even coating may be obtained, the thickness of the coating may be varied, and a thicker coating may be printed than by other processes. The coating may be 10 to 20 times as thick as in letterpress printing. Detailed, fine, and halftone illustrations in single, duotone, multi-color, three-color process, four-color process, full-color process, and special effects may be obtained. If desired, as many as 25 colors may be printed. Flat, metallic, glossy, daylight fluorescent, phosphorescent ink, and combinations of these inks may be applied; opaque, semi-transparent, and transparent inks may be printed. Very fine detailed printing in white and lighter colors may be printed normally over solid dark or darker backgrounds. The process is economical and practical considering the superior results produced, the possibility of both small and long runs, and the fact that many jobs cannot be printed with any other process. It may be employed to supplement other types of printing.

Because of the heavy deposit of ink, the process has striking color impact. The printing plate or printing screen may be prepared by hand or by photographic means. The screen printer may make his own screens* or have them made by any of the specialists catering to the industry. An expression of its versatility is exemplified in the fact that it is used to print all types of signs, Easter eggs, decalcomania transfers the size of a postage stamp to sizes about 36 square feet in area, large outdoor advertising posters, textiles, to finish furniture and toys, electronic circuits, for decorating ceramic tiles and other products, on furs to simulate more expensive furs, mirrors, wallpaper, airplanes, print directly on ice cream, book covers, cosmetic and beverage containers, all types of dials, etc. The industry consisting of the printer, artist, advertiser, salesman, supplier, manufacturer, and consumer is an integrated one so that materials, supplies, and equipment are always available for any job peculiar to the process. See Figure 3. Last but not least, the average printer is an enterprising individual, accepts every new problem as a challenge and follows the axiom "when no other method will solve a printing problem then screen printing must do so."

In this process and industry there is an available ink for any purpose and often the same ink may be used to print on varied materials. The inks may be oil-vehicle inks, synthetic enamel which will resist climatic and atomospheric conditions, water-soluble inks, lacquers, plastics, plain enamels, metallic inks, pure gold inks, ceramic inks, glazes, electrical conducting inks for printing electronic circuits, etching inks or compounds, daylight luminescent or fluorescent inks, phosphorescent inks, half-tone inks, and inks which leave an embossed effect upon the printed surface.

A screen printing ink has many requirements. It must not dissolve the printing plate or medium used to block-out those parts in the screen which are not to print. The ink must not clog the open or design parts of the screen or must not dry in the screen during printing. The ink must not cut or wear out the screen fabric or masking medium making up the design in the fabric. It should be easily deposited with the squeegee and it should print a sharp line or edge. Once printed, it should dry as quickly as possible. It should be

---

*The following book covers various printing plates used by the beginning and advanced screen printer: Kosloff, Albert. *Screen Printing Techniques*. The Signs of the Times Publishing Company, Cincinnati, Ohio.

Figure 3. Some of the varied workers who contribute to the versatile but integrated process of photographic and hand screen printing. (Courtesy of Poster Products, Inc., Chicago, Illinois.)

safe to use and should adhere permanently to the printing surface. Since screen printing is a very individual process the ink should imply upon examination to the consumer that the printing method used is screen printing. It must be easily cleaned off the printing plate or printing screen with safe solvents so that the screen may be reclaimed or be filed away to be used again.

Since the start of screen printing in about 1906 varied factors have brought about the tremendous development of this process. The emerging growth has been especially significant since World War II. Men such as Francis Willet, Charles M. Peter, John Pilsworth, Edward Owens, Roy Beck, Harry L. Hiett, Bert Zahn, Howard W. Parmele, Sr., Robert E. Doran, John W. Key, David R. Swormstedt, Sr., William and George Reinke, F. O. Brant, L. F. De Autremont, and Joseph Ulano who have labored successfully after many disappointments in varied fields have contributed to its development. The early souvenir pennant makers and sign painters who saw its potential developed it as a commercial enterprise. Contributing industries have aided. The organization of the Screen Process Printing Association, International (SPPA) in 1948 in Chicago accelerated an active and energetic industry, has aided to standardize products and motivate good printing, and has encouraged the dissemination of technical and educational information. This association changed its name in 1967 to Screen Printing Association, International (SPA). In 1973 the association established the Academy of Screen Printing Technology, a body of technical authorities representing the highest technological expertise in screen printing. The purpose of the academy members is to write, review, maintain the highest standards for papers under consideration for publication, and to encourage publication of new technical subjects relating to screen printing. The association eliminated old prejudices which often retard the growth of an industry, and interchange of ideas showed that no one had a monopoly on the so-called secrets of the industry, and developed a spirit of research. It generally attempted to solve problems by acting as a unifying agency for the betterment and advancement of each individual in the screen printing industry and the advancement of the graphic arts and thus the general culture of the world. Magazines such as

4

SIGNS of the *Times* and *SCREEN PRINTING* magazine have aided in its development.

Specific products which have made printing easier have definitely aided in its development as an industry. Among these are knife-cut films, inks, block-out or filler materials, hand-prepared printing screens, mechanical methods for printing, mechanized methods of drying varied screen printed matter, and the development of varied photographic printing screens.

Photography has revolutionized and contributed to the growth of screen printing just as it has contributed to the other phases of printing. Many of the photographic processes were adapted from other graphic arts field; others peculiar to the industry were developed as screen printing emerged. The photographic printing screens with their simplified and standardized procedures are enabling the screen printer, craftsman, hobbyist, educator, and student to print reproductions of almost any type of line or solid copy and fine and detailed copy such as that exemplified by halftone printing and color separation work on varied materials and varied shapes.

THE PRINTING PLATE
OR PRINTING SCREEN

The screen printing plate or the printing screen consists of the prepared block-out medium with the design in it applied to the screen fabric which is securely attached to a frame. Although there are other shapes depending upon the shape of the object being printed, the most common shape for the printing screen is flat as illustrated in Figure 1.

The frame may be made of wood or metal; it may be hand made or bought from any screen printing supplier, graphic arts dealer, or art shop. Any soft straight-grained, kiln dried or seasoned wood that is free of knots may be used for the frame. The thickness of the sides may be 1¼ × 1¼ inches*, if screen is to be about 24 × 24 inches in sizes. For larger screens the cross-sections of the sides may be 2 × 2 inches. Very large screens may be made of sides which are 2 × 4 or 2 × 6 inches in cross-section.

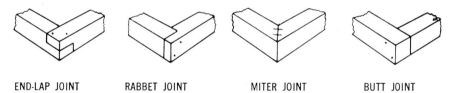

END-LAP JOINT   RABBET JOINT   MITER JOINT   BUTT JOINT

Figure 4. Typical construction of corners for wood frames.

Figure 4 presents practical methods of constructing the frame. Ordinarily, the wooden frame is shellacked. However, it certain inks have to be used which may dissolve the shellac, then difficulty may be encountered in printing. The writer prefers finishing frames by sandpapering the wood well and then rubbing and soaking the wood with a good coat of linseed oil and allowing oil to dry well into the wood. The frame may be fastened to the printing base with push-pin hinges so that one frame may be removed and another one inserted in the same hinge parts, with special hinge clamps, or they may be fastened to printing presses with simple clamps, bolts, or some other simple means. There must be no looseness in the hinge pins, since the colors will not register well in printing.

---

*It is suggested that the reader use a conversion chart where it may be necessary to change U.S. measuring units into Metric system measuring units.

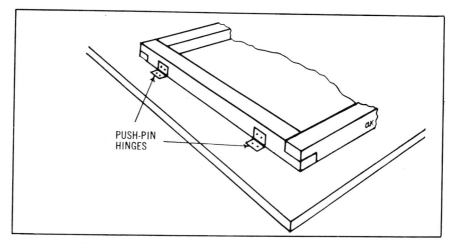

PUSH-PIN
HINGES

Figure 5. Attaching screen directly to printing base or table.

Figures 5 through 11 present various methods of attaching frames to a printing base or table. Figure 9 presents a hand printing unit that may be used for printing objects of varied sizes and thicknesses. The parallel supports, which may be made of metal or wood, allow the screen to be pulled toward and away from the printer. Figures 12 and 13 illustrate a frame that may be used both for hand or machine printing, while Figure 14, shows flat floating-bar frames. The floating-bar frames are employed for stretching very large screens in order to make the screen fabric very tight and for stretching metal fabrics on small and larger screens. However, during the printing of a color the operator should not resort to tightening or loosening the nuts in order to keep register, as it will be impossible to register the colors.

Counterbalanced Screens

Often the printer is forced to use larger printing screens because of the nature of screen printing. Employing counterbalanced screens is one of the ingenious methods employed by the printer to overcome some of his problems such as printing large posters or "gang-up" or print 2, 4 or more positives of one or more designs on one large screen. Although the main purpose of counterbalancing is to keep a screen in a raised position automatically so that feeding of stock or material can be better accomplished, there are other practical reasons for counterbalancing. It frees both hands for feeding and placing material on drying racks or drying machines. This is an advantage especially in feeding large posters. Also, it is safer to use a counterbalanced screen, as counterbalancing prevents the screen from dropping on the printer's or feeder's hand or fingers. The latter experience can be a painful one, particularly when printing with very large screens.

In making a counterbalanced unit, the weights or counterbalancing must be arranged so that a slight pull on the screen will lower it to the base in printing position and releasing the light pressure will allow the screen to return to its raised position for comfortable feeding of stock or objects. A

7

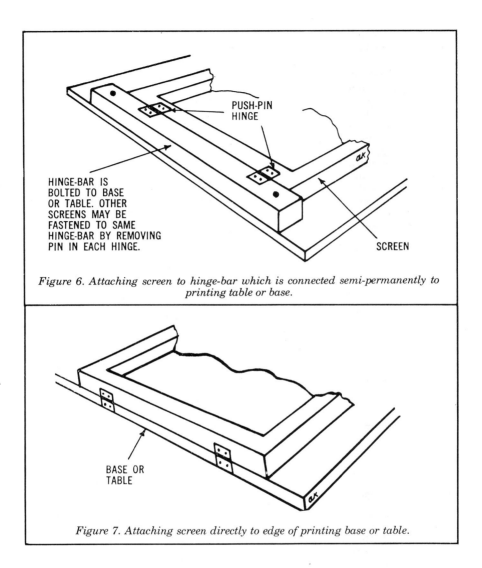

PUSH-PIN HINGE

HINGE-BAR IS BOLTED TO BASE OR TABLE. OTHER SCREENS MAY BE FASTENED TO SAME HINGE-BAR BY REMOVING PIN IN EACH HINGE.

SCREEN

Figure 6. Attaching screen to hinge-bar which is connected semi-permanently to printing table or base.

BASE OR TABLE

Figure 7. Attaching screen directly to edge of printing base or table.

carpenter's level may be used to insure that the plane of the screen is even and parallel to the material that is being printed and to the base of the screen.

Sand makes a good agent for counterbalancing because it gives accuracy in balancing and may be easily obtained. Metal weights or small washers may also be used. Cans, pails, or cloth bags may be employed to hold the weighting material.

The counterbalancing method should not warp the screen. To eliminate distortion of screen or master frame, the tension and stress in counterbalanc-

8

ing should be evenly distributed on two opposite sides of the screen in a centralized location. (See Figures 15 through 19) so that frame or screen is balanced. The rope, wire, or parts attached to the screen should be placed in such a way that the moving or attaching parts will not interfere with the worker's ease of manipulation and pushing or pulling of the squeegee. Those parts in the rope or wire that move over pulleys should be covered with beeswax or a little grease to eliminate friction, to keep rope from wearing out, and to make operation simpler and more efficient. The beeswax may be applied by melting and coating it onto the rope with a brush or impregnating the rope by dipping the rope in the melted wax.

Where counterbalancing arrangements have to be employed, it is advisable to build the unit using a master frame as illustrated. A master frame is a large permanent frame that allows for the easy insertion or attachment of different size screens or printing plates. In attaching smaller screens to the

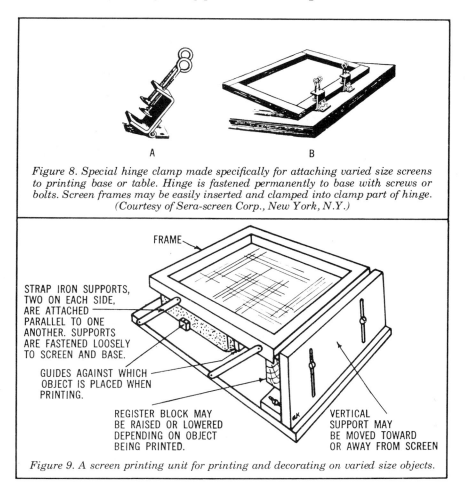

A   B

Figure 8. Special hinge clamp made specifically for attaching varied size screens to printing base or table. Hinge is fastened permanently to base with screws or bolts. Screen frames may be easily inserted and clamped into clamp part of hinge. (Courtesy of Sera-screen Corp., New York, N.Y.)

FRAME

STRAP IRON SUPPORTS, TWO ON EACH SIDE, ARE ATTACHED PARALLEL TO ONE ANOTHER. SUPPORTS ARE FASTENED LOOSELY TO SCREEN AND BASE.

GUIDES AGAINST WHICH OBJECT IS PLACED WHEN PRINTING.

REGISTER BLOCK MAY BE RAISED OR LOWERED DEPENDING ON OBJECT BEING PRINTED.

VERTICAL SUPPORT MAY BE MOVED TOWARD OR AWAY FROM SCREEN

Figure 9. A screen printing unit for printing and decorating on varied size objects.

9

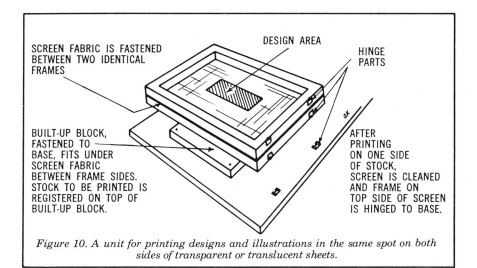

SCREEN FABRIC IS FASTENED
BETWEEN TWO IDENTICAL
FRAMES

DESIGN AREA

HINGE
PARTS

BUILT-UP BLOCK,
FASTENED TO
BASE, FITS UNDER
SCREEN FABRIC
BETWEEN FRAME SIDES.
STOCK TO BE PRINTED IS
REGISTERED ON TOP OF
BUILT-UP BLOCK.

AFTER
PRINTING
ON ONE SIDE
OF STOCK,
SCREEN IS CLEANED
AND FRAME ON
TOP SIDE OF SCREEN
IS HINGED TO BASE.

Figure 10. A unit for printing designs and illustrations in the same spot on both sides of transparent or translucent sheets.

Figure 11. "Magic Hand" hand screen printing unit which will accomodate varied size printing screens. (Courtesy of Naz-Dar Company, Chicago, Illinois).

10

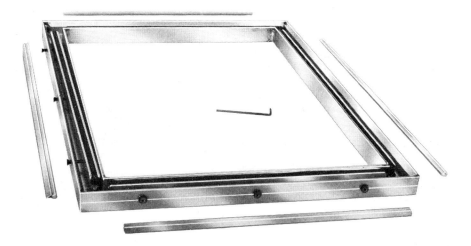

MOUNTING THE MESH | SNAP EACH BAR IN PLACE | TENSIONING THE MESH

Figure 12. "Cam-Lock" screen frame available in varied sizes with a built in device for stretching any kind of screen fabric for all types of precise screen printing. Bottom illustrations show metal mesh cut to a size even with outside of frame. Bars are placed over the fabric and pressed down into channel on sides of frame. Each tensioning bolt is then gradually tightened until mesh is very taut. (Courtesy of Advance Process Supply Company, Chicago, Illinois).

master frame, 1 inch thick strips of wood may be bolted, nailed, or screwed to the master frame and to the smaller screen or the small screen may be attached to the master frame with long bolts and wing nuts in similar fashion to floating-bars in a floating-bar frame. See Figure 20.

Where it is necessary to keep a screen down for longer periods than is normally required in printing, then the operator may attach a simple snap lock to the frame and base. The lock can be opened easily by pressing or pulling the latch in it, depending upon the type of lock that the operator may buy in the local hardware store.

It is suggested that in the unit illustrated in Figure 15 a snap lock be used to keep screen down during printing operation. However, it will not be

11

Figure 13. Bottom view of Cincinnati True-Tension Chase, a commercial screen printing frame, designed for precision printing and for obtaining even tension over entire area of mesh. Any type screen fabric may be attached in the frame which has adjustment screws on all four sides to obtain drum tightness. (Courtesy of Cincinnati Printing and Drying Systems, Inc., Cincinnati, Ohio.

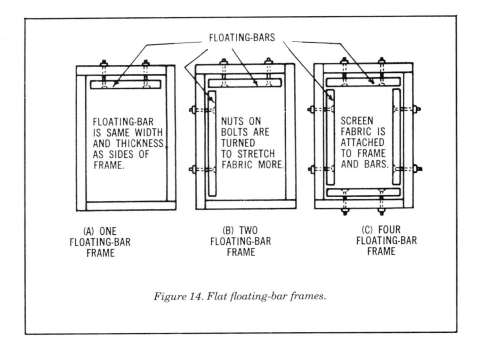

FLOATING-BARS

FLOATING-BAR IS SAME WIDTH AND THICKNESS AS SIDES OF FRAME.

NUTS ON BOLTS ARE TURNED TO STRETCH FABRIC MORE.

SCREEN FABRIC IS ATTACHED TO FRAME AND BARS.

(A) ONE FLOATING-BAR FRAME

(B) TWO FLOATING-BAR FRAME

(C) FOUR FLOATING-BAR FRAME

Figure 14. Flat floating-bar frames.

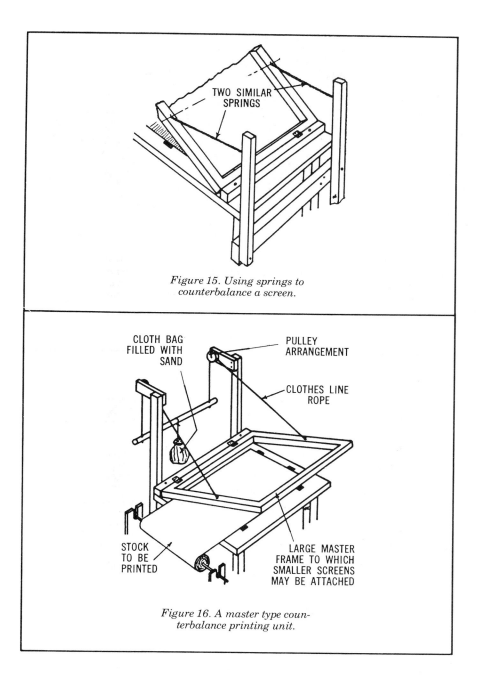

Figure 15. Using springs to counterbalance a screen.

TWO SIMILAR SPRINGS

CLOTH BAG FILLED WITH SAND

PULLEY ARRANGEMENT

CLOTHES LINE ROPE

STOCK TO BE PRINTED

LARGE MASTER FRAME TO WHICH SMALLER SCREENS MAY BE ATTACHED

Figure 16. A master type counterbalance printing unit.

13

necessary to use the lock much if the springs are attached so that they are parallel to the screen when the screen is down or in printing position.

A small screen may be kept in a raised position by using spring hinges for attaching screen to base, although the screen will not be counterbalanced.

Screen Fabrics

Various screen fabrics are and have been employed for screen printing*. Nylon, monofilament and multifilament polyester, metal fabrics, silk, and metallized polyester are common, although organdy, organdy-voile, and bridal netting have and are being used.

The fabric that seemed to answer best the needs of the early printer because of its strength, lightness, and uniformity of weave, was silk bolting cloth which was used originally by millers for sifting various grades of flour. Silk bolting cloth and taffeta weave silk are still employed. The resilient nature of these two silks makes them withstand much wear, resist solvents, and their natural rougher threads are practical for easier adhering of such indirect screens as carbon tissue or pigment papers than adhering to nylon, polyester, or stainless steel.

Because silk was the first practical fabric used, the numbering of other screen fabrics, as they were introduced to the industry, was related to silk. Fabrics for screen printing are specified by numbers, mesh count per lineal inch or centimeter, size of individual mesh opening, and percentage of open area. The mesh count is the number of mesh openings of approximately equal size per lineal inch (or centimeter). Uniformity of mesh spacing, aperture size and uniformity of thread thickness are stressed in silk and in other screen fabrics being manufactured especially for the industry.

Although silk is generally available from about Number 2 to Number 25 from screen printing suppliers, the numbers which have proved most practical for photographic work range from Number 12 to Number 18 inclusive. Ordinarily, the smaller the number, the larger the opening between the threads as illustrated in Figure 21. In other words, Number 12 silk has larger openings than Number 18 and will ordinarily deposit a heavier coat of ink than Number 18. The mesh count for screen fabrics is generally supplied by the manufacturer or supplier of the fabric. The following are ranges of common mesh counts: Nylon — 74 to 385; yellow (anti-halo) nylon — 160 to about 380; monofilament polyester fabric — from about 60 to 400 mesh; and multifilament polyester fabric — (6XX to 21XX) or about 74 to 180 mesh openings per inch.

To designate quality the silk number has a single-X (X), double-X (XX), or triple-X (XXX) after it, for example, 12X, 12XX, 14XX. The "XX" indicates a stronger weave than single-X and double-X fabric is the one that is generally employed for photographic screen printing. Silk comes in varied prices per yard, in widths up to about 60 inches, and in bolt lengths up to about 60 yards. Nylon and polyester fabrics are available in larger widths and in longer bolt lengths. Since the latter two fabrics are used more for photographic printing screens, the printer may make any size photographic screen needed.

---

*The following book covers screen fabrics more completely: Kosloff, Albert, *Screen Printing Techniques*, Signs of the Times Publishing Co., Cincinnati, Ohio.

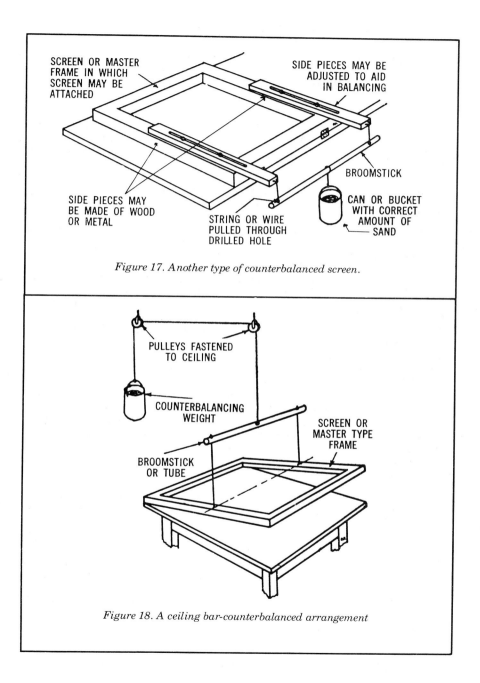

SCREEN OR MASTER FRAME IN WHICH SCREEN MAY BE ATTACHED

SIDE PIECES MAY BE ADJUSTED TO AID IN BALANCING

SIDE PIECES MAY BE MADE OF WOOD OR METAL

STRING OR WIRE PULLED THROUGH DRILLED HOLE

BROOMSTICK

CAN OR BUCKET WITH CORRECT AMOUNT OF SAND

Figure 17. Another type of counterbalanced screen.

PULLEYS FASTENED TO CEILING

COUNTERBALANCING WEIGHT

BROOMSTICK OR TUBE

SCREEN OR MASTER TYPE FRAME

Figure 18. A ceiling bar-counterbalanced arrangement

15

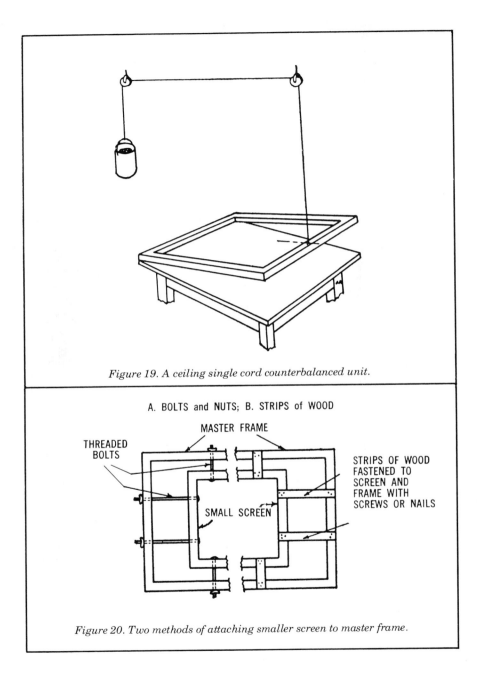

Figure 19. A ceiling single cord counterbalanced unit.

A. BOLTS and NUTS; B. STRIPS of WOOD

MASTER FRAME

THREADED
BOLTS

SMALL SCREEN

STRIPS OF WOOD
FASTENED TO
SCREEN AND
FRAME WITH
SCREWS OR NAILS

Figure 20. Two methods of attaching smaller screen to master frame.

16

SILK NUMBER	11	12	13	14	15	16	17	18
MESH	114	122	127	136	144	152	160	170

Figure 21. Number of silk used for photographic screen printing and approximate mesh of silk number.

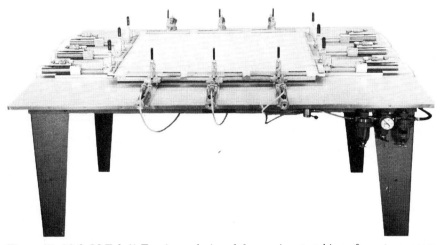

Figure 22. M & M Fabric Tensioner designed for precise stretching of any type screen fabric on various size frames. Fabric may be stapled or adhered with adhesive to screen frame. (Courtesy of M & M Research Engineering Co., Butler, Wisconsin).

Metal screen fabric is also standardized according to numbers, the number specifying the number of strands per lineal inch. Number 2 (coarse) to Number 508 are available, with the following numbers being employed for photographic work: 120, 150, 165, 180, 230, 250. Stainless steel, phosphor bronze, copper wire gauze, and brass wire in the plain weave are used. Although metal screen fabric may be obtained in small size pieces, metal fabrics are available in 36, 41, and 51 inch widths and in lengths up to about 100 feet. The common width for metal fabric is 36 inches.

Metal fabrics generally are used for small size and medium size screens, for electronic circuit printing, and for printing screens that will last for thousands of impressions. However, in attaching the metal fabric to the frame, the fabric may be stretched with a seamer or stretching pliers and one must be careful not to dent the screen, especially in the design area, since metal fabric is not as resilient as silk and the printing plate will be spoiled. Floating-bar frames illustrated in Figure 14 are practical for metal fabrics, since the metal may be stretched after it is tacked, stapled or adhered to the frame and bars. There are commercial stretching devices or units for stretching and attaching metal fabrics to the varied types of frames used in screen printing. See Figure 22.

Attaching Fabric to Frame

Various methods are employed to stretch and attach screen fabrics to the frame. Figures 23 through 26 illustrate some of the methods. Carpet tacks about ½ to ¾ inches in length, staples, the groove-cleat method, and commercial devices are the most common methods of securely fastening the screen fabric to the frame. Staples may be driven directly over the fabric and into the wood or over strips of paper fiber or thin cardboard. (See Figure 24).

TACKS SHOULD BE STAGGERED AND KEPT ABOUT ¾" APART.

STAPLES ARE DRIVEN IN AT AN ANGLE. THIN PAPER FIBER OR CARDBOARD STRIPS MAY BE PLACED UNDER STAPLES.

Figure 23. Position of tacks in tacking screen fabric to frame.

Figure 24. Employing staples in attaching screen fabric to frame with a staple gun. The fiber or carboard strips make it easier to remove staples when it is necessary to change fabric.

Regardless of the method used, the fabric must be taut and perfectly clean before processed film or a coating is applied. Loose fabric on screens will make difficult the registering of colors in the required areas on multi-color jobs, reduce durability of screen, do not print faithful reproduction where accuracy is essential, and produce uneven deposit of ink. Greasy and dirty fabric will prevent perfect adhering of screen printing films and emulsions. Manufacturers and suppliers of fabric and printing screen films and emulsions specify the methods of cleaning and degreasing the varied screen fabrics. For example, metal cloth often has a thin oily coating on it which must be removed with hot water and a strong soap or detergent, with degreasing compounds or solvents. Nylon and polyester must be cleaned and degreased perfectly so that emulsion coatings and films will adhere perfectly to it. Silk may be washed with water (not hot) and a mild soap and rinsed well with water before using.

Fillers for Screen Fabric

Fillers or block-out mediums are substances which close up the unwanted apertures or holes in a printing screen. It may consist of a liquid, film, or paper. The block-out medium may consist of the same material which makes up the design, usually in the center of the screen, and a different filler in the rest of the screen, as in some commercial photographic printing screens. It may be hand-prepared commercial knife-cut film or hand-prepared knife-cut paper in which the design has been cut out and the film or paper applied to the screen fabric. It may consist of a photographic screen printing film, which after processing is applied to the underside of the screen fabric; or it may be a photographic screen printing coating applied directly to the

18

screen fabric. The *underside* of the screen fabric is that side which comes in contact with the material being printed. Generally in photographic work the design is adhered in the center part of the screen and the rest of the screen outside the design area is filled up with a filler.

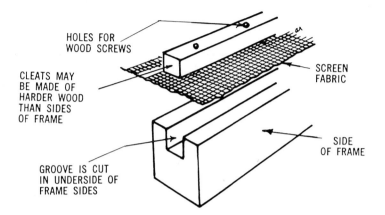

HOLES FOR
WOOD SCREWS

CLEATS MAY
BE MADE OF
HARDER WOOD
THAN SIDES
OF FRAME

SCREEN
FABRIC

GROOVE IS CUT
IN UNDERSIDE OF
FRAME SIDES

SIDE
OF FRAME

Figure 25. The groove-cleat method of attaching screen fabric to a frame. The fabric is held in place while attaching and the cleats are driven down on the four sides to hold and tighten the fabric.

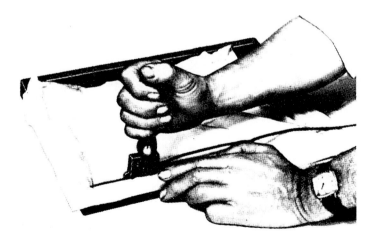

Figure 26. The "E-Z stretch method" employs a special tool and a cord which stretches and attaches the fabric to the frame by pressing the cord over the fabric into the groove on the four sides of the frame. (Courtesy of Naz-Dar Company, Chicago, Ill.)

19

Fillers or block-out mediums are not only employed to block-out the rest of the screen in the areas outside the design area but also in the preparation of some hand-prepared printing plates. The fillers may be applied to the screen fabric by brushing on, either on the top or underside of the fabric, the filler may be applied in squeegee fashion with a flexible piece of cardboard, or by pouring on. They come in various colors and transparent, so that if pinholes do occur after drying, the defect may be easily seen and covered up with a second coating. They are generally available in pint, quart, and gallon containers.

All fillers must be applied easily and must completely fill up the open areas in the thinnest possible one or two coats so as not to leave pinholes. When printing, ink may be pressed through the pinholes onto the material being printed. Any filler applied to a screen must not be dissolved by the ink used in printing and by the various solvents employed to clean the screen. Fillers must be flexible enough so as not to break under the constant pressure of the printing squeegee. They should dry quickly and be removed easily with certain solvents. They should also withstand all types of atmospheric conditions during storage of the printing screen.

There are various types used such as the water-soluble, lacquer type filler, glue, shellac, varnish, collodion, paper, and specially prepared commercial fillers. The latter are very practical, especially for the beginner. Where a printer is not sure that a filler will resist the dissolving action of a specific ink, because of the many inks used, he should make a trial printing before doing the standard printing job. Manufacturer's directions must be followed in using fillers.

To complete the block-out, the corner edges around the sides of the screen should be sealed up with 1 or 2-inch gummed paper tape, or cloth tape, or tape sold by the supplier for this purpose to prevent ink leakage between fabric and frame. This sealing may be done before or after the filler is applied. The tape is applied so that it overlaps the sides and fabric along all inside and outside edges of the screen.

PRINCIPLES OF
PHOTOGRAPHIC
SCREEN PRINTING

Although there are others who aided in the development of photography, practical photography began with the Frenchman, Louis Jacques Mande Daguerre, who by 1837 perfected a method which was developed a little earlier by Nicephore Niepce. Daguerre used light to change a chemical coating on a sheet of copper into a picture. The picture was not visible when the plate was taken from the simple camera which he used. Daguerre, however, developed the method of bringing out the latent or hidden image in the plate. Daguerre's method or *daguerreotypes* made on the metal were pictures that could not be duplicated except by re-photographing.

While Daguerre was experimenting with photographs on metal, duplication of prints was developed by an English mathematician, William Henry Fox Talbot, who was making similar pictures on paper and who developed the negative-positive principle of photography. Talbot employed sunlight to produce positive prints from negatives. Since then with the aid of research and refinement photography has developed into an excellent tool which has greatly contributed to science, health, avocational pursuit, generally to the graphic arts, and has definitely contributed to screen printing.

Photographic screen printing is based on the principle that certain coatings or substances such as gelatin, polyvinyl alcohol, polyvinyl acetate, glue, or albumen when mixed with such salts as potassium bichromate or ammonium bichromate will be changed chemically or hardened when the coating is exposed to light; while those parts of the substances which are protected from the light by an opaque covering will remain soft and may be washed away with a solvent.

Although there are varied methods of preparing photographic printing screens and varied classifications, most of the printing screens fall into three general classes: (1) *direct*, (2) *indirect* or transfer types, and (3) *direct-indirect* or direct-film types. In each type the photographic process consists of placing a photographic positive or negative, which has the image or design on it to be reproduced, against a light-sensitive coating or screen printing film and exposing the whole unit to a source of light. In the indirect or transfer type screen a photographic coating or emulsion is prepared on a support or backing sheet and after being processed so that the emulsion has the desired design on it, the processed emulsion is transferred to the underside of the screen fabric. There are double-transfer and single-transfer screen printing films. In the double-transfer the emulsion is sensitized on its permanent support or backing sheet, transferred to a temporary support, exposed, and

21

then transferred to the screen fabric. In the single-transfer type, the sensitizing, exposing, and etching out or washing of exposed image takes place on the original or transparent permanent backing sheet and then transferred to the fabric.

Indirect or transfer type printing screens are known in the trade by such names as screen printing photographic film, carbon tissue, pigment paper, photographic film, photostencil film, autotype tissue, and by various trade and commercial names.

The direct printing screen is prepared directly on the screen fabric either by brushing the sensitized or unsensitized emulsion onto the silk or metal fabric, by dipping the screen into the photographic emulsion, or by applying emulsion onto the fabric with a coater or squeegee. The emulsion is then dried into the fabric either in complete darkness or in subdued light depending upon the specific formula, completely covering and impregnating the fabric. The dried and sensitized screen is then exposed in contact with a photographic or hand-made positive or negative. After exposure, the screen is washed or etched out in water so that the design parts in the screen are left open and the rest of the areas on the screen are closed up or blocked-out.

In the direct-indirect or direct-film types, generally an unsensitized screen printing film is adhered to the underside of the screen fabric by squeegeeing a liquid sensitizer on the inside or squeegee side of the screen. The sensitizer sensitizes and adheres film to the underside of the fabric. Unlike the indirect screen, the film is processed directly on the screen fabric.

Although there is historical confusion as to whether Charles M. Peter, Al Imelli, T. V. Cook, William Hugh Gordon, or Harry L. Hiett was each successful in being the first to develop the photographic screen printing plate between 1914 and 1915 or whether the West Coast or the Midwest of the United States produced the first photographic plate, it is generally accepted that direct screens were the first photographic screens used. Basically, the principle of photographic screens has not changed. The earliest screen was made by brushing onto the silk of the screen a coating consisting of a mixture of equal warm parts or solutions of gelatin and glue which served as a medium for holding the sensitizer and also as the blocking-out agent for the silk or screen. After this coating dried, a sensitizer was applied over the dried coating. A sensitizer is a substance which makes the coating sensitive to light. The sensitizer consisted of a thin solution made up of the same mixtures as the coating and enough ammonium bichromate was brushed over the first coating to produce an orange tint and the screen was allowed to dry in a darkroom. A hand-prepared negative was clamped in contact with the dried and coated screen and the unit was exposed to the strong light energy of the sun until the exposed parts on the screen turned a bronze color. The exposed screen was then washed off with warm water to dissolve away the unexposed or soft parts.

Generally, the different types of screens have to be exposed in direct contact with a transparent photographic or hand-prepared positive of the required size. However, there are also screen printing films which may be exposed by having the transparent positive projected onto the sensitized film. Those parts in the positive or negative which are opaque will not allow the exposing light to go through; while the transparent parts in the positive will allow the exposing light to pass through and strike the sensitized emulsion.

The three types of screens are used, are not difficult to prepare, and because of the versatility of screen printing, each type serves a practical purpose. The indirect type is available in presensitized and unsensitized forms. The indirect films can be removed easily from the screen and give good general results.

The direct type screen, however, is more durable, since the coating on this screen covers and impregnates the screen fabric producing a reinforced natural or synthetic thin plastic sheet, depending upon the formula used.

The direct-indirect screen, when processed correctly, encapsulates the screen fabric, produces good detail in printing since the product is a film, and is a resistant screen.

Many factors have brought about the development of photographic printing screens. Photographic screens make possible the printing of fine detail, halftone work, three-color process, four-color process, full-color process, and "fake" color work. It will reproduce such art methods as scratchboard technique, air brush, mezzotint, drypoint, etchings, charcoal, and pen and ink drawings. Photography is the quickest and the most accurate of the methods. It makes possible the fitting of the art work or originals of any size to desired specifications by reducing or enlarging the original. It offers short cuts in art work and often some of the art work and design may be eliminated by adapting illustrations from brochures, magazines, by using printer proofs, employing paste-up method, and other advertising media. Photographic printing plates offer the printer a method of employing photographic effects with hand-prepared printing screens and with other printing methods. Photography enables a smaller staff to turn out more work and at the same time replace time-consuming methods. Hand preparation of printing screens, especially large screens is time consuming; photography saves on labor and on cost. Doing the photographic work in one's shop gives the printer a method for offering quicker service to the consumer. If a screen is spoiled, it can be redone with less inconvenience and delay. More than one design may be combined on one positive, as illustrated in Figure 27. After development, the designs may be cut apart to form the varied desired positives. By employing the three- or four-color process photographically, as in halftone printing, photography makes possible by superimposing the three or four colors to produce 4, 5, 6, or more colors. Improvised equipment and an improvised darkroom may be used for starting.

There are direct-indirect or direct-films which may be processed in stages, that is, the direct-film may be processed to the point where it is to be sensitized. In this state the exposed film may be shipped to a distant point or stored for future use. There are also direct screens which may be coated, emulsion coating dried, and screen stored in the dark to be exposed at a future date. Photography offers the printer a method of keeping track of printed jobs by filing away the positives instead of filing or storing screens, should it be necessary to reprint a job. Screens are bulky, require more space, are often a fire hazard, and do tie up equipment and screen fabric which could be used for other purposes. Screens may then be reclaimed and used for other jobs. Modern screen printing films offer durability and are manufactured so that they have dimensional stability. Research by printers, graphic arts establishments, and others is eliminating hindrances and constantly is making available screen printing films and coatings for direct screens, equipment, standardized procedures, and technical aid.

Photographic screen printing developed photographic posterization and also aided in the development of chemical machining. As explained in Chapter 32, photographic posterization is a screen printing process in which a

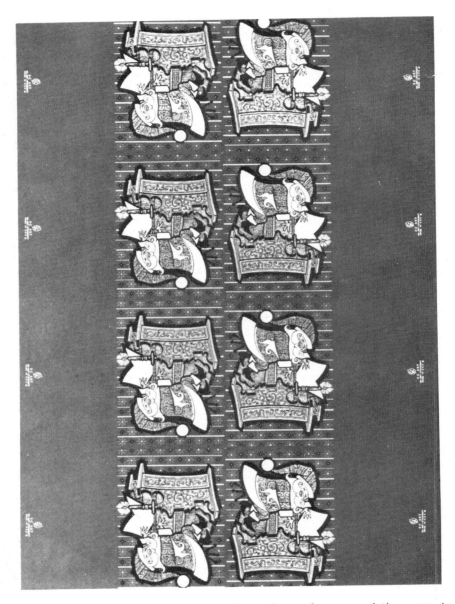

Figure 27. Combining or "ganging-up" eight greeting cards on one printing screen to produce a multi-color job. Each of the colors for the eight cards was printed separately with one screen and a separate large positive was used to produce each printing screen. (Courtesy of Superior Silk Screen Industries, Inc., Chicago, Illinois).

24

photograph may be changed to line copy illustration by printing solid areas from light to dark shades having several tones of the same color or different colors. Chemical machining also known as chemical milling, photofabrication, photoforming, or photoetching, consists of screen printing designs by applying resists and etching away those parts not covered by the resist. This process produces very small parts and intricate contours by chemical etching or removal of material.

The reader must not assume that hand-prepared screens are a thing of the past and should be familiar with each commercial type. Hand screens are generally not as delicate as photographic screens, are essential for certain types of printing and are practical because of the versatility of screen printing, are good for printing very large areas such as the outdoor advertising posters, and will do a creditable job from art work which is not completely finished. Also, a darkroom, photographic equipment, a camera, working area, and experimentation require a financial and time investment. However, the advantages of hand-prepared screens definitely offset the disadvantages.

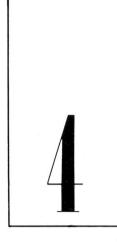

MATERIALS AND EQUIPMENT

Before starting the actual preparation of photographic printing screens, the printer must make sure that he knows every step of the particular process relating to each part of the job and that he has adequate equipment. Although much of the material and equipment may be made by the processor or enterprising beginner, it is advisable that the beginner buy these from screen printing suppliers and graphic arts establishments, since they are inexpensive and specifically designed for the screen printer. Suppliers are located in strategic centers. Everything does not have to be acquired at one time to start but some items may be accumulated as one becomes more experienced and specialized in the field. Before buying expensive items or equipment such as a process camera, the beginner should visit shops and investigate and determine what will fit his specific needs best.

Generally, the beginner will need the following materials and equipment for making photographic printing screens: (1) carbon tissue, pigment paper, a commercial screen printing film, or a similar film; (2) a sensitizer for sensitizing the screen printing film (if film is sold in unsensitized state); or (3) a direct emulsion, if emulsion is to be coated directly onto the screen fabric; (4) about three or four white porcelain-finished, glass, stainless steel, or bakelite trays, large enough for processing the biggest film job; (5) a source of hot, warm, and cold water with a mixing faucet attachment; (6) a photographic thermometer for testing the temperature of solutions; (7) a vacuum printing frame, a photographic contact frame, or an arrangement for holding the sensitized screen printing film or screen in direct contact with the positive during the exposure period (8) a photographic positive or negative with the design on it to be reproduced; (9) a practical light source to which the sensitized screen printing film or coated screen and positive may be exposed; (10) some clean newsprint paper, blotting paper, or even newspaper for blotting the wet film when it is attached to screen fabric; (11) some clean, soft, lintless cloths; (12) an electric fan with a 6-inch blade for drying screen and cooling film when necessary; (13) a screen stretched with the correct screen fabric mesh; (14) standard graduates with large identifying figures on them for accurately measuring the few chemicals when necessary; (15) a completely dark area or darkroom; and (16) if the printer plans to offer complete photographic service so that he may make his own negatives, positives, do copy work, make enlargements and reductions, and do color separation work, then he will need some type of a process camera.

Screen Printing Films and Coatings

There are various photographic screen printing films and coatings for making the actual printing screens used in the trade both in the United States and abroad. The film generally consists of an exactly formulated unsensitized or sensitized coating applied onto a transparent or translucent thin plastic backing sheet or paper. Screen printing coatings which are applied directly onto the screen fabric are also available in unsensitized and sensitized form. The pioneer printer prepared his own film and coatings by mixing specific proportions of colloids such as gelatin, glue with either potassium bichromate or ammonium bichromate granules, sugar, and a few drops of glycerine to give the film flexibility and applying the coating to the silk or a heavy paper. Because of the many painstaking experiments, research, and the attempt to answer needs of the old printer the modern printer may obtain very accurate screen printing products which have been manufactured especially for his needs under rigid, scientifically controlled conditions to give standarized results under normal shop conditions.

He may have films which are unsensitized and may sensitize them at his own pleasure or need; he may have sensitized film which does not require any treatment before exposing; he may have film which may be exposed in direct contact with the positive or films which may be adhered to the screen fabric and sensitized when needed; films which must be processed specifically and films which have slightly more latitude in their processing; coatings which may be applied directly from the container onto the silk in plain daylight; and formulas for coatings which may be easily mixed by the printer. Regardless of the product used, the printer should follow the manufacturer's specific directions in its preparation.

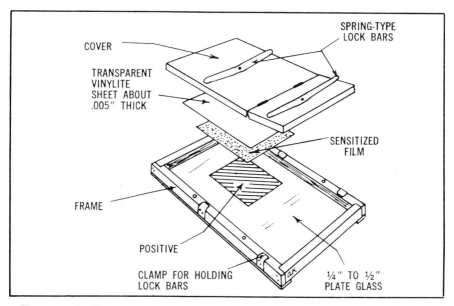

Figure 28. A photographic contact frame for exposing sensitized screen printing film.

27

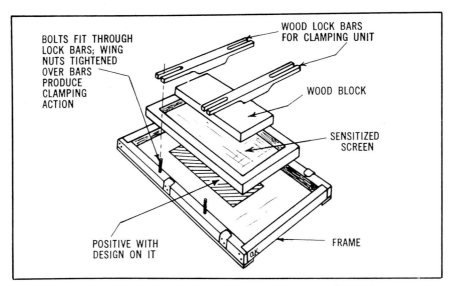

BOLTS FIT THROUGH
LOCK BARS; WING
NUTS TIGHTENED
OVER BARS
PRODUCE
CLAMPING
ACTION

WOOD LOCK BARS
FOR CLAMPING UNIT

WOOD BLOCK

SENSITIZED
SCREEN

POSITIVE WITH
DESIGN ON IT

FRAME

Figure 29. A photographic contact frame for exposing a direct screen.

Sensitizer

A sensitizer is a substance which makes a film or coating sensitive to light so that the coating will be changed chemically or harden when the film is exposed to a correct light source. The sensitizers employed in the making of printing screens are easy to prepare and use. Some of them are mixed or come in stock solutions and the printer just mixes the stock solutions when he is ready to sensitize film. Some come in package form and are easily and quickly mixed in distilled water or any clean water with time consuming weighings practically eliminated. There are sensitizers which are very simply prepared by mixing specific weights of potassium bichromate or ammonium bichromate in given volumes of water. There are prepared commercial sensitizers in package form which have simple directions on container for their mixing. There are more complicated sensitizers which must be mixed as carefully as any chemicals.

Where photographic solutions must be compounded according to a formula, accuracy in weighing and diluting is essential. General chemical mixing cannot be treated lightly if consistent production and quality is to be maintained. Generally working temperature or room temperature is about 65 to 70 degrees Fahrenheit (18 to 21 degress Celsius). Where a darkroom or working area is air conditioned, the temperature is usually in this range.

The sensitizer should be stored according to the directions of the manufacturer or according to the type of sensitizer. Sensitizing solutions mixed from potassium bichromate or ammonium bichromate may be kept a long time, if the sensitizing solution is stored in a dark brown or opaque container in a cool place. Dry bichromate salts may be kept almost indefintely. Sensitizers and other chemical solutions used by the printer must be mixed in quantities that can be stored easily and for such time lengths so that the

28

mixed chemical solution will always be uniform. Since the material part of screen printing is the least part of the expense, chemically pure grades of compounds and chemicals should be used.

A sensitizer, generally is cooled before it is used, especially those employed to sensitize carbon tissue or gelatinous coated tissue. This may be done by keeping the sensitizer in a refrigerator or by running cold water over the container of sensitizer.

It is suggested that the printer use the sensitizer recommended by the manufacturer of the specific film or coating employed. Although sensitizers and chemicals are safe to use, some products may cause irritation to the skin. In such cases one should avoid prolonged contact or use rubber gloves in working with the solution. Also, manufacturers ordinarily include precautions relating to handling in directions.

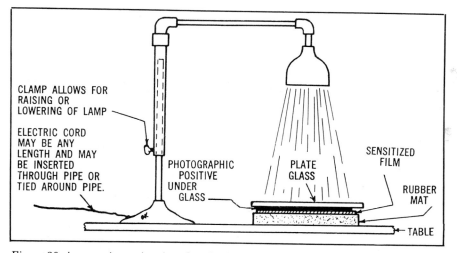

CLAMP ALLOWS FOR
RAISING OR
LOWERING OF LAMP

ELECTRIC CORD
MAY BE ANY
LENGTH AND MAY
BE INSERTED
THROUGH PIPE OR
TIED AROUND PIPE.

PHOTOGRAPHIC
POSITIVE
UNDER
GLASS

PLATE
GLASS

SENSITIZED
FILM

RUBBER
MAT

TABLE

Figure 30. An exposing unit using photoflood lamps or other lamps as the source of light.

Obtaining Contact Between Film and Positive

In order to expose sensitized film correctly, especially in large size films, the film must be in perfect contact with the positive so that sharp, clean lines and dot structures are obtained. Various devices are employed by the printer for exposing film and direct screens. See Figures 28 through 31. Figures 28 and 29 show a practical photographic contact frame designed by the writer which may be used for exposing film and direct screens. It is suggested that rubber foam material that is about ½" to 1" thick be placed between screen and wood block in order to produce perfect contact between positive and screen in Figure 29. It will work well for exposing positives with a printing area up to about 12 × 14 inches. Although these contact frames may be made very large, they become cumbersome and require heavy and thick glass up to an inch or more in thickness in order to prevent glass breakage due to pressure of clamps. Very thick glass also absorbs light and requires longer expo-

29

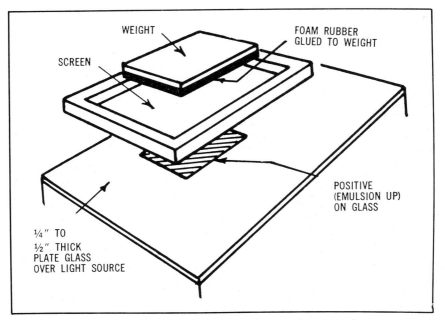

Figure 31. Arrangement of components for exposing a coated screen.

sure time. In using the exposing unit shown in Figure 28, weights may be placed on the edges of the glass to insure perfect contact of the parts.

Where precise contact of film and positive is necessary, especially large size film, vacuum printing frames as illustrated in Figure 32 are used. A vacuum printing frame is an apparatus used for obtaining perfect contact by creating a partial vacuum or by withdrawing the air between the glass and blanket in the frame. The device consists of a frame with a supporting glass which fits perfectly over another frame or arrangement having a flexible rubber blanket. A motor driven pump is attached to the blanket for withdrawing the air between the blanket and glass. The glass is not too thick, since the pressure is the same on both sides of the glass. The film and positive are placed between the blanket and glass, the positive being placed in direct contact with the glass and over the sensitized film.

Vacuum frames (see Figure 32) are available in various prices and sizes from about 17 × 22 inches to about 90 × 300 inches. Some are portable; some are large and are on casters so that they may be moved around. Many process cameras have a vacuum frame as part of the camera equipment built in generally at the back of the camera. Standard equipment with most vacuum frames consist of a motor and pump for drawing out the air, a release valve for releasing the pressure, a gauge for observing the vacuum in pounds per square inch or pressure, and an electrical switch for controlling the mechanism. The frame may be connected to standard electrical outlets. The manufacturer of the specific vacuum printing frame generally recommends the working pressure for best exposure. Generally, from about 18 to 20 cubic inches of vacuum are maintained or about 10 pounds of pressure per square

30

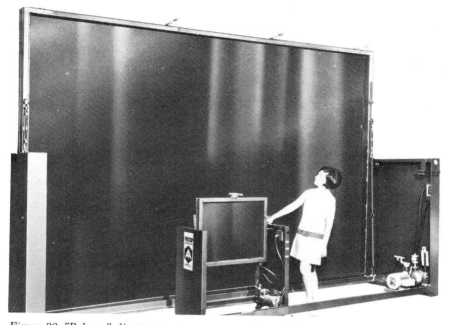

Figure 32. "Polycop" direct-contact vacuum exposing unit for exposing screens in direct contact with positive, available in eight standard mobile sizes from 24" × 30" to 80" × 110". (Courtesy of American Screen Process Equipment Company, Chicago, Illinois).

inch are used. Normal atmospheric pressure is about 14.7 pounds per square inch.

The gaskets between the glass frame and blanket frame should be smooth and clean. It is advisable that the vacuum frame be closed when not in use. The glass must be perfectly clean, both in the vacuum frame or in any of the contact frames, when exposing, since dust may interfere with the fine detail or be the cause of minute pinholes in the final printing screen.

Positives

Both film and direct screens have to be exposed in direct contact with a photographic positive or negative or exposed by projecting the positive onto the sensitized screen printing film. Positives may be made photographically or hand prepared. They are generally made from a photographic negative or may be made directly from an object. A positive consists of a transparent or translucent flexible plastic or rigid glass support upon which the design is photographed, traced, or drawn. A positive is the opposite of a photographic negative. What appears white in photographed original design appears black on the negative. Those parts on the positive which are dark are light or transparent on the negative. The black and white areas on a positive correspond to the black and white spots on an original. Actually the printing screen, which is a reverse of the positive, prints or reproduces positives. Generally, a positive is necessary for each photographic printing plate that is

Figure 32A. Fine Line Vacuum Bag provides an inexpensive method of obtaining a vacuum contact for exposing positives in contact with direct, indirect, or direct-indirect screens. Bag is made of heavy duty transparent vinyl, conforms to any screen shape, and has a valve for vacuum attachment. (Courtesy of Tetko, Inc., Elmsford, New York).

to be prepared, whether the same screen or separate screens are to be used for printing each color. In a three-color printing job three positives are needed, one for each color. However, in color separation work or multi-colored half-tone printing three or four colors may be used to produce more than four colors by superimposing the pigment colors of yellow, red, blue-green and black in printing. Figure 33 illustrates a full-size photographic positive used in the preparation of a very precise printing screen for reproducing electronic circuits.

Positives may also be made by hand, but it is suggested that the special or negative opaque inks recommended for this purpose are used. Although positives may be made with mechanical bow pens and compasses on vellum type or tracing paper or cloth with India ink, best screen printing hand-prepared positives are made with opaque inks and with photographic negative type opaque inks on special transparent or translucent thin plastic sheets available from screen printing suppliers, graphic arts establishments, or art suppliers. Generally, the plastic has a matte finish on one or both sides to better hold the ink or medium for drawing the design. The hand-prepared positive may be made in tracing fashion from the original design or it may be prepared directly on the sheet serving as the support for the design. The opaque inks, which are ordinarily black or red in color, should leave a thin coating yet cover with a complete opaque effect. Light should definitely not pass through the inked lines and areas. A screen printing positive is one which is more opaque than normal positives. There should be contrast in the density of the positive, whether it is photographically or hand-made. The density is the relative opacity or ability to transmit light. Standard film for negatives and positives should be used in order to obtain positives of extreme density and contrast. Although the well equipped screen printing shop may have a densitometer, which is an instrument for determining the relative

32

opacity and transparency of positives and negatives, experience will determine which positives are practical. (See Figures 34 through 38).

Finished art work is required for making photographic positives, since the camera will reproduce each detail. Finished copy or art work in black on white is the best art for photographic reproduction, although colored copy and objects and originals may be reproduced also.

Many printers have special process cameras for doing their own photographic positives and negatives, enlargements, and reductions. The printer who does not have a camera, may have his positives made by a photographic screen printing plate specialist, by photoengraving establishments, by photolithographing establishments, or by commercial photographers. Wherever possible, it is recommended that the positives be photographically made, especially where fine detail is to be reproduced. Positives are made the same size as the final printing screen where the positive is to be exposed in direct contact with the sensitized screen printing film or printing screen. For halftone work, the halftone positive will often be made smaller so the smaller dots are obtained in order that better detail is captured. Then the smaller halftone negative or positive is enlarged to any desired size.

Positives may be made from a negative by contact printing in a photographic contact frame or vacuum printing frame, or they may be made by enlarging onto film in an enlarger or camera. They may be made directly with special film known as "autopositive film" by placing the film in direct contact with the black-on-white design or copy. Hand-made intaglio positives which will reproduce fine detail may also be prepared on transparent plastic

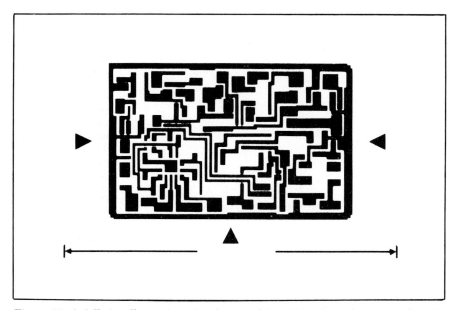

Figure 33. A full-size illustration of a photographic positive (one of seven similar size positives) which was used to prepare printing screens for very precise screen printing of electronic circuits. (Courtesy of Control Process Company, Elk Grove Village, Illnois).

33

Figure 34. Process Densitometer for transmission readings, reflection readings, and ground glass readings. (Courtesy of Eastman Kodak Company, Rochester, New York).

sheets by scribing the design into the surface. The latter two positives are covered fully in Chapter 29 and Chapter 30.

The printer may also make photographic positives from reproduction proofs, from letterpress, lithography, or gravure printing proofs. The proofs may be made on thin paper, and if possible, the printed parts may be sprinkled with bronze or aluminum powder to make the printing completely opaque. The proof paper may then be made transparent by rubbing the back well with caster oil, paraffin oil, machine oil, crude oil, or kerosene.

Where fineness in detail is not essential some printers have made use of photostats for positives. The design is reproduced on thin translucent photostatic paper. The paper is then made more transparent by rubbing the back of the photostat paper well with any of the oils mentioned above.

Sometimes the printer may use a photographic paper negative and then make the positive from the negative. The paper negative may be made by placing a single weight photographic paper in the camera instead of film or by using an enlarger. The photographic paper may be the size of the finished positive or of the final screen print. The advantages of a paper negative is that the screen printer can make desired changes and produce effects with opaque inks which are quite different from the original. The paper may be made more transparent by rubbing the back of it with oil.

Hand-prepared positives may also be made from knife-cut film similar to film used for preparing knife-cut hand-printing screens. This film sheet consists of a transparent or translucent film, deep red or amber in color, coated onto a translucent backing sheet. To prepare the positive the film is taped over the original copy and the desired areas are cut with a sharp knife in tracing fashion through the film but not through the backing sheet. Those

34

areas through which the exposing light is to pass are peeled away; those areas which are not peeled off and are left on the sheet will not allow light to pass through.

Exposing

When a sensitized film or coating is exposed, the film is subjected to the action of actinic light. *Actinic* light is that light which affects a photographic surface in a certain length of time and at a certain distance from the light. Exposing light sources are designed so that the light given off is in a range that will affect the sensitive material which is exposed. The general range for

Figure 35. Three types of safelights for working with orthochromatic photo-sensitive materials. (Courtesy of nuArc Company, Inc., Chicago, Illinois).

Figure 36. Achromatic Magnifier with 5-power color-corrected lens. (Courtesy of East-man Kodak Company, Rochester, New York).

most exposing light sources is between 3200 and 7000* Angstroms. The Angstrom, named after the Swedish physicist A. J. Angstrom, is a unit used to express the length of very short waves. Regardless of the light source, the objective of illumination in exposing is to produce light of even intensity over the whole work area. Manufacturers of exposing equipment strive to carry out this objective.

Although the old printer may have used the sun as a source of light and sunlight still may be used, this source cannot always be depended upon and the intensity of light cannot be controlled. Arc lamps, pulsed-xenon lamps, mercury vapor lamps, blacklight fluorescent tube units, and incandescent type lamps are generally employed to illuminate screen printing film and screens. Some of the above light sources are also used to illuminate copy on process cameras in the darkroom or screen printing shop.

Chapter 25 on actinic light sources explains exposing equipment more completely.

Regardless of the light source, the sensitized plate must be at right angles to the light, exposed for the right length of time, and be a certain distance from the plate. However, if the correct time of exposure for a given film is not known, the printer may easily obtain these data by means of a simple exposure test as illustrated in Figure 39. Uusually, the correct time of exposure of a certain film and the distance from the light source and other data are furnished by the specific manufacturer. To obtain practical time of exposure a piece of sensitized film is placed in the photographic contact frame or vacuum frame as shown and thin strips of opaque tape about ½ to 1 inch

---

*The Angstrom is one-tenth of a millimicron (a ten millionth of a millimeter or .00000001 cm.).

36

wide, are taped over the glass covering the film and leaving about a half inch of the film exposed. During the experimental exposure period the strips of tape are removed from the glass at equal time intervals, say each ¼ minute for fast acting films and 1 minute for slow films, until the whole piece of film is exposed so that some of the film is overexposed and some underexposed. The exposed film is then processed in the regular recommended manner and inspected to determine which time interval or time range produces the best detail and best results. It is advisable that the film be attached to screen fabric and printed to show up the weak, normal, and over exposed areas of the film in actual printing. Of course, the same distance must be used during the exposure and stripping of tape, since the light varies with the distance of light from the sensitized surface. The greater the distance, the longer must be the exposure. When the distance from the lamp is doubled, the exposure time is approximately 4 times as long, everything else being equal and when the distance is tripled, the exposure is about 9 times as long.

Figure 37. Timer, for timing precisely darkroom or other work with minute and second hand, which can be reset to zero. (Clock covers intervals up to 60 minutes). (Courtesy of Eastman Kodak Company, Rochester, New York).

37

Although sensitized film may be brought right up to the black light tubes in exposing, arc lights and especially photo-flood lamps are usually placed at least about 18 to 48 inches (or 46 to 122 cm) away from the sensitized screen printing film. When the film is being exposed wet, as in the wet carbon tissue method, the film must be cooled with a fan, by having the fan blow on the exposed surface of the film or in some other fashion to prevent heat from melting film. Depending on the type of sensitized material and light source, the time of exposure ranges from about 5 seconds to about 30 minutes. The film must not be overexposed or underexposed. Not enough exposure may cause pinholes in the final printing screen or produce a weak film. Overexposure may prevent film from adhering to screen fabric or close up some of the fine detail in the film.

Figure 38. Kodalith Film Processor designed for automatic and controlled processing of films; processor controls temperature and automatically replenishes and recirculates developer. The unit accepts all sizes of Kodalith film and processes most material dry-to-dry in a short time. (Courtesy of Eastman Kodak Company, Rochester, New York).

38

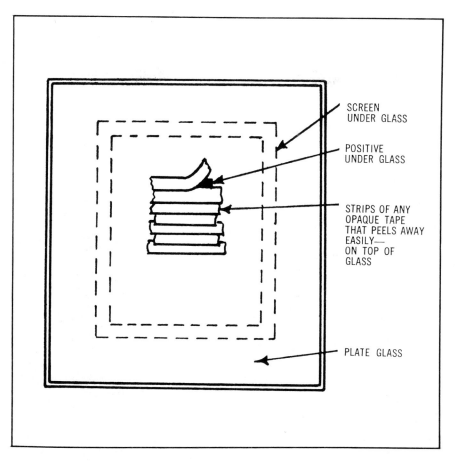

SCREEN
UNDER GLASS

POSITIVE
UNDER GLASS

STRIPS OF ANY
OPAQUE TAPE
THAT PEELS AWAY
EASILY—
ON TOP OF
GLASS

PLATE GLASS

Figure 39. Establishing correct time exposure. (1) Arrange for normal exposure. (2) Press tape strips down on top of glass over area occupied by the photographic positive. (3) During the exposure period, remove tape, a strip at a time, at equal time intervals. (For example, remove one strip at the end of each 15-second period of total exposure. (4) Wash-out screen immediately after all tape strips have been removed. (5) Examine screen to determine which time interval results in best stencil. This will be the standard exposure for exactly duplicated lighting conditions, light source, distance, etc.

The Darkroom

The screen printer or beginner who prepares a photographic screen which uses material that may be processed in ordinary daylight or subdued light or under plain small-wattage incandescent light or the one who prepares a printing screen on occasion may have no necessity for a darkroom. The small shop which has no darkroom is forced to do makeshift work, do the work at night, or send the work out to specialists. However, printers, larger shops, and establishments which are forced to offer a complete screen print-

39

ing photographic service or need to do their own work including process camera work, sooner or later, will install a darkroom.

A darkroom is just what the name signifies — a room or area that may be made entirely or partially dark or light-tight when necessary. Such a room is a practical investment, since it makes it easier to standardize, simplify, and centralize operations in one given area. A darkroom makes equipment and supplies available always when needed, provides storage space for each necessary photographic item, aids in the production of more exact work, makes it possible to do research, and generally aids in the complete photographic process.

The darkroom may be a temporary, semi-permanent, or permanent structure. Temporary structures may have walls fastened semi-permanently to the floor and may be built around a sink or some other main equipment part. Although a printer having knowledge of the use of tools may build his own darkroom, the room is generally built by a commercial contractor, since often it involves building code specifications, plumbing, electrical conduit work, air conditioning, etc. Depending on the equipment, facilities, and size, darkrooms may range in cost from about 100 dollars to thousands of dollars. The printer should preplan the project, keeping in mind the type of work to be done, the size of the room, best location in relation to other processes in the shop, type of plumbing equipment, electrical installations, photographic equipment, ventilation, air conditioning, finishing of walls and floor, miscellaneous equipment, etc. The final darkroom should be the result of visits to other screen printing shops which have darkrooms, the compilation of information from manufacturers of photographic equipment and graphic art suppliers, and the result of general planning to answer individual shop needs.

Depending upon the type of work to be done and the size of equipment to be included, the darkroom may vary in size from about 6 × 6 feet to about 10 × 20 feet in area. If a gallery or process camera is to be in the darkroom, then

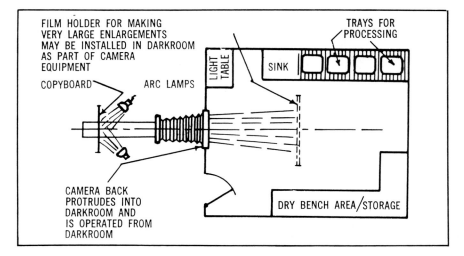

Figure 40. Layout of darkroom in relation to darkroom process camera.

40

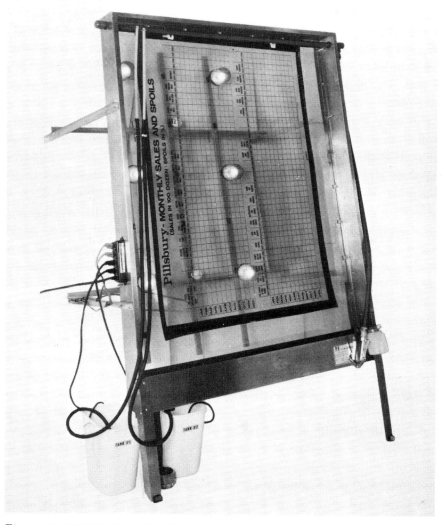

Figure 41. P2V2 Vertical Film Processor for processing and washing out large size photographic film, carbon tissue, screen printing films, and direct method screens. (Courtesy of Atlas Silk Screen Supply Company, Chicago, Illinois).

more floor space may be needed. One of the ways of keeping the darkroom smaller is to install a darkroom process camera so that the back of the camera is built into the darkroom as shown in Figure 40. The spot chosen for the darkroom should be near all the processes that precede it and follow it photographically.

The walls for a permanent structure may be built of 2 × 4 studs and the studs may be covered on the inside or on both sides with plaster board, plywood panels, wallboard, or any other practical paneling. The paneling may be applied with nails and painted on the inside with a suitable color. The walls may be painted a flat black paint, although they may also be painted light gray or light green or another color recommended by graphic arts suppliers to make surroundings more pleasant. The door or doors to the room must be built so that it will be possible to enter and leave without admitting any light to the darkroom.

With the varied available and often inexpensive air-conditioning units many darkrooms are air conditioned to control temperatures and humidity. Where conditioning is not possible, some type of ventilator or an electric blower may be installed preferably near the ceiling to blow out the stale air and fumes. The ventilation must be light-tight or a light trap. Where a darkroom is used much, proper ventilation and atmospheric conditions are essential for more exact processing, for efficient and comfortable working conditions, and for insuring standardization of results. Because dust particles are a hindrance when doing precise work, it is suggested that the incoming air be filtered.

The darkroom should have a "dry bench area" and a "wet area." The room should be equipped with a large sink, installed table-high, or a smaller sink and a large drainboard attached to the sink in such fashion that the liquids and chemicals will drain into the sink and not do damage. The sink may be a porcelain finished one, it may be made of the recommended type of stainless steel for photographic sinks, a lead-lined wood sink, or one made of wood such as cypress. In the wet area the sink or drain should be large enough to hold three or four of the largest processing trays that the printer will normally use.

There should be enough table or counter space for normal working. Also, there should be enough shelves conveniently located for storage of material and for expendable material. There should be enough drawers, of completely light-tight construction for storing the very light-sensitive material.

Regular light outlets and safelights should be conveniently located. Safelights of the type illustrated in Figure 35 are inexpensive and practical, since they allow for the changing of light filters of varied colors for handling different types of films. The safelight should be far enough away but still give enough illumination over a working area.

The equipment found in the screen printing darkroom varies but generally may include a process camera and a photographic printing frame of the contact or vacuum type. Other aids needed in the darkroom are a timer for timing certain processing, thermometer, wastebasket, an overhead wire stretched across the room with spring-clip clothes pins for drying film when necessary, measuring vessels, a scale for accurately measuring the materials and chemicals, a photographic enlarger, although the average process camera may eliminate this, since it can copy, reduce, and enlarge, a print roller or squeegee for flattening down films, and other material such as opaque tape, negative opaque, etc.

A light table or retouching table which has lights under a glass and which may be bought or made is also part of the equipment. In summary, generally it is wise to plan for maximum possible requirements before finally enclosing the darkroom area.

5

DIRECT PRINTING SCREENS

The enormous and varied range of screen printing and decorating on different materials and substrates and in varied industries is in a large part due to the many available practical photographic printing screens. Since World War II photographic screens have been improved in terms of materials and equipment employed for processing and in terms of the needs of an international industry. Today's screen printer should be familiar with as many of the photographic screens as possible. Photographic screens generally may be classified into (1) direct printing screens, (2) indirect or transfer types, and (3) direct-indirect or direct-film screens. There are varied products in each classification and each product in the three types has advantages and disadvantages.

Unlike the indirect or transfer type printing screens which are processed on a temporary support and then transferred to the screen fabric, the direct and the direct-indirect types are processed directly on the screen fabric. The great strides made internationally since about 1965 by direct screens and their increased use* are due to varied factors. There has been a conscientious effort to develop refined and varied coating emulsions and direct-films for the newly developed and precisely woven screen fabrics, other than silk. Methods of stretching the fabrics on specially constructed stretching machines and frames, the durability of direct screen, ease of preparation of direct screens, the processing latitude and economy of these screens, and the accuracy of registration of prints made with direct screens are some reasons for their use and acceptance.

Specifically, a direct screen is one that is prepared by applying a liquid emulsion, generally sensitized, directly on the screen fabric and then processing the emulsion on the fabric to produce the printing screen. Because the emulsion encapsulates and completely surrounds the screen fabric, direct screens are tough and resistant. They print sharp fine line halftones and other detail without ragged edges or serrations, if processed correctly. They produce long runs at high speeds, may be processed on all fabrics and meshes, print all types of inks including water-soluble (depending on the product), print on rough and also on very smooth stock, resist solvents, are safe to use, simple to prepare, and after printing, screen may be reclaimed.

---

*1. Kosloff, Albert, "Photographic Screen Printing Survey," *Technical Guidebook of the Screen Printing Industry*, Screen Printing Association, International, October, 1974; 2. "Survey Shows Use of Photostencils," *Screen Printing Magazine*, Volume 164, No. 3, (10/74), p41.

Varied direct products are available as unsensitized and presensitized emulsions with specific simple directions for their use. The unsensitized emulsions are available generally as a two-package product which consists of the emulsion and sensitizer. Some products are also supplied with a dye to be mixed with the emulsion and sensitizer, which may or may not be used by the printer, in preparing the sensitized emulsion. The dye aids in visible inspection and in washing out of the screen. The unsensitized emulsion has to be sensitized or mixed with the sensitizer by the printer. A presensitized emulsion coating does not have to be sensitized and may be coated directly onto the fabric.

The emulsions may be polyvinyl alcohol solutions, natural gelatinous substances, polyvinyl alcohol-polyvinyl acetate solutions, modified polyvinyl alcohol solutions, or combinations of synthetic products and gelatin products. The sensitizer part of the emulsion may consist of stock solutions of ammonium bichromate, potassium bichromate, or sodium bichromate (dichromate) in liquid or powder form, or of a diazo compound in liquid or powder form. Although the storage of sensitized emulsions depends on the recommendations of the manufacturer, diazo sensitized emulsions will keep longer than bichromate sensitized emulsions. (See Figure 42).

There are also unsensitized emulsion-coated nylon and polyester screen fabric for the preparation of direct screens. These have a very smooth, uniformly thick emulsion coating on one side of the fabric (underside or printing side of screen). After the fabric is correctly and tightly stretched onto the frame, the coating is sensitized and processed in similar manner to other direct screens.

Figure 42. A print made from a direct screen which was coated with a diazo sensitized emulsion and exposed 4 weeks later to a metal halide lamp for 4 minutes at a distance of 5 feet.

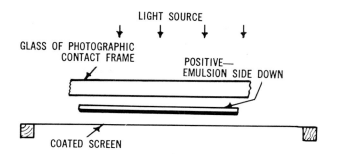

Figure 43. Arrangement of parts for exposing direct screen.

Generally, the processing procedure for direct screens consists of (1) preparation of emulsion, (2) coating of screen fabric, (3) drying coated screen, (4) exposing, and (5) washing out. It is best that processing be done under subdued incandescent light (15 watts or less) or under a yellow light and not in direct daylight or sunlight. Where the printer has to mix the sensitizer with the emulsion, he must do this as recommended in the directions for the product. The sensitizer is added to the unsensitized emulsion in exact proportions by volume or weight as specified by the manufacturer. Usually one part of sensitizer by volume is added or mixed well in 4 to 10 parts of the emulsion, depending on the specific product. Normally, the sensitizer is available as a liquid or as a powder to be dissolved in a specific volume of distilled or plain water to make a stock solution. The sensitized stock solution may be kept up to 3 months, if stored in a dark cool place in a dark brown or opaque bottle. It may be kept longer, if stored in a household type refrigerator. The unsensitized emulsion may be stored for a long time, if emulsion container is well stoppered. Although bichromate sensitized emulsions may keep for about a week, it is best that they be used within 4 to 6 hours. Diazo sensitized emulsions may be stored up to 3 months, and if stored in a refrigerator, may be kept longer, being careful not to freeze the emulsion.

Regardless whether the printer is preparing a direct, indirect, or direct-indirect screen, the screen fabric must be stretched tightly and cleaned and degreased before coating emulsion. The use of the cleaning and degreasing compounds which are available from screen printing suppliers, hardware stores, and often in super markets, should be a standard procedure in the preparation of screen fabric to assure that emulsions will adhere perfectly to the fabric.

The emulsion is generally applied with coaters of the type illustrated in Figures 67 and 68, or with a squeegee to the correct fabric and mesh, squeegeeing one or two strokes or applying the coating on the outside or underside of screen fabric first, then stroking the emulsion once on the inside or squeegee side, allowing the first coating to dry well. The number of coats applied depend on the fineness of the fabric, on the emulsion, and on the type of job to be printed. The ink thickness printed is determined by the type of fabric, the thread thickness, and the open surface of the fabric or mesh. For the average two coats may suffice, the second coat being applied on the underside of the screen. As many as five coats may be applied for a very resistant screen and also to produce a smoother coating on the underside of the screen. Each coat

45

must be dried completely before applying the next one and each coat must dry in the dark.

After the screen is dry, it is exposed, underside of screen in direct contact with emulsion side of positive, as illustrated in Figure 43. Any actinic light ordinarily used in printing shops such as carbon arcs, pulsed-xenon lamps, metal halide lamps, black light fluorescent units, or photoflood lamps may be employed. The exposing time will vary depending on the type of light, distance of light from screen, strength of light, type of copy being reproduced, and on the product being processed. While the manufacturer may recommend an exposure time for his product, it is best to conduct a test to determine the best exposure time and distance from light for the type of equipment one will be using. Coated stainless steel fabric may require more time in exposure.

While it is recommended that the screen be washed out immediately after screen is exposed or within an hour, a diazo sensitized screen may be kept longer.

The exposed screen may be washed out in cold or warm water; however, warm water about 110 degrees Fahrenheit (43 degrees Celsius) is often recommended for washing out. The screen is generally soaked first in water for about 1 to 2 minutes then sprayed with water first on the underside then on the inside of screen. The spraying should continue until design in fabric appears open and definitely clean and sharp. The fabric may then be blotted with newsprint paper. If exposure was done correctly, the washing out period should not be too long. A diazo-sensitized emulsion which has been stored for more than about 4 weeks may take longer to wash out.

Chapters 15 through 23 inclusive deal more specifically with direct screens and their processing.

6

CARBON TISSUE — INDIRECT OR TRANSFER TYPE PRINTING SCREEN

In screen printing photographic work the printer employs three types of mixtures: (1) true solutions; (2) colloidal solutions; and (3) suspensions. As is commonly known, a solution consists of a solvent or liquid and a solute or that part which dissolves or seems to disappear in the solvent. A solid, another liquid, or even a gas may be employed as a solute and dissolved in a solvent. The size of the particles or the material that is dissolved or suspended in the solvent is the distinguishing feature between the above three mixtures.

In a *true solution* the solute or particles break down into the smallest possible particles, as in the case of sugar or salt dissolving in water. A true solution does not separate out or settle upon standing, is the same throughout the solution, and when filtered or passed through a thin membrane will carry the dissolved material with it.

In the mixture known as a *suspension* the particles are suspended in the solvent and are large enough to settle out upon standing, as in the case of the pigments in some screen printing inks.

Colloidal solutions are in between the true solutions and suspensions. The particles of a colloidal solution are neither very small nor very large and are dispersed uniformly through the solution. They do not settle out upon standing, they tend to be cloudy, and in some cases may be seen under the microscope. Substances such as gelatin, glue, gum arabic, egg albumin, or polyvinyl alcohol disperse very uniformly or seem to dissolve in water and yet do not form true solutions. These substances are known by such terms as colloidal solutions, colloidal dispersions, colloidal suspensions, or just colloids. It is interesting to note that the term *colloid* which is derived from the Greek word "kolla" meaning glue, was first used to describe substances such as glue, gelatin, or albumin that would form a compact material when most of the liquid in the substance evaporated out.

Thus, we see that in screen printing colloids refer to substances whose particles will remain in suspension when dispersed in a solution. Once dispersed, these colloids have interesting properties.

Some of the aforementioned materials such as photographic gelatin or polyvinyl alcohol, either separately or in combination with other colloids, are used to make emulsions for photographic screens. When processed in exact proportions and mixed with a sensitizer — a substance that makes the colloid sensitive to light or affected by light — the colloid may be made tough or hard so that it will not be dissolved by water or other solvents.

These colloids may be applied directly to the screen fabric, as was common in the early days of photographic screen preparation, or they may be applied in the form of an even and controlled coating onto a pure paper or plastic backing sheet, as is common today. When this coating or emulsion is completely processed it is transferred from the backing sheet to the screen fabric of the printing screen.

Carbon tissue or *pigment paper* was one of the first used gelatinous substance or colloid for the making of photographic printing screens. Carbon tissue originated and was developed in England in the 1860's by such men as Mungo Ponton, Joseph Wilson Swan, and J. R. Johnson and originally was employed for making printing plates for printing on textiles, wallpaper, and other items. It was and still is produced and used as a resist in the rotogravure and photogravure printing processes. In the late 1920's through the efforts of such men as Harry L. Hiett in the United States and Sidney James Waters of England, carbon tissue began to be employed in the screen printing field. Because the element carbon is found in great proportion in the mixture and because carbon was one of the first pigments used for tissue, this type of colloid has become known as carbon tissue. In the trade, therefore, the gelatinous coating or emulsion together with the backing sheet is known as carbon tissue.

Carbon tissue was and is a common medium for the preparation of photographic printing screens. It may be employed for reproducing line copy, detailed copy, halftone work, color separation work, and is economical. It stresses basic procedures, is practical for preparing screens on silk fabric, and is a good screen for the beginner. Because of its versatility and simplicity of preparation, it may be used in the small shop and in the large shop for printing anything from the size of a postage stamp to that of a large twenty-four sheet poster.

Generally, the tissue consisting of a soluble gelatin, a pigment or dye for coloring, some glycerine, and other ingredients for making the coating pliable and for improving its processing qualities are applied to a strong paper or a very thin transparent plastic backing sheet such as vinylite. Although most printers use the grades of tissue made expressly for the screen printing trade, carbon tissue of good quality made for the graphic arts industry may be used for screen printing. Carbon tissue is sold unsensitized and is available from screen printing suppliers and graphic arts establishments in varied sheet sizes and rolls up to 40 inches in width and 12 feet in length. Thus, the printer has a choice of sizes for preparing any size screen. Although the tissue is available in about 30 colors, most common colors are green, oxide red, brownish black, blue, and black.

Manufacturers of carbon tissue recommend that it be kept in a cool dry place and in the container in which it was sold. Although it is not necessary, large shops which have refrigerators often store tissue in them. Unused carbon tissue should not be allowed to be stored in a very damp warm place for long periods of time, as this may make the tissue insoluble. Good working atmospheric conditions for carbon tissue are about 65 to 70 degrees Fahrenheit (18 to 21 degrees Celsius) with about 55 to 65 percent humidity. If the printer is in doubt as to the qualities of stored carbon tissue, it is suggested that he process a sample of the stored tissue in the usual required manner before attempting a necessary and required job. Generally, tissue does not deteriorate under ordinary shop conditions and may be kept for long periods of time.

General preparation of tissue involves making the tissue sensitive to light by immersing it in a solution made up of water and a given amount of a salt known as potassium bichromate or a salt known as ammonium bichromate. A photographic positive or negative containing the design is placed in contact with the sensitized carbon tissue and the two exposed to a strong light, the light striking the positive side first. The parts of the sensitized tissue which are exposed to light or struck by light are hardened; those parts in the photographic positive which are opaque will not allow the light to penetrate and affect the tissue. The unexposed parts in the tissue which are soft are dissolved away with warm water leaving the design of the positive in the carbon tissue. While still wet the processed tissue may be made to adhere to surfaces such as glass, plastics, metal, paper, fabrics, or silk.

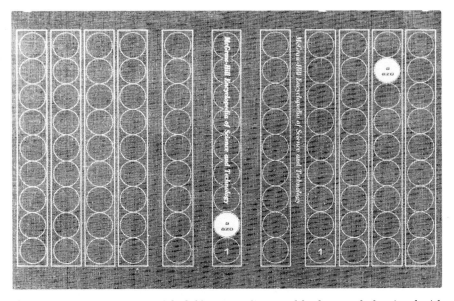

Figure 44. A 20" × 27" piece of dark blue pyroxylin coated book cover cloth printed with yellow and white ink. Photographic printing screens prepared by the "wet" method were used to print the colors. (Courtesy of Superior Silk Screen Industries, Inc., Chicago, Illinois).

Although there are variations to the methods which are used by manufacturers and printers to prepare carbon tissue, the two most common methods that have been standardized are known as the wet-exposure method and the dry-exposure method or just wet and dry method. In the wet method the carbon tissue is in a wet or damp state when it is exposed to light; in the dry method, of course, the tissue is dry when it is exposed. In both methods a temporary support is needed to hold the sensitized tissue while it is being

49

processed. Both methods are known as the "transfer method," since the tissue is prepared on the temporary support first and then transferred to the underside of the screen fabric.

Because any standardized process implies a procedure which generally does not vary and implies certain standardizing of material and equipment during processing, it is imperative that the printer become acquainted with every step in the process and follow the manufacturer's direction for a specific carbon tissue.

Figure 44 presents a screen print produced from a carbon tissue printing screen.

7

WET CARBON TISSUE METHOD

The carbon tissue method is one of the major sources for perpetuating the durable features of the industrial heritage of screen printing. Essentially, the wet carbon tissue method or the wet exposure method of preparing printing screens is a "transfer method." This implies that sensitized carbon tissue is first prepared on a temporary support or directly on the photographic positive containing the design to be reproduced. Then the tissue is exposed, washed out, and transferred from the temporary support and attached to the underside of the screen fabric of the printing screen. The wet method is the most used by printers because it is somewhat less complicated to carry out, since it eliminates several steps and does produce a shorter processing time. Also, since wet sensitized tissue is "slower," that is, it is not affected by light as quickly, as the dry tissue in the dry exposure method, wet tissue may be handled under ordinary incandescent lamp type of illumination.

Screens prepared with this method may be employed for detail printing or solid area printing and for printing with almost any screen printing ink except water-soluble ones. In order to insure consistent uniformity the printer should think through the steps of the process and have all material and equipment necessary before starting the preparation of the plate. The process is definitely not complicated. Generally, the steps involved are: (1) preparation of screen fabric; (2) preparation of carbon tissue; (3) exposing; (4) washing-out; and (5) attaching of tissue to screen fabric.

The following materials and equipment which are obtainable from any screen printing supplier should be available and ready: (1) carbon tissue; (2) photographic positive containing the design; (3) photographic contact frame or a vacuum type frame for holding tissue during exposure; (4) a light source for exposing; (5) sensitizer; (6) opaque masking tape or aluminum foil; (7) two or three glass, porcelain finished, stainless steel, or bakelite trays deep enough and large enough to hold carbon tissue and sensitizer; (8) a water source with a mixing faucet attachment so that hot, warm, and cold water may be readily obtained; (9) a squeegee or roller for squeegeeing or rolling down the sensitized tissue onto the temporary support; (10) a temporary support for holding carbon tissue while it is being processed; (11) wax, if the temporary support has to be waxed and polished; (12) an electric fan; (13) a sheet of glass or thick cardboard to serve as a layer under screen fabric when attaching tissue to fabric; and (14) a screen stretched with the correct type fabric.

51

Preparation of Screen Fabric

The inside dimensions of the screen should be about 4 to 6 inches longer and wider than the stock or material upon which the design is to be printed. Up to the late 1940's silk was used exclusively for screen printing, with some metal fabrics used for specialty work. Silk is a natural multifilament and carbon tissue and gelatin emulsions adhered well to it. Number 12 to Number 18 silk of good quality (about XX quality) may be used with Number 14 silk being employed for most jobs. Number 16 and 18 silks may be employed where fine detail and halftones are to be reproduced. However, equivalent numbered nylon, polyester, and metal fabrics (150 mesh and up per inch) may be used.

If the silk is new, it should be thoroughly washed with soap and water and rinsed off with warm and cold water to remove sizing and other particles. Where a screen is being reused, the printer must assure that all traces of oils, inks, solvents, etc. are completely removed and cleaned off, especially in the areas where carbon tissue is to be adhered, before starting the job.

New nylon, polyester, and metal fabrics should first be roughened very carefully with microscopic abrasive powders or pastes, on the underside of the screen fabric, rubbing with a soft cloth, using little pressure, and then rinsing perfectly with water. The abrasive products are available from suppliers. However, every time these fabrics are reused, they should be degreased with degreasing agents or solutions.

As far as metal fabric is concerned, the pioneer printer held the metal fabric in a direct flame to burn off the dirt and protective oil coating which normally may be found on the new fabric. This was an aid in the adhering of gelatinous emulsions to metal fabric. Since the burning-off process must be done very carefully so as not to distort and damage the fabric, it is recommended that beginners use more modern methods of cleaning and degreasing.

Preparation of Carbon Tissue

Preparation of carbon tissue for exposing involves sensitizing it and squeegeeing or rolling it onto a temporary support. The purpose of sensitizing the carbon tissue is to make it sensitive to light so that desirable parts in the emulsion will be hardened when exposed to light and will not wash away when immersed in hot water. The temporary support, as the name signifies, is used to hold the carbon tissue while it is being processed and exposed.

The sensitizing solution is made by dissolving dry, granulated, or powdered potassium bichromate or ammonium bichromate in water. Although distilled water is used in many shops, any water that is good enough to drink may be employed for this purpose. A 2 to 4 percent solution is generally used. Potassium bichromate is most generally used because it is more economical. Photographic, (C.P.) chemically pure, or (A.R.) analytical reagent type of bichromate is recommended.

When the sensitizing solution is mixed the bichromate is added to the required volume of cold water, making sure that the powder is completely dissolved. Any of the following formulae may be employed: (a) 2½ ounces of potassium bichromate by weight to a gallon of water; (b) 20 grams of potassium bichromate dissolved in 1000 cubic centimeters (1 liter) of water; or (c) approximately three level teaspoons of powder or granules of potassium bichromate per quart of water will make up a correct solution.

52

Although it is not common, inasmuch as the sensitizing solution used is weak, there are some individuals who are susceptible to chemical skin poisoning or chromic poisoning (dermatitis). Therefore, the individual who is susceptible and expects to use and mix many solutions is encouraged to wear rubber gloves.

The mixed sensitizing solution should be stored in a dark colored glass container, should be well stoppered, and kept in a cool place. It is suggested that the sensitizing solution be used when it is about one or two days old. The sensitized stock solution will keep for at least a month, if stored in a cool dry place; it will keep longer if stored in a household type refrigerator. If sediment accumulates in the sensitizer during storage, it is recommended that the solution be filtered through layers of silk. For best results the temperature of the sensitizing solution should be between 40 and 65 degrees Fahrenheit (4 to 18 degrees Celsius). The solution may be cooled in a refrigerator or just by allowing cold water to run over the glass container before being used.

The temporary support most commonly employed for holding the sensitized tissue is a transparent Mylar* or Vinylite** sheet from .002″ to .005″ in thickness, since carbon tissue will release easily from them and these sheets do not require waxing and polishing as is necessary when other plastic temporary supports such as cellulose acetate or cellulose nitrate are used. Some printers also wax and polish vinylite supports. However, the temporary support sheets should be well washed with soap and water and rinsed off well with water before using. These temporary supports may be used over and over. It is suggested, to distinguish the temporary supports from other plastic sheets, that a corner or a "V" be cut in one of the edges of the support.

A photographic positive may be used as a temporary support. However, it is suggested that the positive be coated with a vinyl lacquer. If a positive is coated with other type transparent coatings such as clear spraying lacquer, collodion, lacquer, or even varnish, then the coating will have to be waxed and polished perfectly to prevent the gelatinous emulsion in carbon tissue from sticking to the positive coating. Any good quality wax having a high melting point may be used. The wax for waxing and polishing the coating may be obtained from screen printing supply establishments. The use of the coated positive and the temporary support and the placing of the sensitized carbon tissue in direct contact with the positive during exposure, produces more accurate reproduction and eliminates a photographic contact frame.

The temporary support should be left to chill in cold water before the sensitizing operation is begun.

In sensitizing carbon tissue, cut a piece of tissue about one inch longer and wider than the design in positive, immerse the tissue in the chilled sensitizing solution, gelatinous side up, and immediately rub over surface either with the hand or with rubber glove, if gloves are worn, to remove any air bubbles, to insure even sensitizing, and to enable one to use as short a sensitizing period as possible. It has been discovered that carbon tissue sensitized at about 45 degrees Fahrenheit (7 degrees Celsius) will be considerably faster than carbon tissue sensitized at 75 degrees Fahrenheit (24 degrees Celsius). The time of sensitizing is considered to be from about the moment the carbon tissue is immersed in the sensitizer to the time it is squeegeed

---

*E. I. Dupont de Nemours and Co., Inc., Wilm ington, Del.
**Union Carbide and Carbon Corp., New York, N.Y.

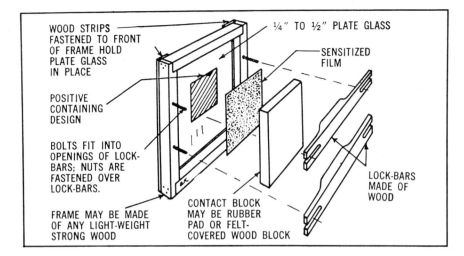

WOOD STRIPS
FASTENED TO FRONT
OF FRAME HOLD
PLATE GLASS
IN PLACE

¼" TO ½" PLATE GLASS

SENSITIZED
FILM

POSITIVE
CONTAINING
DESIGN

BOLTS FIT INTO
OPENINGS OF LOCK-
BARS; NUTS ARE
FASTENED OVER
LOCK-BARS.

LOCK-BARS
MADE OF
WOOD

FRAME MAY BE MADE
OF ANY LIGHT-WEIGHT
STRONG WOOD

CONTACT BLOCK
MAY BE RUBBER
PAD OR FELT-
COVERED WOOD BLOCK

*Figure 45. A photographic contact unit which the processor may make easily for expos-
ing carbon tissue and film type photographic screen printing plates.*

onto the temporary support. The tissue should soak from 1 to 3 minutes.
Prolonged soaking may impair the adhesion of tissue to temporary support.

After the tissue has been sensitized, it is withdrawn carefully and immediately centered over the cleaned or waxed and polished temporary support,
emulsion side down, and squeegeed over the backing sheet of the carbon
tissue into perfect contact with a squeegee or roller, rolling from the center
outward, pressing out the excess sensitizer and making sure that there are no
air bubbles between tissue and support. The excess bichromate solution
should be removed from the back of the backing sheet and the front of the
support should be wiped off also.

Exposing

Place the support and tissue so that the support is in contact with emulsion side of positive. Place support and positive in photographic contact frame
or vacuum printing frame so that light strikes positive, then support, and
finally tissue. Although larger shops employ vacuum frames for this purpose,
the writer has had practical results with the unit illustrated in Figure 45.
However, it is suggested that the printer put a ½" to 1" thick piece of rubber
foam between contact block and sensitized film in Figure 45 to obtain perfect
contact between film and positive.

Before exposing, it is necessary to insure that a "safe edge," opaque
border, or unexposed edge is made along the edges of the tissue so that
backing sheet of carbon tissue will be easily removed during the hot water
wash-out process. This safe edge may be made with opaque tape on the
photographic contact frame glass directly over tissue or directly over positive
as illustrated in Figure 46, or with pieces of aluminum foil as shown in
Figure 47. The aluminum foil tends to keep printing frame and tissue cooler
by reflecting away some of the light energy which has a tendency to melt the
tissue.

54

When the tissue is exposed it is suggested that the light be about 30 inches (76cm) or more away from the contact frame or positive. Manufacturers of carbon tissue recommend that the distance from light source be at least as far as twice the diagonal of the design. See Figure 46. Practical light sources are single carbon arc lamps, "black light" illuminators, pulsed-xenon lamps, double arc lamps, Number 2 photoflood lamps, and sunlight. Practical light sources which have and are being used are the single arc lamp, black light illuminators and mercury vapor lamps. Regardless of what light source the screen printer uses, he will have to standardize exposing procedures on his equipment. If the light employed emanates heat, then the heat must be dissipated by means of a fan blowing against the contact frame or by placing a piece of special heat absorbing glass between light source and tissue. The wet carbon tissue will melt if it becomes too warm during exposure.

Another precaution is to make sure that all parts are clean, especially the frame glass. The glass should be free of dust particles as these may cause pinholes when the tissue is finally processed.

If a single arc 35 ampere white flame type lamp is used, the sensitized tissue may be exposed for about 10 minutes at a distance of about 4 feet. If strong sunlight is employed, 1½ minutes will suffice. A 15 ampere arc lamp will necessitate an exposure from about 12 to 15 minutes at a distance of about 30 inches. If a Number 2 photoflood lamp is used for exposure light,

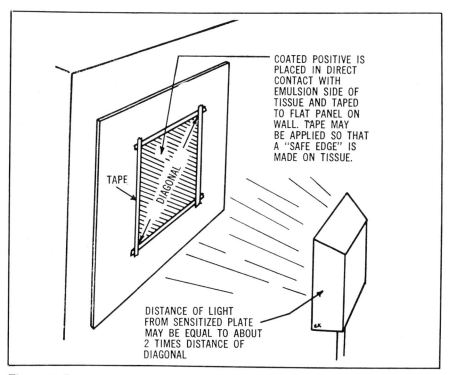

Figure 46. Exposing carbon tissue by placing it under and in direct contact with coated positive.

55

then about 10 minutes exposure may be given at a distance of about 30 inches. Where black light illumination is used the exposing unit may be about 3 inches away from the light source, since the light energy given off is a cool type. Regardless of the type of light and the manufacturer's recommendation some experimenting on the part of the printer will be necessary before he can be sure of a standardized distance of exposure and time.

Washing-Out

After the tissue has been exposed, the temporary support with the tissue is removed and immersed in a tray of water that is about 110 degrees Fahrenheit (43 degrees Celsius). When the colored gelatin in the tissue begins to ooze out at the edges after about one-half minute in the water, the backing sheet may be peeled away carefully. The temporary support should then be agitated slightly to dissolve away the unexposed parts of the gelatin. When all the soluble parts of the tissue seem to have dissolved, the temporary support with the washed-out tissue on it is placed in a tray of cool water that is about 65 to 70 degrees Fahrenheit (18 to 21 degrees Celsius). It is recommended that the tissue be held in the water no more than 5 minutes.

If too long an exposure has been given, the design in the gelatinous coating will cling to the backing sheet making it difficult to remove the backing sheet in the warm water. However, where exposure is long but not too long, printers who do much preparation of this type of screen, generally swab the backing sheet with alcohol before immersing the unit in hot water.

Attaching Tissue to Screen Fabric

After the image on the temporary support is completely washed out, the support is drained and laid flat, tissue side up, on a piece of glass or thick cardboard smaller than the inside dimensions of the screen fabric. The underside of the screen is then centered over the tissue and lowered in contact with the tissue. Excess moisture is blotted out on the inside of the silk with newsprint or blotting paper. The blotter or paper may be laid on the inside of the screen over the tissue part and a hand roller rolled over the paper lightly, repeating the rolling process with clean pieces of paper several times. If no color shows on the blotting paper, it indicates that the tissue is too hard and may break down easily after some impressions are printed. Pressing hard on the roller may destroy fine detail by forcing the gelatinous emulsion through the screen fabric.

After all the moisture has been removed, the frame is weighted down so that fabric will press into tissue and tissue and fabric are allowed to dry.

If it is necessary to hasten drying, a fan may be employed, but it is recommended that heat not be used at this stage.

Normally, there is no trouble and the gelatin will adhere to the fabric. However, if the fabric is too loose, is oily or dirty, or if the carbon tissue has been developed in water that is too hot so that the top layer of the partly exposed gelatin has been washed off, the tissue may not adhere well to the screen fabric.

When the image and fabric are completely dry, the temporary support is gently peeled away; in many instances the support will release itself. If a positive has been used as the temporary support, it also will release, since it

56

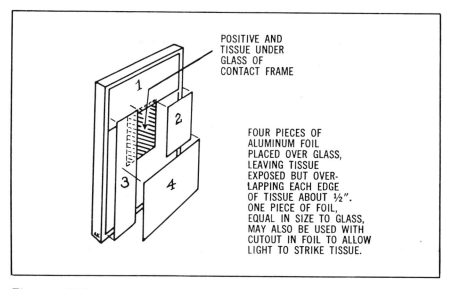

POSITIVE AND
TISSUE UNDER
GLASS OF
CONTACT FRAME

FOUR PIECES OF
ALUMINUM FOIL
PLACED OVER GLASS,
LEAVING TISSUE
EXPOSED BUT OVER-
LAPPING EACH EDGE
OF TISSUE ABOUT ½".
ONE PIECE OF FOIL,
EQUAL IN SIZE TO GLASS,
MAY ALSO BE USED WITH
CUTOUT IN FOIL TO ALLOW
LIGHT TO STRIKE TISSUE.

Figure 47. Making "safe edge" on carbon tissue by placing aluminum foil over contact frame glass.

was waxed and polished to prevent the tissue from sticking to the coated and polished positive. The rest of the screen fabric may then be blocked out with the desired filler, depending on the ink to be printed, and the screen made ready for printing.

Reclaiming Screen

Before reclaiming the screen it is essential that all ink and solvents be cleaned away perfectly from the screen. When cleaning a photographic screen, generally, the cleaning is done from the inside of the screen. When all of the ink has been completely removed and washed out on the inside or top side of the screen, then the underside is dabbed with cotton or with soft lintless cloths that have been dipped in correct solvent and the screen allowed to dry and to be used again.

The gelatinous emulsion or tissue may be removed from the fabric with commercial enzyme type cleaners which digest the film away without doing any harm to the fabric. Generally, these cleaners are dissolved in the right volume of water according to the manufacturer's recommendation and the tissue part of the screen may be soaked over night in the cleaning solution. In the morning the screen is just rinsed off with cold water and the screen is ready for the next job. Another method of removing the gelatinous coating is to wet both sides of screen over image area with hot water to swell and warm the gelatin. Then the screen may be placed on a flat surface and the screen sprinkled sparingly with a film remover powder or enzyme powder over the silk side or inside of screen. The sprinkled areas may then be swabbed with a clean cloth that has been wetted with hot water that is about 90 to 110 degrees Fahrenheit (32 to 43 degrees Celsius). After about 5 minutes, or as soon as enough of the gelatin has been dissolved to break away from the screen, the coating may be washed off with hot water. Uncoated tissue may also be removed by soaking the screen in hot water which has a small amount of bleach added to it. Another cleaning solution for reclaiming carbon tissue screens may be made by dissolving one tablespoonful of sodium carbonate and 2½ ounces of a bleach in a gallon of water. The soaked fabric is then scrubbed off with a suede type brush, rubbing gently with the brush, and being careful not to get the solution on one's clothing, as the bleach solution may form spots on clothing.

Regardless of the method employed to reclaim or remove films and emulsions from fabric, the screen fabric must finally be rinsed off thoroughly with water to assure that no trace of the reclaiming agent is left in the mesh. If any should be left, the reclaiming agent may interfere with the correct adhering of future films or emulsions.

DRY CARBON TISSUE METHOD

As has been mentioned, the carbon tissue method of preparing screen printing plates offers the screen printer both a wet and dry method of making screens. The dry exposure method of preparing carbon tissue does not vary much from the wet method. The main difference between the two is that in the wet exposure method the sensitized carbon tissue is exposed while it is in a damp or wet condition while in the dry method the sensitized tissue is dried and then exposed.

The dry method offers a main advantage — one does not have to guard against the melting of the tissue while it is being exposed. Wet tissue begins to melt at about 82 degrees Fahrenheit (28 degrees Celsius); dry tissue will char at high temperatures but will not melt regardless of the temperature. This is an aid, especially in the hot climates where atmospheric conditions are difficult to control. The dry method may also be employed when the slower exposure of the wet process does not produce sufficient density. Also, the dry tissue may be in absolute contact with the positive or negative and does not have to be separated from the positive by the thickness of the temporary support, as is common in the wet exposure method. More than one positive or negative may be ganged up and exposed in the dry method. This method renders true results and gives a sharp and clean definition of detail and lines. Still another advantage is that enough tissue may be sensitized and dried to last for several days and used as necessary.

Like the wet method, the dry carbon tissue method is a transfer type process and does require a temporary support which is employed for holding sensitized tissue while it is drying and for washing out after tissue is exposed. The temporary support may be any smooth sheet of vinyl or acrylic plastic (Plexiglas or Lucite) about 1/16″ in thickness. Sheets thinner than about .050″ may not be stiff enough to withstand contraction of the drying of the carbon tissue backing sheet. The latter supports are recommended, since they do not require waxing and polishing in order to prevent tissue from sticking to support. Although any colored opaque or transparent sheet may be used, some printers employ white because of contrast created to tissue. Other materials that may be employed for the temporary support are stainless steel, polished brass, tin plate, zinc sheet, cellulose nitrate, or cellulose acetate. However, the latter materials must be thoroughly cleaned, waxed with a ferrotype wax which is obtainable from screen printing suppliers, and polished perfectly with soft cloths before using temporary support.

```
┌────────────────────────────────────────────────────────┐
│              WET METHOD PROCEDURE:                       │
│      1. Sensitizing tissue                               │
│      2. Squeegeeing sensitized tissue onto temporary sup-│
│   port                                                   │
│      3. Exposing WET tissue                              │
│      4. Washing out in hot water and removing backing    │
│   sheet                                                  │
│      5. Attaching developed tissue to screen fabric      │
│              DRY METHOD PROCEDURE:                       │
│      1. Sensitizing tissue                               │
│      2. Squeegeeing sensitized tissue onto temporary sup-│
│   port                                                   │
│      3. Drying and removing sensitized tissue from tempo-│
│   rary support                                           │
│      4. Exposing DRY tissue                              │
│      5. Immersing exposed tissue in cold water and squeegee-│
│   ing it onto temporary support                          │
│      6. Washing out in hot water and removing backing    │
│   sheet                                                  │
│      7. Attaching developed tissue to screen fabric      │
└────────────────────────────────────────────────────────┘
```

Figure 48. Comparison of wet and dry exposure methods.

As illustrated in Figure 48, the main steps in the dry carbon tissue procedure are sentizing of tissue, drying, exposing, wetting and removing backing sheet, developing, and attaching tissue to screen fabric.

Sensitizing of Tissue

Although the sensitizing process is similar to the wet method, in the dry method the sensitizing bath is of a lower concentration, to prevent the tendency of veiling over the finer open parts of the tissue. It is suggested that a 1 to 1½ percent solution be employed for sensitizing. The solution should be chilled either in a refrigerator or by running cold water over the container before immersing tissue in solution. Although granulated or powdered potassium bichromate is generally used for preparing the solution, ammonium bichromate or sodium bichromate may also be employed. It is recommended that once a bichromate solution is used for sensitizing that it not be stored for further use. For the dry method nothing else is necessary but a bichromate salt and water to prepare the solution.

The following formulae may be used for preparing the solution: (1) 2 ounces of potassium bichromate completely dissolved in 1 gallon of water; (2) 10 to 15 grams of potassium bichromate in 1000 cubic centimeters (1 liter) of water; or (3) two level teaspoonsful of the bichromate salt may be completely dissolved in a quart of cool water. The unused sensitizer may be kept for a long time if stored in a dark brown glass container in a cool place or in a refrigerator. The solution should be strained through a piece of silk before using.

60

Either a piece of carbon tissue may be cut that is just large enough for the job at hand or a large sheet may be sensitized and pieces cut from it after the sheet is dried. However, the dried and sensitized sheet must be stored in the dark, darkroom, or between blotters or cardboard. As in the wet method, the tissue should be immersed, gelatinous side up, in the chilled solution and one's hand be rubbed over the emulsion side immediately to insure even and quicker sensitizing. After the tissue is sensitized, which will take from about 1 to 3 minutes, it is placed emulsion side down onto the cool support and squeegeed firmly in contact with the support. The excess moisture is wiped off from the tissue side and from the other side of the support and the tissue is allowed to dry.

Drying

It is recommended that the support and tissue be left alone for about 5 minutes to give the tissue a chance to adhere to the support and to prevent its lifting away when placed in front of a fan. Although the tissue may be dried in a dimly lighted room, it is best to dry it in a darkroom; fluorescent, ultra-violet light, or daylight must be kept away from it. In drying, the flow of air from the fan must be even to prevent one part of the sheet from lifting off while the other is still drying and attached to the support. The sensitized sheet will generally strip off by itself in 30 to 90 minutes depending on atmospheric conditions. However, if it does not then it may be snapped off by inserting the fingernail under one corner. No heat should be employed in the drying of the tissue; just a fan alone should be used. If possible, the drying temperature should not be greater than about 75 degrees Fahrenheit (24 degrees Celsius) to prevent reticulation of the gelatinous emulsion or the formation of a net-like structure in the gelatin.

Exposing and Developing

Although the dry sensitized tissue may be kept for several days, it is best to expose it as soon as possible. In exposing, the tissue is placed in the photographic contact frame or vacuum frame with the gelatinous side in absolute

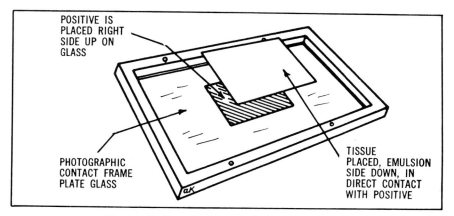

Figure 49. Exposing sensitized dry carbon tissue.

contact with the emulsion side of the positive or negative and the unit locked. See Figure 49. A series of exposures on a single piece of tissue will determine for the processor the practical time and distance of exposure and the desired thickness of tissue. Extreme overexposure will harden the gelatinuous emulsion through to the backing sheet and make it difficult to strip off backing sheet in water before developing. Following are practical exposures; a 3 minutes exposure to a 30 ampere arc lamp at a distance of 30 inches; 12 minutes to a 30 ampere arc lamp at a distance of 40 inches; 18 minutes to a Number 2 photoflood lamp at a distance of 36 inches. For halftone work the tissue may be exposed at the same distance and light source but the time should be decreased about one-third.

After the dry tissue is exposed, it is removed from the contact frame and immediately is submerged in cold water for 1½ to 2 minutes or until tissue flattens out. It is then removed from the water and quickly squeegeed, emulsion side down, onto the clean temporary support.

The support and tissue are then immersed and left in hot water that is about 110 degrees Fahrenheit (43 degrees Celsius) for about 5 minutes and the backing sheet is then stripped off carefully, leaving the emulsion on the support.

The image in the gelatinous emulsion is developed or washed out by rocking the support carefully in the hot water. After the image is developed out, the support with the emulsion is chilled in cold water and the emulsion is then ready for attachment to the underside of the screen fabric.

Some printers wet the exposed tissue by soaking it until it flattens out in a 60 degree Fahrenheit solution (16 degrees Celsius) consisting of water and 25 to 50 percent isopropyl alcohol. Then the tissue is squeegeed in contact with the support. After five minutes and after the excess moisture is wiped off, the backing sheet is swabbed with alcohol and the support and tissue are developed as explained above.

The rest of the procedure is similar to the wet carbon tissue method.

In summary, it must be noted that the dry carbon tissue method, if processed correctly and with care, renders true and very sharp details in printing because the film surface is in direct contact with the positive during exposure of positive with carbon tissue.

DIRECT-INDIRECT OR
DIRECT-FILM PRINTING SCREEN

One of the first photographic printing screens attempted by this writer was the preparation of a direct screen by placing a silk screen on a thin waxed and polished celluloid sheet and coating the inside of the screen over the celluloid with a solution of sensitized gelatin. This was a clumsy way of preparing a screen and after many trials produced a screen that could be used. Today's screen printer is more fortunate; he may choose commercially available products which are easy to prepare, are of uniform formulation, and give excellent results, if prepared according to manufacturer's directions.

The 1960's have produced a printing screen known as a direct-indirect, direct-film, or film-fluid product. This product consists of two parts — an unsensitized film on a plastic or paper support and a liquid emulsion. The direct-indirect film is adhered, sensitized, and processed directly on the screen fabric; unlike the transfer type film, it is not processed on a temporary support. Manufacturers of the direct-indirect screen stress the following advantages for these screens*. The product combines both the durability of a direct screen and the sharp printing qualities of a transfer or indirect screen. The film bridges and encapsulates the mesh, resulting in good adhesion of film to screen fabric. The thickness of the film (which is about .5 to 2 mills) is predetermined and does not depend on coating procedures. A more perfect image is produced with little change of light undercutting, since adhered film is in perfect contact during exposure and does not have a temporary support between it and the positive. An unsensitized film can be adhered to screens hours or days before sensitizing and exposing. If prepared on nylon, polyester, and stainless steel, the film may be reclaimed. While it may be removed from silk, depending on the type of direct-film, the same solvent that will remove the film may damage the silk. Shrinkage during drying period occurs on the inside of the screen which tends to produce better registration of colors during printing. The screen is prepared with a minimum of effort. It may be processed under subdued light, but once the film is adhered and sensitized to the screen fabric, screen and film must dry in light-proof or dark areas.

Any fine or coarse fabric such as nylon, polyester, monofilament and multifilament fabrics, metal fabrics and silk may be used. Red, yellow, and amber color screen fabrics may even produce sharper images. The film will

---

*Autotype Co., Ltd., London, England; Chroma-Glo, Duluth, Minnesota; Establissements Tiflex, Poncin, France; General Formulations, Sparta, Michigan; McGraw Colorgraph Co., Burbank, California; Ulano Products Co., Inc., New York, New York.

adhere to any cleaned and degreased fabric, since the film and emulsion impregnate the fabric. If processed correctly, the screen may be used to print on rough surfaces as well as to produce thousands of finely detailed and large area impressions. Films are available in sheet sizes, in very wide and long rolls, and in such colors as light blue, violet, red, black, and transparent. The dry unsensitized film may be stored in its original container in a dry area.

Preparation of Sensitized Emulsion

As has been mentioned, the direct-film product consists of two parts: the unsensitized dry film and a liquid sensitizing emulsion. Normally, the sensitized emulsion is prepared by the printer. The preparation of the emulsion sensitizer is done simply by adding the supplied liquid or powder sensitizer to the unsensitized emulsion according to manufacturer's directions*. Ammon-

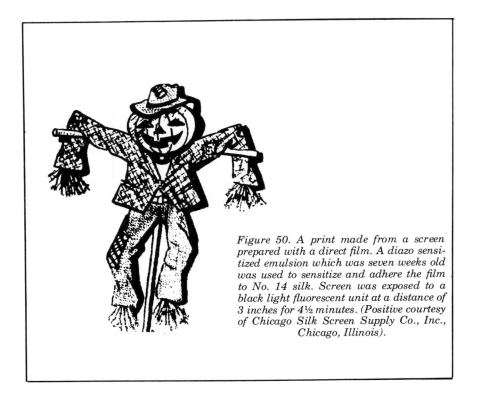

Figure 50. A print made from a screen prepared with a direct film. A diazo sensitized emulsion which was seven weeks old was used to sensitize and adhere the film to No. 14 silk. Screen was exposed to a black light fluorescent unit at a distance of 3 inches for 4½ minutes. (Positive courtesy of Chicago Silk Screen Supply Co., Inc., Chicago, Illinois).

*Examples of some sensitizers are: (1) 4 ounces of ammonium bichromate powder in 1 pint of warm water (113 grams in .47 liters); then use 1 part of sensitizing solution with 5 parts of emulsion by volume. (2) A 30% solution of ammonium bichromate (300 grams of bichromate in 1 liter of distilled water. (3) A 52% solution of sodium bichromate, (4) A 15% solution of ammonium bichromate.

64

ium bichromate, sodium bichromate, or diazo sensitizers are used as sensitizers. A water solution of the sensitizer, of a percentage recommended by the manufacturer of the product is added to the unsensitized emulsion in volumes such as 1 part sensitizer to 5 parts of emulsion or 1 part sensitizer to 6 parts emulsion, depending on the product. The sensitized emulsion must be well stirred and kept in a dark cool area or in a household type refrigerator to increase its shelf life. Diazo sensitized emulsions may be kept for 3 months, longer if stored in a refrigerator. Unsensitized or sensitized emulsions must be kept from freezing.

Although silk fabric was used as illustrated in Figure 50, any screen fabric may be used for this type of screen. However, it must be stretched tightly and precleaned and degreased correctly before adhering film to it.

Once the sensitized emulsion is ready and the screen fabric has been cleaned correctly the printer may continue with the processing steps which consist of (1) sensitizing and adhering film, (2) exposing, and (3) washing out. The same equipment is used for the preparation of this screen as for a direct screen.

Sensitizing and Adhering Film

A sheet of film slightly smaller than the inside dimensions of the screen is cut. Then the film is placed, emulsion side up, on a perfectly flat surface such as glass, plastic, or cardboard. The screen is placed on film so that underside of fabric is in perfect contact with film as shown in Figure 51. A little of the sensitized emulsion is poured in at one end, on the inside of the screen, and the emulsion is stroked slowly just back and forth with a soft squeegee having rounded edges, making sure that good adhesion of film and screen is obtained. Generally only one coat of the sensitized emulsion should be used. The squeegeeing of the liquid emulsion should fill the mesh completely and produce the same color all over the film. Where stainless steel is used for the fabric, one or two extra strokes may be applied and slightly more emulsion may be used.

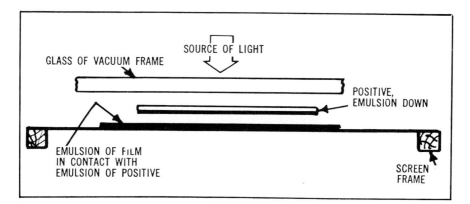

Figure 51. Arrangement of adhered and sensitized direct-film and positive in exposing.

65

Direct-Indirect or Direct-Film Printing Screens

Where the printer is planning to use a screen for extremely long runs, he may apply a second coating, waiting about 1 minute after application of first coat. The second coat is applied on the inside of the screen with one slow stroke, waiting 5 minutes before moving screen.

After the screen has been coated and film adhered the screen is allowed to dry. The writer allows screens to dry more, especially screens sensitized with diazo emulsions, after support or backing sheet has been removed. This extra drying tends to produce a tougher screen.

Drying Screen and Film

The screen may be allowed to dry naturally or with the aid of a fan in the dark. If the screen is to be exposed immediately after drying, the support or backing sheet must be removed from the film, starting the peeling in one corner. After the backing sheet is removed, the screen is ready for exposing.

Exposing

Durability of screen depends on correct exposure to light. The screen is exposed in similar fashion to direct screens, by placing emulsion side of positive in perfect direct contact with film on underside of screen as illustrated in Figure 51. Any actinic light ordinarily used in exposing screens such as pulsed-xenon lamps, metal halide lamps, carbon arcs, black light fluorescent units, or photoflood lamps may be employed. While the exposing time may vary from about 1 to 10 minutes, depending on the type of light, distance of light from screen, strength of light, and on type of copy being reproduced, each manufacturer may recommend an exposure time for his product. However, it is easy to conduct a test to determine the best exposure time and distance from light for the type of equipment one will be using. Stainless steel fabric may require more exposure time.

Washing Out

While it is recommended that screen be washed out immediately or within an hour after screen has been exposed, a diazo sensitized screen may be kept longer, if stored in the dark.

The screen may be washed out in cold or warm water that is about 110 degrees Fahrenheit (43 degrees Celsius). The screen may be soaked in water for about 1 to 2 minutes then sprayed with water, first on the underside then on the inside of the screen. The gentle spraying should continue until design in the screen fabric is clean and sharp. If the exposure has been done correctly, the washing out period will not be too long. Diazo sensitized screens which have been stored for long periods of time may take longer to washout.

After the screen is washed out, it is blotted with newsprint paper or blotting paper, the screen is dried, and the open spots or areas outside the design areas are coated with the excess sensitized emulsion. When this emulsion dries, the screen may be exposed again so that the touched up areas will be as resistant as the rest of the screen.

66

Reclaiming Screens

Each manufacturer may recommend slightly different mediums for removing the film from the screen fabric. It is suggested that the ink be removed and cleaned off thoroughly immediately after printing. Film coating may then be removed from metal fabrics, nylon, and polyester mesh by applying household bleach (sodium hypochlorite) and allowing bleach solution to remain on both sides of screen for about 5 minutes. Silk is not salvaged easily, as the bleach may destroy part of the thread. The soaking of the bleach on the emulsion will soften the emulsion so that a strong spray of water will remove the coating from the fabric. The screen may then be rinsed off well with water and scrubbed with a trisodium phosphate solution and rinsed again. It is suggested that when bleach is used to clean off stainless steel, it be given a one percent acetic acid rinse or a vinegar rinse before scrubbing with trisodium phosphate and rinsing with water. Of course, cleaning and reclaiming units such as commercial automatic screenwashers or water spray pressure washers may be used to clean and remove coating from screen.

Figure 52. A print for a greeting card made from a direct-indirect screen prepared on reclaimed Number 200 white nylon. Direct film was adhered with water alone and screen was sensitized with a diazo sensitizer and processed two weeks later.

Stockpiling Screens

Direct-indirect screens may be stockpiled or partly processed and used as needed. This may be accomplished by adhering the direct-film to the screen fabric with water alone, or with the unsensitized emulsion. To adhere with water, the screen is washed in water and when it is completely wet, screen is placed over the film and film is squeegeed on the inside of screen with a dry soft squeegee. The squeegee is wiped dry and another stroke may be made to assure that no water puddles are left. The excess water is wiped from the edges and screen is allowed to dry.

In applying film to screen fabric with an unsensitized emulsion, the same procedure is used as in adhering a direct-film with a sensitized emulsion. The unsensitized and adhered film is allowed to dry.

The screens may be stored for any length of time but the support or base sheet must NOT be removed from the film until film is to be exposed. When a screen is needed, sensitized emulsion, depending on the type of product, is applied and screen is processed in the usual manner.

Figures 50 illustrates a print made by the writer from a screen prepared with a direct-indirect film. Figure 52 presents a print made from a screen to which the film was adhered with water alone. Screen was later sensitized with a diazo-sensitized emulsion.

ULANO DIRECT -FILM PRINTING SCREEN

In 1928 while Joseph Ulano of Brooklyn, New York, was spraying lacquer on a large tin can to make a spray gun work more evenly, he found that the lacquer coating which formed on the can could be peeled off easily. This incident and much experimentation resulted in his developing hand knife-cut film and in his being responsible for much of the growth of the screen printing industry internationally. His knife-cut films and photographic screen printing films have answered important industrial needs.

For more than a decade (late 1950's and 1960's) Joseph Ulano experimented, developed, and refined screen printing films. One of the films developed during this time and refined later was the Ulano direct-indirect screen printing film known as the Ulano Direct System.* This film is not a transfer type or indirect film; that is, it is not processed on a temporary support or base and then transferred to the screen fabric. It is processed on the screen fabric.

The film consists of a synthetic emulsion on a .002″ thick transparent polyester base. It may be adhered to nylon, polyester, metal fabric, and silk. Very detailed printing and long runs may be obtained, if the film is processed according to directions. The film resists most inks, except water-soluble ones. The direct-film is available with a coating and a liquid sensitizer and may be obtained in sheet sizes and in large rolls. The sensitizer is mixed with the coating when adhering film to the screen fabric, producing a sensitized coating.

Regardless what type of screen fabric is being used, the fabric must be thoroughly cleaned and degreased so that film or emulsion will adhere perfectly. Cleaning compounds and degreasing solutions are available from screen printing suppliers, including Ulano, should the printer need them. The film may be adhered to a range of screen fabrics from fine to coarse. It produces prints without ragged or serrated edges, yet a tough screen is obtained, since the coating solution encapsulates the fabric. A darkroom is not required; processing may take place in subdued light or under yellow light.

The same equipment is used in the preparation of this screen as in preparing direct screens. The processing steps consist of (1) sensitizing of coating, (2) adhering film, (3) drying and peeling of plastic base, (4) exposing, and (5) washing out.

---

*Ulano is a registered trademark of the Ulano Products Company, Inc., New York, New York.

Before starting preparation of this screen, it is suggested that the printer have the following ready: (1) Ulano direct-film; (2) sensitized coating; (3) a screen with cleaned and degreased fabric stretched tightly; (4) a sheet of glass or plastic that is about ¼ to ½ inch thick and larger than the film to serve as a built-up layer; (5) a soft squeegee with rounded edges; (6) an electric fan; (7) an actinic light source for exposing screen; (8) a vaccum frame, a direct method exposing unit, or any set-up that will produce perfect contact between film and positive; (9) a positive with design to be reproduced; (10) a source of hot and cold running water with a mixing faucet arrangement; (11) newsprint paper (not newspaper) or blotting paper; and (12) soft clean lintless cloths.

Preparation of Sensitizer and Sensitized Coating

The sensitized coating is made from a viscous coating and a liquid sensitizer. However, the liquid sensitizer may be made by mixing a 20 percent solution of ammonium bichromate (200 grams in 800cc of distilled water). The sensitized liquid is added to the coating to produce the sensitized coating. One part of ammonium bichromate solution is added to 5 parts of the coati ng by volume to make it sensitive to light. Before using the sensitized coating, it is best to wait a few hours after coating has been mixed. The sensitized coating can be kept for 2 weeks under room temperature. It will keep up to 3 months if stored in a refrigerator and protected against freezing and strong light. Changes in viscosity of the stored sensitized coating do not influence the adhering of the film.

Adhering Film to Fabric

A piece of film, smaller in size than the inside dimensions of the screen, is placed emulsion side up, on a built-up layer such as glass or plastic, as illustrated in Figure 53. Pieces of tape longer than the film edge are applied on the open screen between film and frame, on two opposite sides, on the squeegee side of the screen. Then a bead of sensitized coating is poured along the tape. Using a soft rubber rounded-edged blade squeegee, slightly wider than the film, the coating is applied through the screen over the film in one uniform stroke with light pressure. The printer should wait about 3 to 5 minutes before moving the frame to allow the sensitized coating to react with the film for adhering. The tape may then be removed and any excessive coating in the corners is also removed.

In making screens for extremely long runs, the sensitized coating is applied in one stroke and after waiting one minute, a second stroke is applied, allowing 3 additional minutes before starting drying.

For adhering film to steel mesh, one stroke of the coating is applied. Then the screen and film are left alone for 15 minutes, and without changing position of screen, a second stroke of the coating is applied. The printer should then wait 3 additional minutes before moving the frame.

Drying and Peeling of Plastic Base

Drying is done at room temperature in a dark area with screen in a horizontal position, squeegee side up, using a fan to hasten drying. After

70

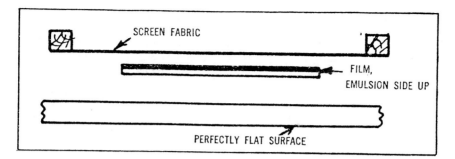

Figure 53. Arrangement of parts for sensitizing and adhering film to screen fabric.

about 15 minutes, the plastic base may be removed. If every step in the processing has been done correctly, the base will peel off easily. Although warm air up to 86 degrees Fahrenheit (30 degrees Celsius) may be used in drying, one must be careful that dimensional stability is not affected by too warm a temperature or too fast drying. The plastic base may be left on the sensitized film for a maximum of 24 hours before exposure and will prevent settling of dust on film. The base should be peeled off immediately before exposing.

Exposing

A soft blanket vacuum frame, a direct method exposing unit, or a photographic contact frame of the type illustrated in Figure 29 may be used for exposing screen and positive. Although the film has wide latitude, underexposure may cause poor adhesion of film to fabric and poor resistance in printing. When the film and screen are definitely dry, the screen is exposed, making sure that the plastic base is peeled off immediately before exposing. Any actinic light source such a pulsed-xenon lamp, carbon arc, mercury vapor lamp, or black light flourescent tubes may be used. The exposure time and distance of screen from light source may vary considerably, depending on the light source, strength of light and distance of film from light. To obtain correct exposure to light it is suggested that a test exposure or "step wedge" be made for local conditions and equipment. The parts for exposure are arranged as illustrated in Figure 54.

Washing Out

After the screen is exposed, it should be washed out with water that is between 76 and 112 degrees Fahrenheit (25 to 45 degrees Celsius). However, cold tap water may also be used. The screen, which is in a vertical position, is first rinsed on the squeegee side and then sprayed with a gentle spray on the printing or underside of screen until particles not hardened by light are dissolved completely and until all openings are clean. The washout time, depending on the size of the screen, may take from about 3 to 7 minutes.

After washing out, the screen is dried in a horizontal position, squeegee side up, drying with a fan at room temperature until the film is completely

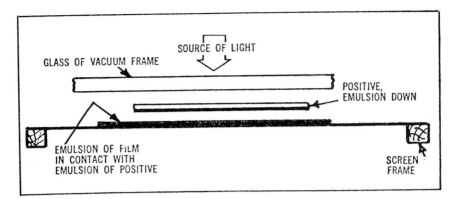

Figure 54. Arrangement of film and positive in exposing.

dry. Warm air may be used for drying, if register is not a serious problem. Water-soluble filler is used to block out the open areas of fabric outside film areas. The applied filler may be dried with the aid of a fan.

Reclaiming Screen

Before reclaiming screen, it is important that the ink used in printing be cleaned off thoroughly with the correct solvent immediately after printing. Varied methods may be used to reclaim the screen. The screen filler may be removed with warm water. Chemicals recommended for removal of direct emulsions may be used for removal of film and coating. A high pressure water spraying unit may remove the coating. A 4-to-6 percent sodium hypochlorite solution (bleach) can be applied with a nylon type brush to both sides of the fabric on synthetic and on metal fabrics. The solution is allowed to remain on the fabric for 5 minutes and then is rinsed off throughly with water. Another removal procedure is to immerse the screen in a film removal bath or in a reclaiming tank containing reclaiming solutions.

Repeated cleaning of film during varied printings can be carried out without distorting printing details. Fabric should be degreased before reusing screen fabric.

Figure 55 presents a print made with a Ulano direct-film as explained in this chapter.

Figure 55. A print made from a screen prepared with a direct-film on No. 14 silk and exposed to a carbon arc lamp for 5 minutes at a distance of 5 feet.

ULANO PRESENSITIZED SCREEN PRINTING FILMS

With the development of screen printing the preparation of photographic printing screens is becoming a more exact science because more is being expected and required of printing screens. However, each manufacturer expects the printer to use the product as specified in the manufacturer's directions in order to meet the following requirements. Printing screens must be durable, flexible and tough, must last for a long storage period, and must be capable of being adhered to wire gauze, silk, or synthetic screen fabrics. They should be able to print on varied surfaces and materials normally used in screen printing. It should be possible to prepare the screen easily under normal shop conditions without requiring complex processing.

Hi-Fi Red, Hi-Fi Green, Blue Poly 2, Blue Poly 3, Super Prep, RX-200, RX-300, XPM-2, and XPM-3,* nine presensitized photographic screen printing films, have attempted to answer the above prerequisites. While Hi-Fi Red may be used on silk, it is manufactured especially to be used on metal screen fabrics. Hi-Fi Green and Super Prep are intended for all purpose screen printing. The Blue Poly films may be used for all types of printing and adhered to any screen fabric. The RX and XPM films are designed specifically for high resolution printing in the electronics field. Because they are presensitized, these films do not have to be sensitized by the printer before they are prepared. This tends to eliminate errors which may develop in sensitizing, especially when sensitizing is being done by a novice. The films can be handled under subdued incandescent light and do not require a darkroom for processing. The films will keep indefinitely if stored in their original tube or container and covered in such a way that no light strikes the film. However, films should be protected from heat, humidity extremes, and from buckling.

Each of the films is manufactured on a stable transparent plastic backing sheet. Each of the films is always exposed through the plastic backing sheet. The films are sold with a developer which is made from two powders, powder "A" and powder "B." Ulano A and B developer is sold premeasured in pint, quart, and gallon foil packets, which protect the powders under all climatic conditions. Hi-Fi Red film also comes with a special solvent called a "Conversion Solvent." The purpose of this solvent is to obtain full strength and unusual durability after Hi-Fi Red film is adhered to the screen fabric. However, depending on the screen fabric to which the film is to be attached, heat may also be used to obtain full strength and durability or to convert the film.

---

*J. Ulano and Company, Inc., New York, New York.

74

Hi-Fi Green and Blue Poly films do not require the conversion step; these films are somewhat easier to process.

As is true with processing most photographic screens, it is best for the printer to have the following materials and equipment ready before starting preparation of screen: (1) a piece of any of the films that the printer plans to use; (2) developer consisting of two powders — powder A and powder B; (3) a glass jar in which to mix the developer; (4) a tray for holding developer and for developing exposed film; (5) an actinic light source for exposing film; (6) a vacuum frame or photographic contact frame for holding film and positive during exposure; (7) a mixing faucet with a source of hot and cold water; (8) a screen with the screen fabric perfectly cleaned and stretched and of the desired mesh (Number 12 through 18 fabrics or higher or their equivalent are practical); (9) some newsprint paper, not newspaper; (10) a built-up board, slightly smaller than the inside dimensions of the frame, to serve as a layer upon which the developed and washed film is placed when it is adhered to the screen fabric; (11) a source of heat for converting the Hi-Fi Red, if conversion solvent is not to be used, or conversion solvent for making the screen more durable before screen is to be used; (12) some naphtha or benzine; (13) a sheet of cardboard to cover tray holding developer; (14) some soft clean cloths; (15) tongs or tweezers; and (16) some cotton.

The steps in preparation of the film consist of (1) exposing film; (2) developing exposed film; (3) washing out film; (4) adhering film to screen fabric; and (5) converting film (Hi-Fi Red).

Before starting, the printer should make sure that the fabric has been stretched correctly and has been cleaned and degreased. New nylon and polyester fabric may be given a mechanical cleaning treatment with 500 mesh silicon carbide. This is done by wetting the fabric and sprinkling the silicon carbide grit on the underside of the screen or that side to which the film will be adhered. Using a wet rag, the underside of the fabric is scrubbed for about 2 or 3 minutes. The grit should then be rinsed off with a strong water spray. Since the grit particles are almost microscopic in size, they will not clog even the finest mesh.

Every time, before a film is to be processed and adhered, new and used fabrics must be degreased. This may be done by wetting the fabric with cold water and sprinkling powdered trisodium phosphate on both side of the fabric. Both sides of the fabric are then scrubbed with a soft brush. After scrubbing, the screen is rinsed throughly with a strong spray of water and screen is allowed to drain and dry. If trisodium phosphate is not available, automatic dishwater powders, containing alkaline salts may be used. These are soluble and may be rinsed. However, trisodium phosphate is preferred, since dishwater compounds are subject to change.

While other factors enter into the correct preparation of a photographic screen, the most important step is the standardization of correct exposure to light. Since a presensitized film is affected by light, the best light source and the best conditions should be employed.

Practical sources of light for exposing are carbon arc lamps (preferably a motor driven one for constant output), mercury vapor light, quartz iodide lamp, metal halide lamp, and black light fluorescent lamps. The film is arranged for exposure as illustrated in Figure 56. Exposure time and distance of film from light will vary, depending on the type of light, strength of light, and distance of film from light. While exposure time may vary from about 3 minutes to 7 minutes and distance may vary from 4 inches to 40 inches, shop conditions for exposure must be standardized. The printer can easily make an exposure test by placing 4 to 6 pieces of the film, one piece being placed next to the other, placing positive over them, and locking the pieces and positive in a vacuum frame or contact frame. Then black paper, masking film, or opaque tape is placed over the pieces. As each piece is exposed for a certain time interval, say ½ to 1 minute, the black paper or tape is removed from piece Number 1 after the first ½ minute, then from piece Number 2 after 1 minute, etc. After the pieces are each developed and washed out, the best exposure can be chosen for standardized procedure. (See Figure 39.)

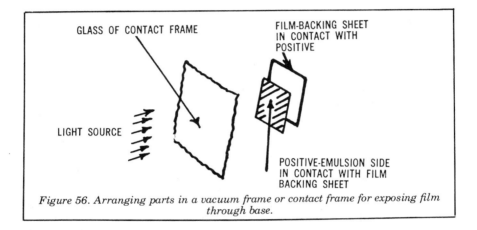

GLASS OF CONTACT FRAME

FILM-BACKING SHEET IN CONTACT WITH POSITIVE

LIGHT SOURCE

POSITIVE-EMULSION SIDE IN CONTACT WITH FILM BACKING SHEET

Figure 56. Arranging parts in a vacuum frame or contact frame for exposing film through base.

Developing Exposed Film

It is best to develop film immediately after exposure. The developing solution is prepared by pouring the premeasured powder A into a pint, quart or gallon of water (not over 75 degrees Fahrenheit; 24 degrees Celsius) as specified in the directions. The water should be stirred or shaken until the powder A is definitely dissolved. Then powder B is added to the dissolved powder A solution, making sure that both powders are dissolved. The mixed developer is poured into a glass, porcelain-finished, stainless steel, or a polyethylene tray.

Developing solution should not be used for a longer period than one day. Although the developer may change color slightly after the first piece of film has been placed in it, the changing color does not harm the developer; it indicates that chemical action is taking place. However, after the first piece is developed, the tray should be covered with a piece of clean cardboard to prevent light from reaching developing solution. Sensitizer of film washed out in developer is affected by strong light. If film is developed in spoiled developing solution, the film will crinkle, wrinkle, and float off the plastic backing sheet.

The actual developing consists of immersing film, emulsion side up, in solution. The film should be covered quickly with the developer by rocking the tray and the rocking should continue for about 1½ minutes. While solu-

76

tion may turn color it will not affect the film negatively; however, if solution turns brown, it is a sign of decomposition. Too long development time tends to loosen film from the base.

Washing Out

After developing, the film is washed out with a mild spray of water that is 90 to 100 degrees Fahrenheit (32 to 38 degrees Celsius). Washout should not be done any longer than necessary. The whole surface of the film should be washed out including the areas outside the design areas. Control of water temperature for washout is important for making consistent films. After washing, the film is rinsed with cold water, lowering the water temperature while continuing the washout. It is best to adhere the film immediately and not leave film lying around.

Adhering Film to Screen Fabric

As is common with other film, it is best to have a built-up layer or contact layer to obtain perfect contact between film and screen fabric. A glass plate makes an excellent one, since it is easy to clean. The wet film is placed, film side up, on the built-up layer which is smaller in area than the inside dimensions of the screen, and the screen is placed over the film in position and pressed down lightly over film. With screen in position over and in contact with film, newsprint paper is used to blot over film. Printed newspaper should not be used, as the ink in the paper can cause problems. Undue pressure should not be used in blotting. Enough changes of newsprint should be used to remove excess moisture from the film. The film which is best adhered to a damp screen should be allowed to dry naturally.

After the film is dry, the plastic backing is peeled off. If the film is completely dry, the sheet will strip off easily. If there is much resistance to peeling, more time should be allowed for drying. Heat should not be used in drying.

While the open parts of the screen may be filled in with a filler after the plastic sheet has been peeled off, another method is to apply the filler on the back side of the screen also covering the plastic support. The filler will dry along with the film and when filler and film are completely dry, the plastic support may then be peeled off.

Conversion of Hi-Fi Red Film

To obtain full strength and maximum durability, Hi-Fi Red film must be converted. The conversion or strengthening may be accomplished in either of the following ways: By applying heat to screen, by employing a special solvent, or by using solvent with heat application.

The best temperature for conversion ranges from 325 to about 350 degrees Fahrenheit (163 to 177 degrees Celsius). Although varied forms of heat may be used, the best method is to employ an electric pressing iron. For ironing silk and metal screen fabrics the iron is adjusted to the same temperature that is used to press woolen materials. The screen is placed film side up and the film is ironed until the film is converted or until the film changes in color.

77

In using the solvent method, good ventilation must be used as the solvent is toxic. Also, it is suggested that the solvent not be handled with bare hands to avoid absorption of solvent through the skin. Only a little of the solvent has to be applied; it should be applied quickly. A practical method of solvent application is to saturate a piece of cloth that is held between tongs or tweezers and the solvent is applied to the inside of the screen evenly and all over the film. The screen is then allowed to dry. Since the solvent evaporates slowly, it is best to leave the screen until the following day. However, the drying may be hastened, if a fan is allowed to blow over the solvent area after the solvent has been on for about 10 minutes. A fan will decrease the drying time to about an hour.

In the combination solvent and heat method for converting synthetic fabrics with film on them, the solvent is applied and the screen is then placed on a smooth surface such as glass and the fabric is ironed with an iron set at "synthetic."

Reclaiming Screens

Before starting reclaiming of screen fabric, it is imperative that the ink has been removed and cleaned off immediately after printing. Processing directions for the various screen printing films also include directions for reclaiming or removing of film from screen fabrics. Three general reclaiming methods are recommended for removal of films treated in this chapter. (1) In this method both sides of the screen fabric are wetted with hot water and screen is allowed to stand for about 5 minutes. Then using a brush and hot water, the film generally may be cleaned out of the fabric. This method may be used or tried for cleaning off all fabrics.

(2) This second method employs enzyme products for reclaiming. These are available from the film manufacturer or from screen printing suppliers. In this method, the screen is wetted on both sides and an enzyme powder or solution is sprinkled liberally on both sides of the fabric. The screen is then covered with a squeezed out wet rag and allowed to stand for 5 minutes. Then the film is hosed off with hot water. After cleaning off the enzyme, the screen should be wiped off with white vinegar or with a 5 percent acetic acid solution to neutralize or inactivate the enzyme and to prevent it from attacking the next film which may be adhered to the reclaimed fabric. The fabric must then be rinsed off thoroughly with water.

(3) The third method is used to reclaim more stubborn screens which have been processed on metal, nylon, or polyester fabrics. This method employs sodium hypochlorite (household chlorine bleach) solutions. The solution is applied on both sides of the fabric which has first been wetted with hot water. The screen fabric covered with the solution is allowed to stand for 5 minutes. Then using a brush and hot water the film may be cleaned out of the fabric.

Where the printer may be in doubt about a reclaiming method, it is suggested that he first try the first and second methods, since these will not damage natural silk.

In summary, it must be stressed that the film thickness and strength can be varied by exposure and development time. Since every actinic light gives slightly different results, it is vital that the user find out exactly what his particular equipment will do by making a set of test screens. An important part of test screens is also finding out the best method of reclaiming screens.

McGRAW COLORGRAPH
PRESENSITIZED PHOTO FILM

In order to standardize procedure of screen preparation and to assure uniform results, new presensitized products are being offered to the screen printing industry. One such product is the McGraw Colorgraph presensitized stencil film.* This presensitized screen printing film is easily processed and will print any type of ink that is normally printed with carbon tissue type screens. It is a gelatinous type film. If processed correctly, it will reproduce very fine detail, including halftone work. It can be adhered to the fabrics normally used in the screen printing trade. The film is processed with inexpensive solutions normally found in the average screen printing shop or solutions available from the corner drug store. It should not be handled in daylight but may be handled under subdued tungsten illumination or under yellow light. Film should be stored in a cool place and protected from light.

In using this film, the printer can expose his jobs at one time and then process the film at his convenience. However, once the film is exposed it should be kept in the dark or in opaque envelopes, especially if the printer plans to keep the film for some time after exposure. The film comes on a stable plastic base and because of this minimizes register problems in multicolor work. It is available in varied sheet sizes and in rolls wide enough and long enough for any size screen. The film should be stored in a cool place in its original container.

Materials and Equipment Needed for Processing

Before starting the processing, one must make sure that the screen mesh is tightly stretched and perfectly clean. Number 12 to Number 18 screen fabric or equivalent mesh may be employed. New or used screen fabrics should be cleaned with a solution of trisodium phosphate, thoroughly washed with hot water and then rinsed with a dilute solution of muriatic (hydrochloric) acid. The acid is made by adding 1 liquid ounce of acid to 1 gallon of water. After the acid rinse the screen fabric should be washed thoroughly with hot water and the fabric dried. Synthetic fabrics should be abraded slightly by rubbing the fabric surface with wet Number 300 to Number 400 sandpaper so that fabric will better receive the processed film.

Besides the prepared screen, the printer will need the following simple materials and equipment which are ordinarily found in the average screen

---

*This film is one of a group of several products manufactured by McGraw Colorgraph Co., Burbank, California.

printing shop: (1) Colorgraph presensitized photofilm; (2) a source of light for exposing film; (3) a 2 percent potassium bichromate solution or a 1 percent (2 volume) hydrogen peroxide solution to be employed as the developer; (4) a 50 percent alcohol solution; (5) a photographic contact frame, vacuum frame, or arrangement for exposing photographic positive in perfect contact with presensitized film; (6) a piece of ¼-inch thick soft foam plastic or foam rubber to serve as support, larger in size than the film but smaller in size than the inside dimensions of the screen; (7) a piece of unbleached muslin; (8) a photographic positive bearing subject to be reproduced; (9) two glass, bakelite, or photographic trays for holding developer and water; (10) an electric fan and (11) a sink with a source of warm and cold water with a mixing faucet arrangement.

The procedure consists of exposing film, developing, washing out, and attaching processed film to screen fabric.

Exposing

Before exposing film in contact with positive, the printer must make sure that the positive is perfectly opaque in the opaque areas and that transparent areas on positive are definitely transparent. Also, that the glass on the photographic contact frame or vacuum frame is free of dust. Dust particles may cause pinholes in the processed film.

The film is arranged for exposure with the emulsion side of positive placed over film, positive touching the plastic base of the film (dull side), so that in exposing, the light strikes the positive first, the base side next, and finally the film side. There must be perfect contact between positive and film. Vaccum frames or photographic contact frames may be employed for this purpose. Carbon arc lamps, daylight fluorescent tubes, black light, or mercury vapor lamps may be used as the light source. The exact exposure time may be determined by an exposure test as shown in Figure 39. However, a 35-ampere carbon arc lamp at a distance of 5 feet from the film will require 3 to 4 minutes for exposure. A 15-ampere carbon arc will require 4 to 5 minutes at the same distance. For standardization procedure it is suggested that the printer, after exposing test, have the film processed, attached to screen fabric, and test-printed.

Although the film is normally processed after exposure, the exposed film may be stored up to a period of two weeks before processing, providing that it is not subjected to high temperature or high humidity. However, a better procedure for storing film is to expose it, wash out film, and dry film. The dry film may be stored in complete darkness for an indefinite period. Then when film is ready to be adhered to screen fabric all that is required is to soak film in warm water from 3 to 5 minutes. This method is especially practical when the processing is done in one area or climate and film is mailed to another area.

Developing

The film may be washed out in tap water (not distilled or perfectly pure water) after exposure and attached to the screen fabric without going through the developing step. However, if a strong film and/or fine detail is desired the film should be developed in a developer. The developing solution may be either a 2 percent solution of potassium bichromate or a 1 percent (2 volume) solution of hydrogen peroxide. The 2 percent potassium bichromate solution may be made by dissolving 2½ ounches by weight of potassium bichromate powder in 1 gallon of water (71 grams in 3.785 liters or in 3785 cubic centimeters of water).

The exposed film may be developed either by placing the film in a tray containing enough developer to cover film or by placing the film on a flat level surface, emulsion side of film up, and a small quantity of the developing solution poured on and spread over the film to wet the emulsion completely. In either method the film is developed for 2 minutes.

After developing, wash out film by flooding film with water that is 105 to 115 degrees Fahrenheit (41 to 46 degrees Celsius) until all unexposed gelatin is removed. After the image appears to be completely clean and open, the washing is continued for 1 minute. Then chill film with cool water that is 70 degrees Fahrenheit or cooler (21 degrees Celsius); and finally flood film with a 50 percent alcohol solution and allow film to stand for 1 minute.

The alcohol employed ordinarily is an isopropyl type. The writer uses an inexpensive rubbing alcohol. However, if the latter alcohol is employed, it should not have any additives in it such as perfumes, etc. While the use of alcohol is not essential, its use does speed drying without affecting adhesion of film to screen fabric. It also minimizes the possibility of gelatin running into openings and causing scum. When attaching film to metal or synthetic screen fabrics, a 10 to 20 percent alcohol solution is used, depending on the detail to be reproduced.

When the gelatin is wet, it is soft; when dry, it is thin, firm, and pliable. The softness in the wet stage is purposeful, since it aids in obtaining better adhesion. However, when the screen is attached to the film no blotting on the inside of the fabric or rolling is necessary.

Attaching Film to Screen Fabric

To attach film to screen fabric, place film, emulsion side up, on a soft ¼-inch thick foam plastic or foam rubber sheet that is covered with an unbleached muslin. Hold screen over the film and lower screen into contact without rolling or blotting. Leave screen alone and allow it to dry. It is not necessary to blot or roll over the areas on top of film with rollers or paper to make film adhere to fabric. A fan may be used to hasten drying. If humidity is very light, a fan with warm air may be used to hasten drying toward the end of the drying period.

When the film is thoroughly dry, the plastic film base is removed by peeling, and the rest of the screen is blocked out and made ready for printing.

Reclaiming Screen

After printing, the ink must be perfectly cleaned with the correct ink solvent and the screen may be reclaimed. This may be done easily by using the reclaiming powder or agent available from the manufacturer of the film or by using any good quality enzyme type film remover generally available for reclaiming gelatin screens. To remove the film, wet the screen fabric over the area on both sides with hot water. Place screen on a flat surface and sprinkle sparingly with remover powder over the silk side or inside of the screen. The sprinkled areas are then swabbed with a cloth that has been wetted with water that is about 100 degrees Fahrenheit (38 degrees Celsius). After about 5 minutes or as soon as enough of the gelatin has dissolved, the film may be washed off with hot water. The reclaiming powder must be washed away completely so that absolutely no traces are left. It is suggested that the printer wash the screen fabric with a weak acetic acid solution or household vinegar. After screen fabric is rinsed off perfectly with water the fabric is ready to receive another film.

ACTIVE MICROPHOTO SCREEN PRINTING FILM

The improved photographic printing screens with their simple procedures and standardized results are enabling the printer to reproduce almost any type of copy. Research in this field is constantly producing advantageous materials and techniques for the screen printer. One such material is the *Active Microphoto Film which was developed by Oscar Whitman.

The film consists of a plastic transparent backing sheet coated with an unsensitized blue colored gelatinous coating or emulsion. The shiny side of the film is the emulsion side; the dull or matte side is the backing sheet. The film is available in varied sizes up to rolls 36 inches wide and 300 inches long. It may be employed for the same type of printing jobs as screens prepared with carbon tissue. It may be exposed in direct contact with a photographic or hand-made positive or negative containing the desired design or image. The film has the advantage of using its backing sheet for the support in processing and thus eliminates a temporary support. The film does away with long exposure and does not require special chemicals for processing.

Generally the following are the steps in the preparation of the film; (1) Sensitizing film; (2) drying film; (3) exposing; (4) washing out; (5) attaching to screen; (6) removing backing sheet.

Before beginning the processing it is advisable to have the following ready: (1) A piece of film about two inches longer and wider than the positive to be employed; (2) a transparent photographic or hand-prepared positive; (3) a piece of cardboard larger than the film; (4) some masking tape; (5) a practical source of light for exposing screen printing photographic film; (6) a 3 or 2 inch soft hair brush for applying sensitizer to film; (7) a photographic contact frame or a vacuum contact frame or an exposing arrangement; (8) a screen stretched with Number 12 to Number 18 silk, depending upon the detail of copy to be reproduced; (9) newspaper or blotting paper; (10) potassium bichromate powder or granules of chemically pure grade or an equivalent grade for preparing the sensitizer; (11) a source of hot and cold water; (12) a sink or tray large enough for film to be processed and (13) a fan for drying the film, if it is desired to hasten drying.

Preparation for Sensitizer

The sensitizer is prepared by dissolving one ounce by weight of potassium bichromate powder in one quart of cold water (28.3 grams in 946 cubic

---

*Active Process Supply Company, New York, New York.

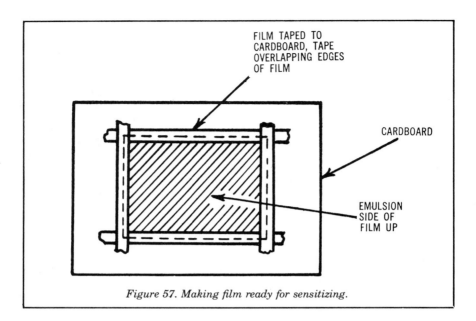

FILM TAPED TO
CARDBOARD, TAPE
OVERLAPPING EDGES
OF FILM

CARDBOARD

EMULSION
SIDE OF
FILM UP

Figure 57. Making film ready for sensitizing.

centimeters of water) or similar proportions, depending upon the amount of sensitizer to be used. Any tap water that is fit to drink may be used. If the sensitizer is stored in a dark brown bottle and kept in a cool place, it is good for at least two weeks.

After the potassium bichromate has dissolved completely in the water, the film may be sensitized. It is wise to chill the sensitizer by running cold water from a faucet on the container in which the sensitizer is kept before sensitizing the film.

Sensitizing Film

The film may be sensitized in the light; however, it must dry in a dark place or in a darkroom. Before sensitizing, the film may be taped to a piece of cardboard with masking tape, the tape overlapping the four edges of the film and cardboard, emulsion side of film up, as shown in Figure 57, allowing tape to overlap film about ¼ to ½ inch.

The film is sensitized by dipping a soft brush into sensitizer and applying sensitizing solution over film over the whole emulsion area, first in one direction and then in the other direction. The excess solution from the brush should be removed and the stroking with the brush should be continued until no surplus sensitizer is left on the film. The film should be left to dry in the dark. A fan may be employed to hasten drying.

Exposing

When the film is dry, it is removed from the cardboard and made ready for exposure to a strong light. The film may be exposed to a Number 2

84

photoflood lamp or to an arc lamp. Good contact between film and positive is essential. In exposing, the emulsion side or right side of the positive is placed in direct contact with the backing sheet side of the sensitized film as illustrated in Figure 58 so that the exposing light will strike the positive first, then the backing sheet of the film, and last the film. The film and positive may be locked in a photographic contact frame, in a vacuum frame, or clamped together between one piece of sponge rubber and a sheet of clean and clear plate glass.

If a Number 2 photoflood lamp is employed as the exposing light, about 1 minute will suffice for time of exposure, keeping the lamp at a distance of about 20 inches from the film. If a 35-ampere arc lamp is used, the exposure time is about 30 seconds at a distance of about 20 inches from the film. The film must not be overexposed, as overexposure will harden the film and it will not adhere to the silk. On the other hand, underexposure will produce a weak film.

Washing-out

After the film has been correctly exposed, it is placed in a sink, on a tray, or on a glass, emulsion side of film up, and the emulsion is sprayed with a

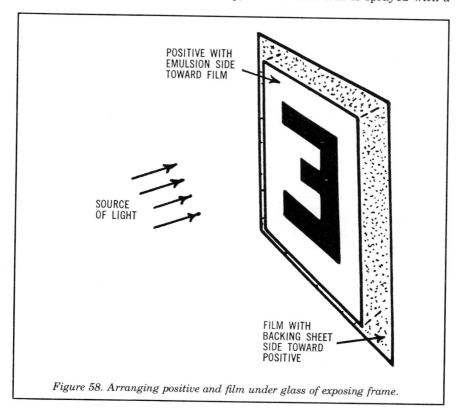

POSITIVE WITH EMULSION SIDE TOWARD FILM

SOURCE OF LIGHT

FILM WITH BACKING SHEET SIDE TOWARD POSITIVE

Figure 58. Arranging positive and film under glass of exposing frame.

| 25 | 30 | 35 | 40 | 45 | 50 | 55 | 60 | 65 |

Figure 59. A print made from a screen prepared with Active Micro Photo Screen Process Film.

gentle spray of water that is about 105 to 110 degrees Fahrenheit (40 to 43 degrees Celsius). The film may also be washed out or etched by submerging it, emulsion side up, in a tray of warm water (about 105 to 110 degrees Fahrenheit or 40 to 43 degrees C.), and the tray rocked gently back and forth. When the image washes out and the design appears clean and sharp on the backing sheet the film is rinsed with cold water. Image should wash out in a few minutes.

Attaching Film to Screen

Before attaching film to screen fabric, it is important that silk be cleaned and degreased thoroughly with a good detergent and detergent washed off with plenty of water. For cleaning nylon a 10 percent solution of cresylic acid or a 20 percent solution of caustic soda may be scrubbed on both sides of the fabric with a medium hard nylon brush. The hands and dyes should be protected, should any splashing occur. After brushing, all traces of the cleaning solution should be rinsed off thoroughly with water. Caustic soda or cresylic acid should not be used on silk.

After the film is completely etched or washed-out, it is laid, emulsion side up, on a piece of newspaper or blotting paper in order to give the paper a chance to absorb excess water. Then the film is placed, emulsion side up, on a piece of cardboard or glass slightly larger than the film but smaller in size than the inside dimensions of the screen, and the underside of the screen is brought in perfect contact with the film. The screen is then blotted with one's hand using newspaper under the hand. This blotting is repeated until all the moisure has been removed.

Removing Backing Sheet

After the screen has dried, either naturally or with the aid of a fan, the backing sheet will peel off very easily by starting the peeling of the sheet in one corner. However, the printer must make sure that the film is completely dry before peeling off the backing sheet. After the film is attached, the rest of the screen may be blocked out, the screen taped, and made ready for printing.

The film may be removed from the screen fabric in the same manner as any other photographic screen. Commercial photographic cleaners, available from screen printing suppliers, may be used also, providing the screen is cleaned and the ink is completely cleaned off immediately after printing.

Figure 59 presents a print made from a screen that was prepared with a Microphoto screen printing film.

86

ULANO SUPER-POLY-X SCREEN PRINTING FILM

Change is a tradition in the American way of life and in American industry. Change that is the result of much search and research aids in self-repair and self-direction. It produces new ideas, new processes, and new products.

The Ulano Super-Poly-X* screen printing film is one of the newer unsensitized ready-to-use films that is exposed after being sensitized. This blue-green transfer type film has a short exposure time, may be used for printing the finest line and halftone jobs, and adheres to nylon, polyesters, silk, and metal cloth. The film consists of an unsensitized emulsion which is semi-permanently cemented to a thin transparent 2 mil (0.05mm) polyester base or backing sheet. The adhesive coating between emulsion and base allows controlled peeling of the base when necessary, does not interfere with processing, and aids in holding the film to backing sheet during processing and developing. The emulsion also has a protective outer coating that prevents sticking, finger marks, and allows for safer storage and processing under humid conditions and fluctuations in temperature. After printing, film may be removed from silk, nylon, polyester, and metal fabrics.

The product offers enough latitude so that thin, average, and thicker films may be produced, depending on the job to be printed. It is practical for machine printing, long runs, and also for manual printing. While it can be processed without a darkroom, without air conditioning, and with the average equipment found in a screen printing shop, it should be processed under subdued light. The film should be protected from daylight, direct sunlight, actinic light sources, and fluorescent tubes, and should be stored in a cool dry place. If possible, it should be stored in the original wrapping and in the tube in which it came. Of course, ideal storage and working conditions, which may be obtained in air conditioned areas, are about 68 degrees Fahrenheit (20 degrees Celsius) and 55 to 65 percent relative humidity.

Once the film is sensitized, it may be kept up to 1 to 2 hours, depending on temperature and humidity conditions, in complete darkness before exposure. After this time continuing "dark hardening" reduces the resolution and increases film thickness. Only ammonium bichromate (or dichromate) is used for most of the formulations of this product, since other bichromates do not mix with alcohol, which is part of the sensitizing formula. Fresh sensitizing solution should be made every working day. The film will reproduce any type

---

*Ulano Products Company, Inc., New York, New York.

of detail that is normally reproduced by screen printing and will print any type of ink except those containing water or those which are hygroscopic. The prepared screen will print more impressions, if it is possible to keep it in the printing room a full day before printing. The film is available in sheets of varied sizes, and rolls up to 44 inches wide by 288 inches long (112cm by 730cm).

It is best to have the following materials and equipment ready before starting: (1) a sensitizing stock solution made from chemically pure ammonium bichromate crystals and distilled water; (2) Ulano Super-Poly-X film; (3) ethyl alcohol, methyl alcohol, or isopropyl alcohol; (4) a screen stretched tightly with cleaned and degreased nylon, metal cloth, polyester, or silk screen fabric that is equivalent to Number 12 to 18 silk or higher; (5) a photographic vacuum frame, contact frame, or an arrangement for exposing film in perfect contact with the photographic positive; (6) a photographic or hand prepared positive; (7) an actinic light source to which sensitized film is exposed; (8) a tray large enough for sensitizing film; (9) a source of hot and cold running water with a mixing faucet arrangement; (1) newsprint paper not newspaper; (11) clean cloths; (12) an electric fan; (13) built-up layer; and (14) a soft squeegee.

Sensitizing Film

Although there are five different methods of sensitizing this film, most screen printers sensitize the film in a tray employing a 50 to 60 pounds Kraft wrapping paper, one that is not waterproof and has a smooth surface, as an aid in sensitizing. Any other absorbent paper ($150g/m^2$) will suffice. The other four methods are the semi-dry method, the screen printing method, whirler method, and the water method.

This chapter presents the following three methods for sensitizing: (1) wet method (chromate-alcohol-paper method); (2) semi-dry process; and (3) water method (water-chromate-plastic method). The chromate stock solution for the first two methods consists of a 9 percent ammonium bichromate solution made with distilled water (90 grams to 1 liter of water, or 3 ounces of ammonium bichromate powder to 1 U.S. quart). The stock solution for the third method (water-chromate-plastic method) consists of a 2 percent bichromate solution (20g to 1 liter of water, or ¾ ounces to 1 U.S. quart of water). Since no alcohol is used in the latter sensitizing solution, the printer may use ammonium bichromate, potassium bichromate, or sodium bichromate.

Bichromate stock solutions (those not containing alcohol) can be kept in a brown stoppered or opaque bottle in a cool place for several months. It is suggested that the individual who is allergic to bichromates wear rubber gloves when working with bichromate sensitizers.

The sensitizing solutions for the first two methods — wet and semidry — consist of one part bichromate and 3 parts alcohol. The alcohol in the solution prevents melting of the film emulsion. If possible, the temperature in the working area should not exceed 72 degrees Fahrenheit (22°C) to aid in prevention of melting of emulsion. Isopropyl alcohol, methyl alcohol (wood alcohol), and denatured ethyl alcohol may be used. Denatured alcohol mixtures remain stable for a long time and are good for any method of application, especially for tray sensitizing. While isopropyl alcohol may also be mixed with a bichromate, it is not as stable as ethyl alcohol and will stay mixed in a

88

bichromate solution for about ½ hour. Methyl alcohol is excellent; however, it must be used with good ventilation and the printer must follow the manufacturer's directions in its use. The alcohol used must be one that stays clear and does not turn brown. An alcohol that is at least of 97 percent concentration should be used, although, if the sensitizing bath should turn brown during sensitizing, it can still be used. If the tray containing the bath is covered, the solution can be used for a prolonged period. It must be noted that alcohol is not added to the water method, since this method is generally used in air conditioned rooms in which the temperature is controlled. Once the film is sensitized it should be kept in complete darkness.

The correct bichromate concentration, the correct sensitizing time, and the right exposure make the ideal film which is hard on the bottom of the film and has a soft top making adhering to screen fabric easier.

Wet Method (Chromate-Alcohol-Paper Method)

This method of sensitizing uses a 50 to 60 pounds Kraft wrapping paper (150g/m²) as an aid in sensitizing the film. However, any paper that is not waterproof and has a smooth surface may be employed. In sensitizing, sufficient cool sensitizer is poured in a tray. The temperature of the sensitizer should be between 61–68 degrees Fahrenheit (16–20°C). Then a piece of paper that is somewhat larger in width and length than the film, is immersed in the solution. After the paper soaks up the solution and sinks to the bottom of the tray, the film is placed, emulsion side up, on top and in contact with the paper, and film is soaked or sensitized for 90 seconds. Then the film is turned over so that emulsion side of film is in contact with the paper, forming a sandwich with emulsion between the paper and film backing sheet as illustrated in Figure 60. The film and paper are removed from tray and both

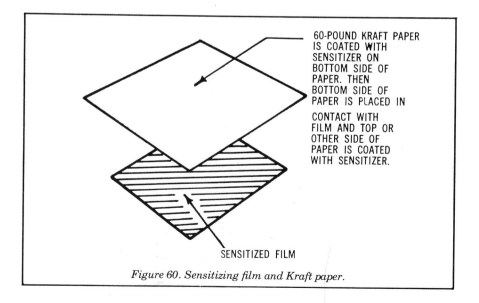

60-POUND KRAFT PAPER IS COATED WITH SENSITIZER ON BOTTOM SIDE OF PAPER. THEN BOTTOM SIDE OF PAPER IS PLACED IN CONTACT WITH FILM AND TOP OR OTHER SIDE OF PAPER IS COATED WITH SENSITIZER.

SENSITIZED FILM

Figure 60. Sensitizing film and Kraft paper.

pieces are placed on a glass or plastic sheet, base of film up, and excess sensitizer is removed with a squeegee. A damp cloth is used to wipe off any of the sensitizer left on the film backing sheet. The film and paper are placed on a few sheets of newsprint paper, film base up, and film is exposed. See Figure 61. The total sensitizing time should not be less than 3 minutes to permit penetration of sensitizer into paper.

Exposure

The sensitized film may be exposed to a carbon arc lamp, pulsed-xenon lamp, mercury vapor, or to actinic fluorescent tubes (blacklight), as illustrated in Figure 99, making sure that the parts are in perfect contact and that there is no dust on the positive, film base, or on exposing frame glass. Dust may produce pinholes in the print. Exposure is made so that light strikes frame glass first, then the positive, then base of film, and finally the emulsion. Too much pressure should not be used to prevent the damp film from being squeezed and prevent loss of detail. Depending on the light source, the exposure time may vary from 30 to 120 seconds and distance of film from light may vary from about 12 inches to 48 inches (30 to 120cm). However, it

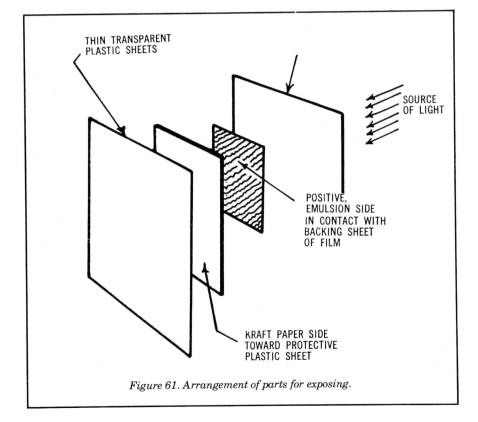

THIN TRANSPARENT
PLASTIC SHEETS

SOURCE
OF LIGHT

POSITIVE,
EMULSION SIDE
IN CONTACT WITH
BACKING SHEET
OF FILM

KRAFT PAPER SIDE
TOWARD PROTECTIVE
PLASTIC SHEET

Figure 61. Arrangement of parts for exposing.

is suggested that screen printer make an exposure test or exposure "step-wedge" as suggested in Figure 39. After the test, the best exposure or exposures will be evident when the film is washed out. It is also recommended that film representing the two or three best exposures are adhered to screens for test printing.

Washout

The exposed screen is washed out with water that is 110 to 120 degrees Fahrenheit (45° to 50°C). Where Kraft paper is used, the paper should release from the emulsion or be peeled off easily within 15 to 20 seconds without much resistance. The washout can be accomplished by using a mild water spray, keeping film slightly tilted. Warm water is sprayed on the film until the unexposed or soft parts of the top coat dissolves. It dissolves quickly, if processing has been done correctly. The washing is continued until all details are perfectly clear. A hard spray should be avoided, since it may damage detail and halftone dots. The washout is continued for about one minute more until the water that is draining is perfectly clean. Then the film is rinsed thoroughly with cold water.

The film may also be washed out by placing it in a tray containing water and rocking film gently, changing the water several times. Then rinsing the film under cold water thoroughly.

Ahdering Film to Screen Fabric

The film should be adhered to the screen fabric immediately after being washed out. The film will adhere perfectly, if the fabric has been cleaned and degreased immediately before adhering. However, an overexposed film will show less adhesion.

A built-up layer such as glass, plastic, or cardboard which is smaller than the inside dimensions of the frame and about ¼ inch thick should be used between film and screen fabric to produce perfect contact of film to fabric. The film is placed, emulsion side up, on the built-up layer, and the screen which should be dampened before adhering, is placed over the film in one operation. After the screen is in place, the inside of the screen is blotted carefully and uniformly with newsprint paper (not printed newspaper), changing the paper several times until the newsprint remains dry. If a roller should be employed for blotting over the newsprint, care must be used not to employ too much pressure. After the film is adhered, it should remain in a horizontal positon for at least 5 minutes.

Drying and Peeling of Base

Cold air from a fan may be used to hasten drying of film on the inside of screen, keeping screen in a horizontal position. Although the film may be dried in a vertical position, to achieve extremely sharp edges the film should be adhered and dried in a horizontal position. The screen should not be moved until the film is completely dry. After about 10 minutes, and while base or backing sheet is still on, a filler may be applied on the underside of the screen, over the plastic base and the open areas of the screen fabric. The filler and film are then dried in one operation with a cool air fan.

When the film is dry, the plastic base is peeled off, starting the peeling in one corner. Should there be too much resistance to the peeling, the film should be allowed to dry longer. If there are residues in the open parts of the film after peeling (these may be residues of the cement), they may be removed with a soft lintless cloth that has been dipped in a solvent such as naphtha or benzine.

Reclaiming Screen

Before reclaiming screen, all the ink must be removed completely and immediately after printing. In reclaiming silk, both sides of the fabric are wetted with hot water and an enzyme solution is rubbed with the palm of the hand or with a brush uniformly over the whole film. Then the film is covered with wet rags which are allowed to remain on the fabric for at least 20 minutes or as recommended by the enzyme manufacturer. The film is then removed with hot water so that all of the enzyme solution or particles are washed away. After removal of enzyme, the fabric must be washed or neutralized with a 4 to 5 percent acetic acid solution or with white household vinegar and then screen is rinsed thoroughly with cold water. In using enzymes for film removal, the printer should follow the directions of the enzyme manufacturer.

To remove film from nylon, polyester, and metal fabrics, a 20 percent solution of caustic soda (sodium hydroxide) or a 4 percent solution of sodium hypochlorite (bleach) may be used. The solution is applied with a brush on both sides of the film and is allowed to remain on for about 15 to 20 minutes. Then the screen is rinsed thoroughly with hot water. After rinsing, the fabric is neutralized with acetic acid or vinegar in similar fashion to reclaiming silk with enzymes.

Semi-Dry Method of Sensitizing Film

This is the second method of sensitizing this film. In this sensitizing process, the film is placed emulsion side up, on a flat rigid base such as glass or plastic. Then a sensitizer consisting of one part of ammonium bichromate (9 percent stock solution) and 3 parts of alcohol is poured on film, and a brush or paint roller is used to distribute the sensitizer uniformly over film emulsion. The film should be brushed up and down and from left to right for about 3 minutes to assure proper penetration of sensitizer into film.

The film may be partially dried with the aid of a fan until film feels almost dry to touch. Film should not be over-dried, as it will curl. Fine talc powder is applied over the whole film surface and the film is turned over, film side down, against a piece of paper or plastic. Any sensitizer that remains on the plastic support is wiped off with a damp cloth and film is exposed immediately. After exposing and washing out, the film is adhered to the screen fabric.

Water Method (Water-Chromate-Plastic Method) of Sensitizing

The sensitizing solution for this method, the third method, does not contain alcohol. The method is the same as that used for carbon tissue (wet method). The screen printer will need a .005″ thick transparent polyester sheet or another plastic — not paper. Sensitizing solution is made by mixing any of the following bichromates: ammonium bichromate, potassium bichromate, or sodium bichromate, mixing a 2 to 2½ percent solution with distilled water.

The film is sensitized by immersing in the sensitizing solution that is about 50 degrees Fahrenheit (10 degrees Celsius) for 90 seconds. Then the film is removed and is placed, emulsion side down against a piece of the cool plastic support. The excess sensitizer is removed carefully with a squeegee on base side of film and a damp cloth is used to remove the excess solution remaining on the temporary plastic support. The film is then exposed, exposing so that light strikes plastic support first. After correct exposure, film is washed out and adhered as explained for the first method of sensitizing.

Figure 62 presents a full-size print made with a screen sensitized by using Kraft paper and the wet method of sensitizing.

JANUARY

S	M	T	W	T	F	S
						1
2	3	4	5	6	7	8
9	10	11	12	13	14	15
16	17	18	19	20	21	22
23	24	25	26	27	28	29
30	31					

FEBRUARY

S	M	T	W	T	F	S
		1	2	3	4	5
6	7	8	9	10	11	12
13	14	15	16	17	18	19
20	21	22	23	24	25	26
27	28					

MARCH

S	M	T	W	T	F	S
		1	2	3	4	5
6	7	8	9	10	11	12
13	14	15	16	17	18	19
20	21	22	23	24	25	26
27	28	29	30	31		

APRIL

S	M	T	W	T	F	S
					1	2
3	4	5	6	7	8	9
10	11	12	13	14	15	16
17	18	19	20	21	22	23
24	25	26	27	28	29	30

MAY

S	M	T	W	T	F	S
1	2	3	4	5	6	7
8	9	10	11	12	13	14
15	16	17	18	19	20	21
22	23	24	25	26	27	28
29	30	31				

JUNE

S	M	T	W	T	F	S
			1	2	3	4
5	6	7	8	9	10	11
12	13	14	15	16	17	18
19	20	21	22	23	24	25
26	27	28	29	30		

JULY

S	M	T	W	T	F	S
					1	2
3	4	5	6	7	8	9
10	11	12	13	14	15	16
17	18	19	20	21	22	23
24	25	26	27	28	29	30
31						

AUGUST

S	M	T	W	T	F	S
	1	2	3	4	5	6
7	8	9	10	11	12	13
14	15	16	17	18	19	20
21	22	23	24	25	26	27
28	29	30	31			

SEPTEMBER

S	M	T	W	T	F	S
				1	2	3
4	5	6	7	8	9	10
11	12	13	14	15	16	17
18	19	20	21	22	23	24
25	26	27	28	29	30	

OCTOBER

S	M	T	W	T	F	S
						1
2	3	4	5	6	7	8
9	10	11	12	13	14	15
16	17	18	19	20	21	22
23	24	25	26	27	28	29
30	31					

NOVEMBER

S	M	T	W	T	F	S
		1	2	3	4	5
6	7	8	9	10	11	12
13	14	15	16	17	18	19
20	21	22	23	24	25	26
27	28	29	30			

DECEMBER

S	M	T	W	T	F	S
				1	2	3
4	5	6	7	8	9	10
11	12	13	14	15	16	17
18	19	20	21	22	23	24
25	26	27	28	29	30	31

Figure 62. A full size print made with a screen which was prepared using the wet method and paper to sensitize the film.

93

DIRECT POLYVINYL ALCOHOL
PRINTING SCREENS

The influences which have been at work in contributing to the growth of screen printing are numerous and have come from varied sources. Sometimes it has been an ordinary dormant property of a material used in another industry which produced an important answer to some complex problem. The polyvinyl alcohol direct printing screen is an example of this.

Polyvinyl alcohol printing screens, commonly known as PVA screens in the trade, are prepared from the man-made plastics material of the same name which first made its appearance synthetically in Germany in about 1924. Because polyvinyl alcohol is not affected by fats, oils, greases, and such solvents as alcohols, ethers, esters, ketones, and hydrocarbons of the aliphatic and aromatic types, polyvinyl alcohol is used in many places and products outside the screen printing industry. Although PVA is employed for other uses such as coating paper, sizing textiles, for adhesives, as ceramic binder, emulsifier, etc., it was not until World War II that the screen printing industry became aware of its contribution to screen printing.

Some forms of polyvinyl alcohol can be used to emulsify or disperse materials such as vegetable, acid, minerals, oils, waxes, resins, etc. Specifically, and to identify it chemically, we are concerned with the PVA tradenamed "ELVANOL",* partially hydrolized and of medium viscosity. However, the property of polyvinyl alcohol which concerns the screen printing industry directly is the ability of coatings of polyvinyl alcohol which have been dissolved in water with potassium bichromate or ammonium bichromate to become insoluble in water after the coating is exposed to strong light energy or ultra-violet light. In other words, PVA coatings, films, or emulsions having a given percentage of potassium bichromate or ammonium bichromate in them will be affected or changed by light. Those areas so affected are not soluble in water. This principle is used to produce direct photographic polyvinyl alcohol screens or screens that are prepared directly on the screen fabric. Thus, this method, often referred to as chromium tanning, produces the desirable quality of PVA — that of making the light exposed film non-soluble in water and other solvents. Polyvinyl alcohol as used for this screen preparation consists of very fine white powder.

These polyvinyl alcohol screens, because they have dimensional stability and long life, are especially practical in ceramic and textile printing, in circuit or electronic printing, and in any situation where a very tough non-

---

*Trademark, E. I. du Pont de Nemours and Co., Wilmington, Delaware.

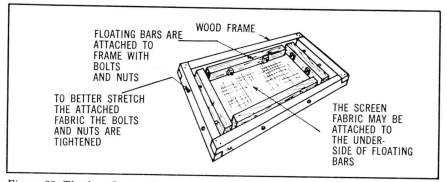

FLOATING BARS ARE
ATTACHED TO
FRAME WITH
BOLTS
AND NUTS

WOOD FRAME

TO BETTER STRETCH
THE ATTACHED
FABRIC THE BOLTS
AND NUTS ARE
TIGHTENED

THE SCREEN
FABRIC MAY BE
ATTACHED TO
THE UNDER-
SIDE OF FLOATING
BARS

Figure 63. The four floating-bar screen printing frame which is especially practical for attaching and stretching metal screen fabrics.

solvent film or coating is desired. They may be used anywhere where it is necessary to produce screens that are water resistant, easy to prepare, for printing on crackle type finished surfaces, and screens that will last for thousands of impressions. The screens may be employed both for hand printing and machine printing. They will produce very fine detail but because the screen is prepared directly on the screen fabric a very fine serrated edge may be noticeable in printing detail which is equivalent to about 6 point type. The ragged edge may be eliminated by applying more coatings on the screen fabric. However, this type of screen, if processed correctly, is very tough, since an impregnated and reinforced plastic screen is obtained — the screen fabric acting as the reinforcing agent, and the PVA acting as the impregnating agent. If one desires, an inert powder of the finest grind may be added to the formula to further strengthen the screen. The powder serves as a filler and has a tendency to aid in developing out the screen. However, the inert powder is not essential.

These printing screens may be prepared on any screen fabric — silk, metal, nylon, or polyester that has been correctly cleaned and stretched. It is suggested that about Number 140 to about 300 fabric mesh be employed; Number 12 to 18 silk of good quality may be used. Depending upon the detail to be reproduced, Number 14 and 16 silks are more practical. For metal and synthetic fabrics it is suggested that the foating-bar type frame illustrated in Figure 63 be employed to attach and stretch the fabric. Because this type of screen has been used more with abrasive type inks, metal fabrics have been employed more than silk, and the screens generally have been small in size.

Screens may be prepared under ordinary shop conditions. The easiest method to use in preparing this direct plate is to coat the screen directly with the light sensitive PVA solution. Another method that may be employed is to coat the screen with an unsensitized PVA solution and then to brush the coated and dried screen with a saturated solution of potassium bichromate or ammonium bichromate and allow the bichromate covered coating to dry in the dark or in a darkroom.

Generally, the following are the steps in the preparation of PVA direct screens: (1) Cleaning of screen fabric; (2) preparation of PVA solutions; (3) coating of screen; (4) exposing; (5) developing of screen and (6) printing and relcaiming of screen.

95

Cleaning of Screen Fabric

Before preparing any direct printing plate, it is necessary to make sure that the screen fabric is clean. If silk is employed, make sure that the screen fabric is well cleaned with soap and water, soap rinsed off well, and the screen allowed to dry before coating on the PVA solution. Silk may also be cleaned with vinegar and then rinsed well with warm water. Allow screen fabric to dry before applying coating to it. The silk will also become tighter in drying and this is an advantage in coating the screen, since a very tightly stretched fabric is desirable.

If a metal screen fabric is employed, the protective coating such as oil on the fabric may be cleaned off in any of the following methods: (1) The screen may be immersed in a 5 to 10 percent solution of glacial acetic acid for about five minutes, rinsed off well in hot water and brushed on both sides with a brush that is similar to that employed for cleaning suede; (2) the metal cloth may be held and moved uniformly over an ordinary gas burner or a Bunsen burner (being careful not to overheat and metal fabric) and then brushing off the cleaned surface with a brush; or (3) by using general degreasing agents such as trichlorethylene or tradenamed products similar to it to clean or degrease the metal fabric and then washing off the fabric with hot water.

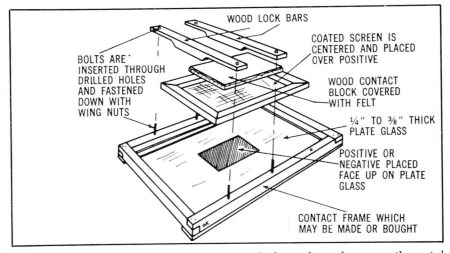

WOOD LOCK BARS

COATED SCREEN IS
CENTERED AND PLACED
OVER POSITIVE

BOLTS ARE
INSERTED THROUGH
DRILLED HOLES
AND FASTENED
DOWN WITH
WING NUTS

WOOD CONTACT
BLOCK COVERED
WITH FELT

¼" TO ⅜" THICK
PLATE GLASS

POSITIVE OR
NEGATIVE PLACED
FACE UP ON PLATE
GLASS

CONTACT FRAME WHICH
MAY BE MADE OR BOUGHT

Figure 64. Suggested photographic contact unit which may be used to expose the coated and sensitized polyvinyl alcohol screen.

Preparation of Polyvinyl Alcohol Solution

The solution employed to coat this type of printing plate consists of certain proportions of polyvinyl alcohol; potassium bichromate or ammonium bichromate; water and, if desired, coloring matter. Specifically, the formula used may be any of the following: 1 ounce (28.35 grams) by weight of polyvinyl alcohol fine powder dissolved perfectly in 10 to 11 ounces (295.7 to 325.3 cc) of water to which is added ¼ ounce (7.1 grams) of granulated potassium bichromate or ammonium bichromate and an inert coloring matter. Since they are inert as far as the formula is concerned, the coloring matter employed may be five to ten drops of green or blue stamp pad ink. The coloring matter is not essential but it does aid in coating the screen and in developing. A formula with which the writer has experimented and which produces a very tough screen, since it not only impregnates but also fills the screen mesh is the following: 1 ounce (28.35 grams) of PVA dissolved completely in 10 liquid ounces (296cc) of water to which is added ¼ ounce (7.1 grams) by weight of potassium bichromate or ammonium bichromate, and ⅛ to ¼ ounce (3.5 to 7.1 grams) by weight of the finest ground inert powder. These powders which are obtainable from screen printing suppliers, especially those who manufacture inks, may be of any color except black. Another formula consists of 2 ounces (56.7 grams) by weight of PVA powder dissolved in 12 to 13 liquid ounces (355 to 384cc) of water to which is added a little less than a liquid ounce (.85 ounce or 24cc) of a saturated solution of potassium bichromate or ammonium bichromate, and if desired, five to ten drops of blue or greem stamp pad ink. An earlier formula which is still used consists of polyvinyl alcohol 11.5 percent by weight which is dissolved in water (87.5 percent by weight) to which is added 1 percent by weight of granulated ammonium bichromate or potassium bichromate.

To mix the ingredients, slowly pour the correct amount of PVA powder into the required amount of water that is of room temperature or colder, stirring the powder in the water to dissolve the lumps which ordinarily form. An ordinary glass jar may be used for this. A stirring rod, a piece of glass rod, a spoon, a small egg beater, etc., may be used to dissolve the powder and to stir the solution. The solution is non toxic and will not in any way harm the utensil employed for mixing. The utensil used may be washed off with hot or warm water.

Any water that is fit to drink and that does not have any sediment in it may be used in the preparation of the formulae.

A simpler way to avoid formation of lumps is to allow the correct weight of polyvinyl alcohol powder to soak in the required amount of water for about 24 hours at room temperature or until the powder dissolves. A solution of PVA which has no sensitizing agent in it such as ammonium or potassium bichromate will last indefinitely, providing the container is well-stoppered to avoid loss of water through evaporation and thus cause variation in concentration and viscosity of the solution. All that is necessary is to add the required amount of sensitizer or bichromate to the required amount of solution.

To complete the dissolving of the powder, heat the jar containing the PVA solution in an enameled pot which has water in it, being very careful not to boil the PVA solution. It is advisable not to bring the temperature of the mixture above 185 degrees Fahrenheit (85 degrees Celsius). When all the PVA is completely dissolved, add the potassium or ammonium bichromate crystals or sensitizing solution and make sure that the bichromate dissolves completely in the solution. If an inert powder is used as part of the formula, then one must be assured that the powder is well stirred into the mixture. If some of the solution has evaporated, (generally it does not do so in the preparation) the correct amount of water may be added to compensate for the evaporation. When all the ingredients are uniformly and completely dissolved the mixture should be strained through a piece of silk or metal fabric or a piece of clean cloth. After the solution is strained and while still warm, it is ready to be applied to the cleaned screen fabric. The solution may be used over and over. By keeping the prepared PVA solution in a well-stoppered dark container in the refrigerator the mixture may be stored for longer periods of time. The writer has used one such mixture for 23 weeks.

Coating the Screen

Although coating may be done under ordinary light, it is best to do the coating in subdued light. In applying the solution to the screen fabric the coating may be applied in any of the following methods: (1) By pouring the solution over the underside or face side of the screen; (2) by dipping the underside of the screen into the prepared PVA solution, or (3) by brushing the solution onto the fabric.

In the first method a spoon, glass, or cup may be used to pour the solution on in the required area or over the whole surface, holding the screen at a slight angle and allowing the solution to pour over the fabric. The excess may be run into a clean pan and reclaimed and used again. To obtain a coat of uniform thickness use the sharp edge of a piece of cardboard and draw the edge over the coated side immediatly in squeegee fashion.

In the dipping method, the PVA solution is poured into a shallow tray which is slightly larger than the screen and just the underside of the screen is dipped into the solution, being careful not to form any bubbles. If any of the solution seeps through the openings in the screen cloth, squeegee down carefully on the inside of the screen to make the coating uniform.

In brushing the solution onto the fabric, employ a camel hair brush that is about two inches wide and brush solution onto the screen fabric, applying a uniform coating, starting at the top of the screen and working toward the bottom. When using the pouring and brushing method, a slightly heavier or thicker PVA solution may be used. Be very careful not to allow bubbles to form, since bubbles develop into pinholes when the screen is developed.

Another method that the screen printer may use in applying the PVA solution is to squeegee it on evenly on the underside with a squeegee and immediately stroke the squeegee back and forth on the inside of the screen. The important thing is to make sure that the screen fabric or the required area in the screen is well covered with the solution. Generally, the coating should not be too thin or too thick.

Allow the screen to dry in the dark or in a darkroom either naturally, or, if one is in a hurry, with the aid of a fan. The screen should dry at a temperature of about 85 to 90 degrees Fahrenheit (29 to 32 degrees Celsius), although no heat should be applied in the drying operation. Screen should not be touched when it is drying and should be kept in or near horizontal position. Once the screen is beginning to dry it becomes more sensitive to light, therefore it should be kept in the dark.

Some shops employ whirlers or whirling devices to insure an even distribution of the coating over the entire or desired part of the screen fabric. The whirling devices are in most cases homemade and are similar in their action to that of a phonograph turntable. Whirling devices may also be obtained from photo engraving or photo lighography equipment suppliers. Small screens fastened to the whirling device may be whirled at about 250 to 350 revolutions per minute for about 15 minutes; larger screens should be whirled at lower rates of speed. The important feature of the whirler is that there is no vibration in rotation and that the rotation be uniform. However, whirlers are not essential for making this screen.

After the coating has dried completely the screen is exposed to a strong light equivalent to about 1,500 candlepower. A 35 ampere single or double arc lamp, an indoor type of black light, two to four Number 2 photoflood lamps, or sunlight may be employed for exposing. Black light is a practical light source for this type of screen. When exposing, the positive or negative must be in perfect contact with the dried coated fabric and the exposing unit is arranged as illustrated in Figure 64. This unit may be bought or made by the printer. It is suggested that ½" to 1" thick foam rubber be placed between contact block and screen in Figure 64 to produce more perfect contact between screen and positive. Make sure that the plate glass of the photographic contact frame is perfectly clean and free of dust as dust particles may show up as pinholes when the screen is finally developed. Time and distance of exposure will vary somewhat. When being exposed to an arc light, the unit should be kept about 3 feet from the lamp, allowing 2 to 7 minutes for exposure, depending on the size of the screen. About 20 to 30 minutes may be allowed for exposure when exposing to a black light unit at a distance of about 2 feet. Two Number 2 photofloods may be kept about 2½ feet from photographic contact frame and exposed from about 20 to 25 minutes. In

Figure 65. Prints from polyvinyl alcohol direct screen printing plates which were prepared from handmade intaglio positives. The screen for printing the head of General Douglas MacArthur at the left was prepared on Number 140 copper wire screen fabric.

99

direct, strong, uniform sunlight the screen may be exposed for about 7 to 10 minutes.

Washing Out PVA Screen

To develop or etch out those parts of the screen which were protected by the opaqueness in the positive and which were not hit by light energy, the screen may be immersed in warm water that is about 110 degrees Fahrenheit (43 degrees Celsius) for about 1½ minutes or until the image or design is washed out clean. Don't keep the screen in water any longer than necessary to insure complete opening of the image. Or the screen may be developed by pouring water on the underside of the screen or by spraying water on with a hose or mixing faucet. The mixing faucet is better, since it allows for adjustment of water temperature. When the image appears clean, wash off with cold water and remove excess moisture by dabbing inside and underside of screen with soft clean cloths or with paper towels. Allow screen to dry in front of an electric fan, with coated side facing fan.

If pinholes develop during development or after drying, it is suggested that a thicker or heavier solution of PVA be used. If desired, the screen may also be reinforced in certain areas with a suitable filler such as nitrocellulose or lacquer type of filler.

Figure 65 shows some prints made from direct polyvinyl alcohol screens as explained in this chapter.

Reclaiming Screen Fabric

It is not practical to reclaim PVA silk screens. The solution that is strong enough to reclaim the silk in many cases will make the fabric unusable for practical purposes. Each prepared silk PVA screen was boiled directly in water by the writer for two hours while he was experimenting with varied formulas; hardly any of the coating was removed. However, where it is essential to reclaim nylon, polyester, and even silk, the screen may be boiled in about a 20 percent caustic solution, then scrubbed with a type of brush used to clean suede or with a nylon brush.

Metal fabric screens may be reclaimed by boiling the screen for 2 to 5 minutes in a 15 to 20 percent caustic solution and scrubbing with a suede brush using hot water. Another method is to soak the screens in a solution of one part hydrogen peroxide and three parts water at a temperature of 120 to 130 degrees Fahrenheit (49 to 54 degrees Celsius). The remaining particles of the screen may then be burned off. Metal screens may also be soaked in a 3 percent hydrogen peroxide solution for about an hour, then scrubbed with hot water, and the remaining particles burned off in a direct flame such as a gas burner or Bunsen burner.

POLYVINYL ALCOHOL-POLYVINYL ACETATE PRINTING SCREEN

16

Screen printing manufacturers and suppliers have been cognizant of specific needs of the industry and have developed commercial type screen printing films and coatings especially for specialized printing. For example, the printing on ceramic surfaces has motivated the development of the direct polyvinyl alcohol-polyvinyl acetate printing screen.* Because tough, inert, and long lasting photographic printing screens are needed to resist the fine abbrasive action of the ceramic ink particles, the polyvinyl alcohol-polyvinyl acetate screen can be used for all general and specialized screen printing.

When a solution of plasticized polyvinyl acetate is added to a solution of polyvinyl alcohol, a mixture is produced that is easier to apply to screen fabric than a polyvinyl alcohol solution alone would be. The mixing of the two solutions eliminates the necessity for using a whirling device for coating and drying the coated screen. Also, the prepared screen has less tendency to develop pinholes, is more flexible, gives longer service, and prints fine detail. The prepared printing screen consists of a plastic impregnated silk, nylon, or metal screen fabric that has dimensional stability, flexibility, and toughness. If the screen is prepared correctly, a tough screen is obtained that resists abrasion, action of dyes, ketones, ethers, alcohols, oils, greases, all types of inks, etc., thus obtaining a screen that can be employed for a type of printing that is more difficult to produce.

The printing screen is easy to prepare. The following three stock solutions are used to make the sensitized coating emulsion: (1) a polyvinyl alcohol solution; (2) a solution consisting of polyvinyl acetate and dibutyl phthalate; and (3) an 18 percent potassium bichromate or ammonium bichromate solution which serves as the sensitizing solution. Besides the three solutions, the printer will need the following common materials and equipment to prepare this screen: (1) A perfectly clean and tightly stretched screen with a Number 12, 14, 16, or 18 or equivalent screen fabric; (2) a squeegee, emulsion coater, or sharp edge of a piece of cardboard for applying emulsion onto cleaned screen fabric; (3) a carbon arc, black light exposing unit, or any practical actinic light source for exposing the prepared printing screen; (4) a vacuum contact frame, a photographic contact frame, or a unit of the type illustrated in Figure 66; (5) a photographic positive containing design or copy to be reproduced; (6) a sink with a source of hot and cold running water; (7) glass jars or polyethylene containers for storing the varied solutions; (8) a plain

---

*E. I. du Pont de Nemours and Co., Wilmington, Delware.

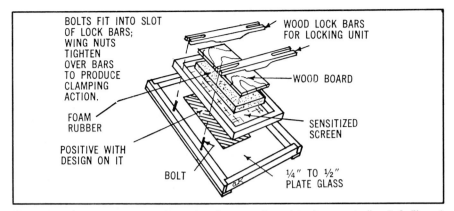

Figure 66. Component parts of exposing frame and sensitized screen in "exploded" position to show relative placement for exposure.

electric fan; (9) a photographic thermometer; (10) a darkroom, dark area, or cabinet in which to dry the coated screen; (11) some blotting paper, newsprint paper, or paper towels.

The general procedure for preparing this screen consists of: (1) Preparing or mixing the ingredients which make up the sensitized photographic emulsion; (2) coating the cleaned screen fabric with the emulsion; (3) drying the coated screen; (4) exposing the screen and photographic positive to a light source; (5) washing out or developing the exposed screen.

Polyvinyl Alcohol Solution

The polyvinyl alcohol (PVA) used for the preparation of this screen is of the same type that is used to prepare the sensitized polyvinyl alcohol printing screen explained in Chapter 15. The polyvinyl alcohol solution consists of 1 part, by weight, of polyvinyl alcohol powder, which is dissolved in 4 parts, by weight, of water. While distilled water is generally best, any clean and clear water may be used. The correct amount of weighted powder is poured slowly into the water in a glass jar. The powder and water may be stirred with a glass stirring rod, a fork, or with an electric mixer, if a large quantity of solution is being prepared. The writer prefers to allow the weighed powder to soak in the required water overnight. It then can be stirred easily to complete the dissolving process. If the polyvinyl alcohol solution is stored in a clean glass-stoppered jar, the solution will keep indefinitely. If scum forms after a long storage period, the scum may be removed or the polyvinyl alcohol strained through screen fabric and the clean or strained solution used.

Polyvinyl Acetate Solution

The polyvinyl acetate solution is made by adding 1 part, by weight, of dibutyl phthalate to 11 parts, by weight, of polyvinyl acetate solution. The dibutyl phthalate is a plasticizer which is added to the polyvinyl acetate to overcome the inherent brittleness of acetate films or coatings. The polyvinyl

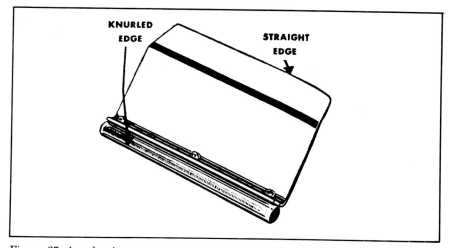

KNURLED EDGE

STRAIGHT EDGE

Figure 67. An aluminum commercial coater for applying emulsions to screen fabrics. The first coat is applied with the straight edge of coater; the second coat may be applied with the knurled edge.

acetate solution (which is similar to that employed in industry for adhesives and coatings) is thick and white. The adhesive property of the acetate solution aids in producing an excellent impregnated fabric or metal screen. The parts are weighed first and dibutyl is added to the white acetate solution. The acetate-dibutyl mixture should be stirred for about 25 minutes or until the butyl is completely dissolved in the acetate. The mixture will keep, if stored in a glass container in a cool place. However, it should not be stored in a refrigerator.

Sensitizing Solution

The third solution, the sensitizing solution, is made by dissolving 18 parts, by weight, of granulated or powdered potassium bichromate or ammonium bichromate in 82 parts of distilled water, by weight. This will produce an 18 percent solution of sensitizer. When the sensitizing solution is added to the other solutions it makes the mixture react to light. Hot water should be used and the solution should be completely clear before it is added to the other solutions. The sensitizing solution will keep indefinitely, if stored in a cool dry place in a dark bottle that is well-stoppered.

Preparing the Coating Solution

To prepare the emulsion for coating, add 5 parts, by weight, of the prepared polyvinyl alcohol solution to 12 parts, by weight, of the mixed polyvinyl acetate-dibutyl phthalate solution. When the two solutions are stirred well, add 6 parts, by weight, of the 18 percent sensitizing solution to the two mixed solutions (polyvinyl alcohol and polyvinyl acetate-dibutyl phthalate solution). It is recommended that the completely mixed sensitized emulsion consisting

103

Figure 68. Metal emulsion scoop coaters for applying uniform thickness of emulsion coatings to fabric on screens. Coater available in sizes up to 12 feet. (Courtesy of Advance Process Supply Company, Chicago, Illinois).

Figure 69. A print made from a screen on No. 12XX silk. Fabric was covered with one coat of sensitized polyvinyl alcohol-polyvinyl acetate solution.

104

of the three solutions be strained through a piece of screen fabric tc eliminate air bubbles before the screen is coated.

The mixed polyvinyl alcohol-polyvinyl acetate-phthalate solution without the sensitizing solution is very stable and will keep for long periods of time. Once the sensitizing solution has been added to these two solutions, the sensitized emulsion consisting of all the solutions will keep for about one month, if stored in a cool place, but not in a very cold place.

Coating Screen

It is best to do coating under subdued light or under a 15-watt incandescent light. While coatings are not very sensitive to light when the coat is in liquid form, they are sensitive when they are dry on the screen fabric. The solution may be applied by squeegeeing with a squeegee; it may be applied with special coaters or troughs available from screen printing suppliers (see Figure 67 and Figure 68) with the sharp smooth edge of a piece of cardboard or polyethylene, with brushes, or with a sprayer. Some printers prefer to apply the emulsion coats on the outside or underside of screen fabric. While others prefer to apply the first coat on the inside of the screen and the second coat on the outside. Applying all coats on the outside has a tendency to produce slightly sharper printing and to eliminate serrated edges in printing. The coating solution is applied by pouring some of it at one end of the screen fabric and squeegeeing it back and forth evenly and carefully with a squeegee or coater. Air bubbles must be eliminated, as each air bubble may become a pinhole. The excess emulsion at the edges of the screen may be wiped off with a paper towel or a soft cloth.

After the coating is applied, the screen should dry in a horizontal position in complete darkness at a temperature of 70 to 80 degrees Fahrenheit (21 to 27 degrees Celsius). Drying may be accelerated with the aid of a fan; heat should not be used. After the first coat is completely dry, a second coat may be applied in similar fashion to the first coat. If a very tough screen with a thicker printed impression is desired, a third coat may be applied. However, each coat must dry completely, before the next one is applied. Screen surfaces must not be touched after coating.

Exposing

The dry coated screen is arranged and exposed as illustrated in Figure 66. The photographic positive is placed so that it is right side up on the plate glass. The photographic positive bearing the design must be in perfect contact with the coated screen. The time of exposure will vary depending on the type of light, detail of design, the distance of light from screen, and the strength of the light. Strong carbon arc lamps that are about 36 inches (91.44cm) away from the screen will require about 4 to 6 minutes exposure; black light will require the same length exposure as illustrated in Figure 69.

Washing Out

The exposed screen is washed out or developed immediately after exposure by immersing screen in cool or luke warm water for 1 to 2 minutes. It is then washed out by using a pressure spray of cold water to the outside of the screen. Warm water up to 110 degrees Fahrenheit (43 degrees Celsius) will speed the operation. The screen should not be kept in contact with water any longer than is necessary for washing out design. When the design appears clean and sharp in the screen, the screen may be blotted carefully on both sides of the fabric with blotting paper or newsprint paper. The screen should then be allowed to dry. A fan without heat may be used to hasten drying. The areas outside the image areas (that may be uncoated) may be coated or blocked out with the same emulsion that was used originally to coat the screen.

Reclaiming Screen

Since the coating on this screen is quite inert and resistant, it is not practical to reclaim screens made of silk. The solvents that will destroy the emulsion may damage the silk. However, a metal screen may be reclaimed by boiling the screen in a 15 to 20 percent caustic solution for 3 to 5 minutes, then scrubbing the screen with a brush and hot water and rinsing thoroughly in water. Another method that may remove the emulsion is to soak the screen for 5 minutes in a solution containing 1 part hydrogen peroxide and 3 parts water at a temperature of 120 to 130 degrees Fahrenheit (49 to 54 degrees Celsius). In either of the methods, the traces of material left on the metal fabric should be burned off in an open flame and the screen rinsed off thoroughly in water. However, the burning of metal fabric in a flame cannot be overdone, since it may destroy the properties of the metal fabric.

Figure 69 presents a print made from a screen which was prepared on Number 12XX silk. Instead of a positive, opaque paper cutouts were placed in direct contact with the coated screen and exposed. The fabric was covered with one coat of sensitized polyvinyl alcohol-polyvinyl acetate solution. The emulsion was squeegeed once or twice on both sides of the screen fabric and was processed as explained in this chapter.

17

ENCOSOL DIRECT EMULSION

Encosol* emulsion for direct coating of screens incorporates a diazo sensitizer.** This product was developed by the Azoplate Corporation, Murray Hill, New Jersey, who introduced the first commercially available diazo-sensitized emulsion in 1963. Prior to that all direct emulsions had to be sensitized with bichromate products which reduced the shelf life of sensitized emulsions. Diazo sensitized emulsions produce screens with a virtual absence of "sawtooth" effect, excellent resistance to a wide variety of solvents as well as inks containing water. Screens made with these emulsions are intended for printing under high humidity conditions, precision printing, and for long production runs. Diazo sensitized screens may be stored under darkroom conditions for months prior to exposure.

The emulsion can be coated on nylon, polyester, metal cloth, and silk. Very fine or coarse fabric may be coated. However, silk cannot be easily reclaimed without damage to the fabric. As with other direct emulsions, optimum performance can be obtained, if proper processing methods are used in the screen preparation prior to coating.

The emulsion produces an extremely tough screen and does eliminate sawtooth or ragged edges. Once coated, the screen may be stored up to 6 months, if screen is not exposed to high temperature or actinic light in storage. Normal temperature and fluctuations do not affect exposure time and exposure time may be shortened by decreasing the distance between screen and light source. "Dark hardening," common with bichromate sensitized products, is almost eliminated. The unsensitized emulsion may be stored indefinitely under normal atmospheric conditions, if emulsion is not allowed to freeze or get above 85 degrees Fahrenheit (29 degrees Celsius). When the emulsion is sensitized it will remain stable at room temperatures for periods up to 6 months; it will keep up to 12 months, if stored in an ordinary refrigerator. This writer has used one sensitized emulsion for one year which was kept in a refrigerator.

Screens which are correctly coated with the sensitized emulsion may be stored under darkroom conditions for periods up to one year prior to exposure. This allows the printer to coat screens in slack time and to expose them as needed.

The product is available in four types of formulations. One of these — a special formulation — may be used for adhering and sensitizing direct-indi-

---

*Naz-Dar Company, Chicago, Illinois.
**Patent No. 3,246,986

107

rect films. Each of the formulations is available in separate containers but packaged as a unit consisting of the unsensitized emulsion, sensitizer, and a special dye concentrate. Since everything is already measured, it is easy for the printer to prepare the emulsion for coating.

The procedure in the preparation of this screen consists of (1) preparing sensitized emulsion, (2) precleaning screen fabric, (3) coating, (4) drying coated screen, (5) exposing, and (6) developing or washing out. It is suggested that the printer read the directions through thoroughly and have materials and equipment ready before starting. It is best to sensitize emulsion and do the coating in a darkroom or under subdued light (less than 15 watts incandescent light).

Preparing Sensitized Emulsion

The bottle containing the sensitizer is filled with water and shaken well making sure that the sensitizer is dissolved. Then the sensitizer is poured into the emulsion and stirred well with a plastic or wooden paddle. After the sensitizer is thoroughly mixed in the emulsion, the sensitized emulsion is ready to be used. The sensitized emulsion now may be stored in a dark area at room temperature or in a household refrigerator. The addition of the dye to the sensitized emulsion is optional; however, it may make visual inspection of screen easier.

Precleaning Screen

It is important to clean and prepare the screen fabric in order to assure good adhesion of sensitized emulsion to fabric. There are commercial degreasing and cleaning solutions available from the supplier of Encosol and other suppliers recommending precleaning of fabric. In using degreasing solutions, both sides of the fabric are wetted with warm water. Then the degreasing agent or liquid is poured on both sides of the wet screen and fabric is scrubbed thoroughly on both sides with a nylon brush. After scrubbing, the fabric should be rinsed with hot water to remove all traces of degreasing or cleaning solution before coating.

Coating

The coating should be done under subdued light, using special coaters available for this purpose, or with rigid strips of plastic material, stainless steel, or aluminum. The outside of the screen fabric or that side which will come in contact with the stock is coated first. Some of the emulsion is poured along one edge and the emulsion is applied in squeegee fashion, using about four strokes of the coater, and employing strokes in opposite direction, assuring that the emulsion penetrates to the inside. Then the screen is turned around and the inside of the screen is scraped with one or two even slow strokes allowing the emulsion to encapsulate the fabric. Any excess emulsion remaining around the edges may be removed with pieces of cardboard or plastic.

Monofilament meshes up to about 200 mesh and finer may not need extra coats. On coarser meshes and for special applications where thicker coatings are necessary, additional coats may be applied on the outside of the screen

108

fabric. Each coat must dry perfectly before applying the next one. Also, additional coats will require longer exposure time. Although the screen is ready for exposure after drying, it may be stored up to about 6 months in the dark at normal room temperature.

Drying

After the screen is coated, it may be dried either in a horizontal position, vertical position, or at an angle, with warm air from a fan being directed toward the outside of the screen. Each coat must dry thoroughly in the dark before applying the next sensitized coat. Although dried and coated screens may be stored in the dark and used at a later time, the screen may be exposed as soon as it is perfectly dry.

Exposing

To obtain fine image definition and resistance in printing correct exposure is very important. This product has a wide latitude for exposure and it is safer to overexpose than to underexpose the screen. In exposure there must be perfect contact between positive and screen and even illumination over the entire design area. A direct method exposing unit, a vacuum contact frame, a photographic contact frame of the type illustrated in Figure 64 or 66, or the cement method explained in Chapter 20 may be used to hold positive in perfect contact with screen. Everything else being equal, Encosol will require a longer exposure than bichromate sensitized emulsions.

Correct exposure time can be obtained by placing strips of clear film over coated screen, exposing, and removing each strip at intervals of one minute. The exposure range of the best time will be obvious. If the printer uses the full amount of the dye in the emulsion, correct exposure may be determined after development or washing out, when no difference is noticed in color or shade between the area exposed through the clear film and the surrounding area. If the area exposed through the film shows a lighter shade than the surrounding area, this indicates that screen was underexposed. Generally, while this sensitized emulsion will require a longer exposure than bichromate sensitized emulsions, exposure time can be shortened by decreasing the distance between the screen and the light source.

Developing or Washing Out

Developing or washing out should be done under subdued light. Although if screen is wetted within one minute after exposure, washing out may be done under ordinary daylight. The screen may be placed in a sink and a low pressure spray of cold or warm water (105 degrees Fahrenheit or 40 degrees Celsius) may be applied with a hose on both sides of screen. After washing out for one minute, the pressure may be increased. When the design appears clean and sharp, the excess water should be blotted from the screen using paper towels or newsprint paper. If compressed air is available, it may be advantageous to remove any particles and excess water which may cling to the screen. Where compressed air is not available, the screen may be dried with the aid of a fan, after blotting.

Figure 70. A print made from a screen which was coated with an 8-weeks old sensitized Encosol emulsion on No. 283 nylon. Coated screen was exposed 2 weeks later to a blacklight fluorescent unit at a distance of 4 inches for 4 minutes.

Reclaiming Screen

Before starting reclaiming of screen fabric, it is imperative that the ink used in printing be removed completely and thoroughly from the screen with a suitable solvent. Screen may then be reclaimed by immersing it in full strength bleach for about 15 minutes and washing screen off throughly with strong warm water spray. If pressure washers are available, a 2 to 3 minutes bleach application on both sides of the fabric will suffice with final removal of bleach with warm water pressure at full blast.

Nylon, polyester, or metal screen fabric can be reclaimed with the above procedures. Natural silk coated with direct emulsions cannot be reclaimed without some damage to the silk.

Figure 70 presents a print made by the writer from a screen as explained in this chapter. Emulsion used for coating was 8 weeks old. Coated screen was stored for 2 more weeks and then exposed.

110

SCREEN STAR DIRECT UNSENSITIZED AND PRESENSITIZED PHOTOGRAPHIC EMULSION

18

Since the introduction of screen printing, direct printing screens, or screens which are prepared by coating the screen fabric directly with emulsions, have developed under three general classifications: (1) those prepared with gelatinous coatings; (2) those prepared with a combination consisting of gelatinous and synthetic substances; and (3) those prepared with purely man-made or synthetic coatings. The solution Screen Star* photographic emulsion is essentially a synthetic adhesive resin which was formulated under the guidance of Henry Joseph and M. Spielvogel for easy screen preparation. When the emulsion is mixed with an ammonium bichromate solution or a diazo solution (which serve as the sensitizer) the mixed sensitized emulsion can be used for coating directly onto screen fabrics and for preparing practical printing screens. It can be coated onto such fabrics as silk, metal cloth, any of the synthetic cloths, organdy, and other fabrics normally employed in the industry. The processed screen may be employed for printing lacquers, vinyls, oil-base inks, water-base inks, flock adhesives, and even magnetic ink containing iron particles. A well prepared screen is resistant to common solvents used in the industry and to water. In spite of the high viscosity of the emulsion, the coating is easily applied, dries naturally, but dries quicker with the aid of a fan. The sensitized emulsion reproduces fine detail and solid large areas and produces a tough impregnated printing screen that may be used for printing on almost any surface. Either cold or warm water may be used to wash out the exposed screen.

This product is available in an unsensitized and in a presensitized formulation. The presensitized emulsion does not have to be mixed with a sensitizer by the screen printer before using. The emulsion is coated directly onto the screen fabric from the original container. Screens coated with the presensitized emulsion may be stored for weeks in the dark before exposing and washing out without losing their effectiveness. The writer prefers to store these types of screens in complete darkness in black opaque envelopes or containers. However, presensitized emulsions are generally stored for definite periods: for example 3 months, 6 months. Therefore, the screen printer must make sure that he does not use a spoiled presensitized emulsion.

The unsensitized product may be stored for very long periods, if stored in well-stoppered containers, in cool places, under ordinary atmospheric conditions. Both types are used in similar fashion for the preparation of printing screens. However, the preparation of the unsensitized product will be covered, since the making of printing screens with the presensitized emulsion does not require preparing a sensitized coating.

---

*Bond Adhesives Co., Jersey City, N.J.

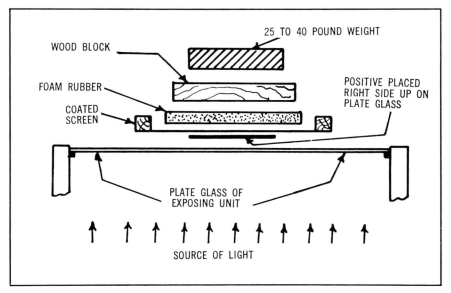

Figure 71. Arrangement of parts for exposing screen.

The preparation of the unsensitized emulsion is simple and consists of the following steps: (1) preparing sensitizing coating; (2) coating screen fabric; (3) exposing; and (4) washing out exposed screen. The ordinary materials and equipment needed for preparing a screen with this emulsion are (1) Screen Star photo emulsion; (2) an ammonium bichromate solution or a diazo sensitizing solution; (3) a photographic or hand-prepared positive; (4) simple measuring utensils; (5) a screen with the desired screen fabric; (6) an arrangement for exposing photographic screens or any photographic contact frame that may be used for exposing direct screens; (7) a light source to which screen may be exposed; (8) a scraper, a coater, or squeegee for applying emulsion to screen fabric; (9) a source of water; (10) an electric fan for hastening drying of coated screens; and (11) some newsprint paper.

Preparing Sensitized Coating

A sensitized coating consists of the unsensitized emulsion to which a sensitizer has been added. If the Screen Star product the printer is using will be sensitized with a bichromate sensitizer, then he will add 1 part of the sensitizer to 5 parts of the emulsion by volume. If the product is one that is to be diazo-sensitized, then 1 part of the diazo solution is added to 7 parts of the emulsion. Each of the sensitized emulsions will produce a dried coating that is sensitive to light.

The ammonium bichromate solution is made by dissolving 4 ounces by weight of chemically pure or photographic ammonium bichromate in 1 quart of water (or 119 grams in one liter of water). Distilled water or any clean or clear water that is fit to drink may be used. The ammonium bichromate

112

solution will last a long time if stored in a well-stoppered dark colored or amber bottle. The emulsion by itself will also keep indefinitely if stored in a capped container. The emulsion should not be allowed to freeze. After long storage periods the emulsion should be stirred well before using. However, once the emulsion is mixed with the sensitizing solution the mixture will keep for about two weeks, if stored in a tightly covered amber colored bottle. The writer prefers to keep such solutions in polyethylene squeeze type bottles and store them in the dark. After the sensitizing bichromate solution is added to the emulsion, the mixture must be thoroughly stirred. Mixing should be done under ordinary lighting conditions. Should there be any air bubbles in the mixture, it is suggested that the mixed solution be strained through several layers of clean screen fabric.

The shelf life of the sensitized emulsion can be increased by mixing emulsion with a diazo sensitizer supplied by the manufacturer of the emulsion. The diazo sensitized emulsion will remain usable from 2 to 4 months, if stored in the dark at room temperature, or until the emulsion becomes too thick to pour from the container. If stored in a refrigerator, emulsion will last for about 5 to 6 months.

Thus, screens coated with diazo sensitized emulsions can be stored in the dark at room temperatures for a period from 3 to 6 months.

Figure 72. A print made from a screen prepared on No. 12 silk with two coats of emulsion and exposed for 2 minutes to black light.

Coating Screen Fabric

Depending on the thickness of the coating desired, two or three coats may be applied. The screen fabric should be clean and taut. Dirty, greasy, and oily screen fabric will prevent any emulsion from sticking to the fabric, especially metal and synthetic fabrics. The coating may be applied onto coarse or fine mesh. If a sharper detailed print is desired, then the first coat may be applied on the outside or underside of screen. The first coat is best applied by squeegeeing the emulsion on the underside, stroking slowly once or twice, with a soft rounded squeegee and then immediately stroking once on the inside of the screen fabric. This coat must be allowed to dry perfectly and

113

Figure 73. The three color detailed designs were mechanically printed directly onto the cylindrical metal container with screens prepared as explained in this chapter.

the second coat is then coated on the outside of the screen fabric. Each coat is applied by pouring enough of the solution at one end of the screen fabric and squeegeeing the solution a few times with a scraper, coater, squeegee, or sharp edge of a cardboard until a smooth coat is obtained. All coating may be done under ordinary light conditions; not under fluorescent light. However, each coat should dry in semi-darkness or, better still, in complete darkness, depending upon the facilities in the working area. A fan may be employed to hasten drying of coats. If a third coat is needed, it is applied over second dried coat. The dried screen should be stored in darkness or in an envelope until it is exposed, since the dry coating is more sensitive to light than the solution.

Exposing

It is best to expose a screen that has been coated with a bichromate sensitized emulsion as soon as it has dired or on the same day. However, screens coated with diazo sensitized emulsions may be stored up to about 3 months, if kept in complete darkness. Exposing lights such as carbon arc, pulsed xenon lamps, blacklight fluorescent units, and other lights normally employed in screen printing shops, including sunlight, may be used for exposing. The exposing arrangement illustrated in Figure 71 is practical for this type of screen where a blacklight fluorescent unit is available. Regardless of light source used, the important point to remember is to make sure that there is perfect contact between the coated screen and the positive containing the design to be reproduced. Good contact may be obtained by using a sheet of foam rubber about ½ to ¾ inch thick, as illustrated in Figure 71. The time of

114

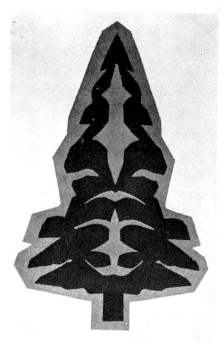

Figure 74. A two-color greeting card, printed from screens which were prepared by coating Number 196 nylon screen fabric. The coated screens were exposed and processed four weeks after they were coated.

exposure varies depending upon the light source, the type of copy in positive, and the distance of screen from light. Where a blacklight unit is employed the screen should be about 3 inches from the light and exposed from 1¼ to 4 minutes, depending upon the detail to be reproduced. See Figure 72. However, a sample exposure trial will easily standardize exposure time and distance for the screen printer.

Washing Out Exposed Screen

The exposed screen may be washed out or developed either in cold or warm water. Both sides of the screen should be wetted first and a water spray used to develop out the design. The writer has had practical results by spraying a high pressure spray on the outside or that side of the screen fabric which was in direct contact with the positive. When the design appears clean and sharp the screen is allowed to dry.

The washed out screen is dried by blotting excess water first with newsprint paper and then setting screen aside to dry. Drying may be hastened with a fan. If necessary, the rest of the screen fabric may be blocked out or filled in with the excess emulsion left over from the coating.

Reclaiming Screen

It is suggested that the screen printer test the reclaiming qualities of any emulsion by applying the emulsion onto a sample of the same screen fabric

115

that he intends to use before spending time and effort on reclaiming. As is common with most practical direct synthetic type screens, the very same qualities that make these direct screens desirable for printing different type of inks also make the printing screens inert to most reclaiming solutions.

However, metal screens may be reclaimed with a caustic solution such as sodium hydroxide solution. The solution may be applied on both sides of the screen fabric, allowing it to soak into the emulsion, and then scrubbing carefully with a brush to remove the coating. Printers must wear rubber gloves when working with caustic solutions.

Synthetic fiber screens may also be reclaimed if the emulsion is not too old. It is not practical to reclaim silk, since it may be destroyed in the reclaiming solution.

Figures 73 and 74 present prints made from screens prepared as described in this chapter. Figure 74 was printed with a screen prepared with a diazo sensitized emulsion.

AZOCOL DIRECT PHOTOGRAPHIC SCREEN PRINTING EMULSION

Azocol direct photographic screen printing emulsion* was introduced in 1963 to answer needs of the screen printing industry. This product consists of a coating which is applied directly onto fine or coarse screen fabrics generally employed in the screen printing industry. The product employs a sensitizer which is not of the dichromate type and which does not tend to change the quality of the basic emulsion in prolonged storage. Correctly prepared screens will last for thousands of impressions, resist solvents generally used in screen printing, produce fine detail and sharp lines in printing, and eliminate serrated or ragged edges even on coarse meshes.

The screens are easy to prepare and once coated may be stored for months before exposing. This implies that a printer may coat as many screens as he desires and store the coated screens in complete darkness under room temperature (of about 70 to 75 degrees Fahrenheit; 21 to 24 degrees Celsius) for periods up to 6 months, providing simple precautions are observed such as prevention of exposure of coated screen to actinic light and to abnormally high temperatures. However, high temperatures and humidity have no effect on the exposure time of the screen. The stability of the coating on silk, nylon, and other synthetic fabrics is about equal; on stainless steel it is a little less; and on bronze gauze it is more limited. Emulsion coated fabrics such as nylon, metal cloth, and polyesters may be reclaimed.

The product consists of an unsensitized basic emulsion and a sensitizer which is added to the emulsion before using. There are two types of emulsions available: One type is for the preparation of screens for the printing of oil-vehicle inks, enamels, lacquers, epoxy type inks, and the like; the second type emulsion is intended for printing of aqueous adhesives or dyes employed in textile printing and for dye printing medias.

The shelf life of the unsensitized emulsion is about eight months from date of shipping. While accidental freezing will not harm the product, it is suggested that one should avoid conditions which lead to extremes of temperatures. The sensitized emulsion, after mixing, will keep for approximately two months at about 80 degrees Fahrenheit (27 degrees Celsius). The viscosity changes of the sensitized emulsion at room temperature are minor within this two-month period. The sensitized emulsion will keep for shorter periods as the storage temperature increases; however, the coated screens will keep very well even at increased temperatures. On the surface this may seem

---

*Colonial Printing Ink Company, East Rutherford, New Jersey.

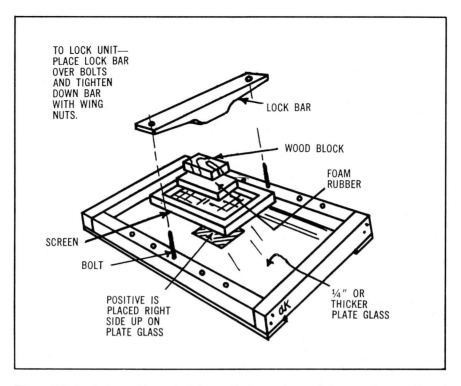

Figure 75. A photographic contact frame that may be used for exposing small and medium-size screens.

contradictory but the manufacturer advises that this is typical of the new class of sensitizers employed. The sensitizer has a remarkable stability as supplied and when applied to the carrier and dried down to a film. Water, which is the main vehicle in the basic emulsion lowers the stability of the sensitizer and this is the reason for the somewhat decreased shelf life of the working emulsion. Sensitized emulsion can be stored in standard household refrigerators for at least four months. Before using refrigerated emulsion, it is suggested that emulsion be allowed to reach room temperature.

The printing screen requires the same type of preparation and equipment as is normally required for most direct screens. The screen is prepared by coating the screen fabric, exposing the dried and coated screen, and developing or washing out in water. The materials and equipment needed are: (1) Basic Azocol emulsion; (2) special sensitizer supplied with basic emulsion; (3) screen which has correctly stretched, cleaned, and prepared fabric; (4) a non-metallic squeegee or coater for applying sensitized emulsion to screen fabric; (5) a vacuum frame or a photographic contact frame of the type illustrated in Figure 75 or other practical arrangement for exposing screen; (6) photographic positives; (7) an actinic light source such as carbon arc lamp, black light fluorescent unit, pulsed xenon lamp, mercury vapor lamp, or commercial cold cathode type exposure unit; (8) a source of hot and cold running water with a mixing faucet arrangement and (9) a stiff nylon brush for cleaning screen.

The product consists of an unsensitized basic emulsion, a sensitizer, and a dye additive. The small bottle containing the sensitizer is filled with water and shaken well until sensitizer is completely dissolved. The sensitizer is poured into the emulsion and mixed well by stirring with a wooden or plastic paddle or spoon. The dye additive is not necessary but may be added to the sensitized emulsion in order to better show the contrast of the image in processing. The sensitized emulsion should be covered when it is not in use. Although not imperative, it is suggested that emulsion be kept for at least two hours after sensitizer is added before the screen is coated. This aids the sensitizer to mix with the colloidal solution.

Coating Screen Fabric

Before coating screen, the screen printer must assure that the screen fabric was correctly stretched, prepared, and cleaned. Nylon, polyester, and metal cloth should be prepared as for other direct screens. However, the manufacturer of the emulsion does have a cleaning solution which is recommended for this purpose. This solution is diluted one part by volume of solution to three parts water. The fabric is scrubbed with a stiff nylon brush, scrubbing on both sides with the cleaning solution. Then the screen is flushed with hot water (140 to 160 degrees Fahrenheit; 60 to 71 degrees Celsius) until all traces of the solution are gone. When the screen is dry, it is ready for coating.

Nylon, polyester, and metal screens may also be cleaned and degreased by scrubbing a 20 percent caustic soda solution on both sides of the screen fabric with a brush and allowing solution to react on the screen for 15 to 20 minutes. Then solution is swabbed and neutralized with household vinegar, allowing vinegar to remain on fabric for about 15 minutes, and then completely washing vinegar off with water.

Figure 76. A two-color print of a greeting card consisting of a solid background color with message in contrasting bright color to be printed over background. Screen for printing both colors was prepared from handmade positives on No. 12 multifilament polyester fabric.

The sensitized emulsion is applied under subdued light to the fabric with a squeegee or a coater. It must be noted that coaters made of mild steel, copper, and zinc should not be used; applicators made of stainless steel and aluminum and, of course, all plastics are suitable. The coating is applied by pouring the emulsion onto one edge of the underside of the screen and then squeegeeing emulsion upward with a squeegee slightly smaller than the inside dimensions of the screen, coating the entire surface. The procedure is repeated on the inside of the screen, squeegeeing from the bottom to the top of the screen and from top to bottom. Drying time can be shortened by employing a fan and heat or any air directed toward the coated surface such as that from a hair dryer. The screen should be dried horizontally, outside or bottom side of screen downward to allow emulsion to flow out evenly. When the first coat is dry and if a second coat is to be applied, especially on coarser meshes, it is coated on the outside or underside of screen. On fine meshes a second coat may not be necessary. The dried and coated screen may be exposed immediately or the screen may be stored in the dark for several months and exposed as needed. The writer prefers to store smaller size screens in perfectly opaque bags under normal atmospheric conditions.

Exposure

Since the toughness and general qualities of the printing screen are dependent upon correct exposure, exposing should be done carefully, but not necessarily differently than for other types of direct screens. Over exposure does practically no harm, provided there is perfect contact between positive and screen and positive is the usual quality needed for screen printing work. Under exposure will reduce the life of the screen. When in doubt, it is better to overexpose this screen than to underexpose it.

Everything else being equal, exposure for this emulsion is somewhat longer than for other type emulsions. However, the screen can be brought nearer to the light source; although the distance from the light source such as an arc lamp should not be less than the length of the diagonal of the screen. The screen can be placed about 3 to 6 inches from a black light fluorescent tube unit or from a cold cathode type exposure unit of the type illustrated in Figure 99.

Correct exposure time may be determined by placing a narrow strip of clear film over the properly coated and dried screen, then exposing through clear film at equal time intervals, using 1 minute time intervals for high output arc lamps (90 amperes) and 2 to 5 minute intervals for smaller units. Proper exposure can be determined after washing out film when it is noticed that there is no difference in color between the area covered by the film and the area that was not covered by the film.

Developing or Washing Out

The developing or washing out of the parts of the screen which were not exposed to light may be performed in subdued daylight or under ordinary incandescent light. This is accomplished best by placing exposed screen in a tank of warm water that is about 100 degrees Fahrenheit (38 degrees Celsius) for 2 minutes. The screen is then washed out by directing a sharp spray of warm water against both sides of the screen. When image appears clear and sharp, excessive water may then be blotted off with newsprint paper and

120

Figure 77. A fine detailed print printed in one color with a screen prepared by coating emulsion on number 306 nylon. (Courtesy of Azoplate Corporation, Murray Hill, New Jersey).

screen dried with a fan. Where screen has very fine detail, it is suggested that after washing out, the open areas be blown with a stream of compressed air removing excess water and microscopic particles which may cling to the open areas.

Since this emulsion is quite inert, the reclaiming solutions which will remove it may destroy silk. However, nylon and similar synthetic cloth can be reclaimed, if desired. This may be done by soaking the screen in a solution of full strength of bleach (poured directly from the container), for about 15 minutes and then brushing out remaining particles with a stiff nylon brush under running water. Wire cloth is reclaimed in similar fashion, except that the screen can be soaked for a longer period. For screens that are too large for tray immersion, bleach may be applied to both sides of screen with a nylon brush until surface is completely wet, allowing solution to remain on fabric for 15 minutes. Decomposed coating may then be removed with a fine spray of hot water. Water pressure cleaners used for cleaning and reclaiming printing screens may also be employed to reclaim this screen.

Figures 76 and 77 present two prints made from screens prepared as described in this chapter.

NUMBER 32 E-Z DIRECT METHOD

This emulsion, Number 32 E-Z direct emulsion,* was formulated for the preparation of printing screens intended for printing with all types of screen printing inks including ceramic inks. The coating emulsion may be applied to all types of screen fabrics either fine or coarse. Screens prepared correctly with this emulsion will last for long production runs. It prints fine detail and halftones (see Figure 78 and 79) and correctly prepared screens will not show serrations in printing. The unsensitized emulsion may be stored indefinitely under ordinary amospheric conditions. After printing, the screen may be re-claimed.

Preparation of Coating Emulsion

The emulsion is sold unsensitized. The coating emulsion is made by adding sensitizing solution to the synthetic emulsion. The sensitizing solution is made by applying 4 ounces by weight of ammonium bichromate or sodium bichromate powder in one quart (32 ounces) by volume of water, or 113 grams in 946 cubic centimeters of water. For maximum shelf life, the sensitizing solution should be stored in a well-stoppered amber bottle in a cool place. The coating emulsion is made by adding one part of sensitizing solution to 5 parts of emulsion by volume. The two solutions should be mixed well by stirring in one direction with a glass, plastic, or stainless steel rod. While the sensitized emulsion will keep for longer periods, it is suggested that just enough solution be mixed for periods not longer than ten days. The sensitized emulsion may be stored in polyethylene type squeeze bottles.

Preparation of Screen Fabric

Before coating, the screen fabric should be prepared and cleaned for the application of this emulsion in the same fashion that it is prepared for the coating of other direct emulsions. Silk should be washed well in hot water and soap and rinsed thoroughly with water. Nylon may be cleaned with any of the methods employed for cleaning this fabric. One of the methods employed by the manufacturer is to scrub the nylon well with a cloth that has been dipped in bleach and then rinse the fabric perfectly with water. Metal fabrics should be degreased and cleaned thoroughly before applying emulsion. Fabric should be allowed to dry before coating emulsion on it.

---

*Naz-Dar Co., Chicago, Illinois

122

Figure 78. A print made from a screen prepared on No. 185 nylon as explained in chapter. Special effect wavy line positive was cemented to coated screen and both were exposed at 4 feet to a 17-ampere arc lamp for 3 minutes. (Photographic negative courtesy of Caprock Developments, New York, N. Y.)

Coating Screen Fabric

The coating emulsion is applied to the cleaned fabric by pouring some of the sensitized emulsion along one edge of the underside of the screen and squeegeeing the solution back and forth with a squeegee or with the sharp edge of a cardboard until a smooth and uniform coating is obtained. The coating may be done under subdued incandescent light or subdued daylight. Once the coating is applied the screen should dry in the dark. Drying may be hastened with an ordinary electric fan; heat should not be used. Drying of one coat takes about 10 minutes. The second coat may be applied in similar fashion, on the underside of the screen, after the first coat has dried completely. For most printing jobs two coats will suffice. However, if a tough, long lasting screen is desired, a third coat may be applied. Each coat must dry thoroughly.

Exposing

The coated screen may be exposed to any type of actinic light ordinarily used in screen printing — such as a carbon arc, black light fluorescent tube unit, mercury vapor lamp pulsed-xenon lamp, sunlight, and in an emergency, even a Number 2 photoflood lamp. The first four types of light are most practical. The time of exposure may be easily obtained by a trial exposure. Carbon arc lamps at 4 feet distance from the screen will take about 1½ to 6 minutes, depending on the type of arc lamp; black light fluorescent tubes will take 4 minutes when screen is exposed about 4 inches away from unit. Since exposure is an important part of the processing of the printing screen, it is suggested that the printer standardize his time and distance for his particular conditions. It is important that there be perfect contact between positive and screen. The positive should be arranged as illustrated in Figure 80. A vacuum contact printing frame, a photographic contact frame of the type shown in Figure 80 may be employed, or the "cement method" may be used in exposing film positives with screens.

Cement Method of Exposing

Where the screen printer has no access to a vacuum frame or a photographic contact frame, the cement method of exposing may be used for exposing small and medium size screens. In this method of exposing, a film positive is used and a good quality rubber cement solution is applied to the film positive and to the coated and dried screen fabric. The rubber cement used is thinned with cement solvent, using one part of solvent to one part of cement. Enough cement is brushed on the side of the film that is to come in contact with the screen and on the underside of the screen fabric. Immediately when the cement is dry (cement dries quickly), the screen is placed on cement-coated side of film and a piece of a newsprint paper is placed on the inside of the screen over the positive area. Using a soft cloth or cotton, the cloth is rubbed over the paper covering the positive area, until the fabric is in perfect contact with all of the positive. The screen is exposed then in the usual manner. After exposure, the film positive is peeled off, the excess cement is removed from the screen fabric by rubbing off cement with one's finger or by cleaning off cement with a cloth dipped in cement solvent, and the screen is washed out or developed in water.

Washing Out

The screen may be washed out in cold or warm water by spraying with a mixing faucet on both sides of the screen until the image appears perfectly

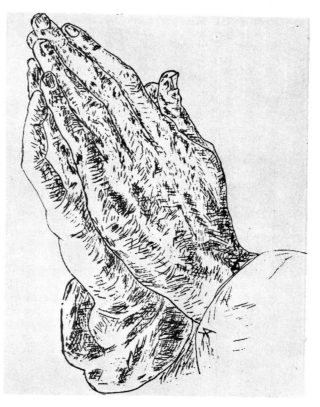

Figure 79. Line print of hands was made from a screen prepared on No. 196 nylon screen fabric. A clear, transparent, rigid plastic acrylic sheet made as a drypoint etching plate by the writer served as the photographic positive. Screen was exposed for 4 minutes at 4 inches away from a blacklight fluorescent tube unit.

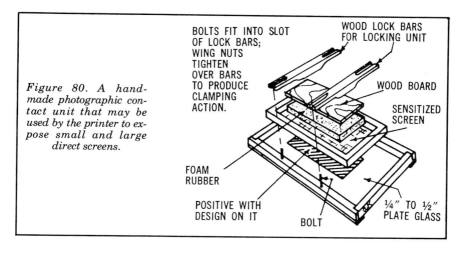

Figure 80. A handmade photographic contact unit that may be used by the printer to expose small and large direct screens.

BOLTS FIT INTO SLOT OF LOCK BARS; WING NUTS TIGHTEN OVER BARS TO PRODUCE CLAMPING ACTION.

WOOD LOCK BARS FOR LOCKING UNIT

WOOD BOARD

SENSITIZED SCREEN

FOAM RUBBER

POSITIVE WITH DESIGN ON IT

BOLT

¼" TO ½" PLATE GLASS

125

sharp and open. The screen may also be washed out by allowing screen to remain in water until all traces of the unexposed parts of the screen are washed away; although, this method will take longer for washing out.

After washing out remove excess water by blotting with newsprint paper and allow screen to dry naturally or with the aid of a fan. Do not use heat for drying. Fill in the rest of the screen with a blockout solution or with some of the excess emulsion, should this be needed, and the screen is ready for printing.

Reclaiming Screen Fabric

Although this inert type of emulsion is generally not removed from most screens, since screens may be used for thousands of impressions, the fabric may be reclaimed. This may be done by saturating a piece of cloth in hydrogen peroxide (an ordinary 3 percent solution obtained from the local drug store), and rubbing over both sides of coated screen. Solution should be allowed to remain on screen until the coating begins to dissolve. The coating is then washed away with water and scrubbed at the same time with a hard type nylon brush. A second application of hydrogen peroxide may be applied, if necessary. It must be stressed, as with the reclaiming of most screens, that the ink used in printing must be cleaned off thoroughly, before starting the reclaiming operation.

Another method of removing emulsions from screen fabrics such as nylon, polyester, or metal cloth, after removing all traces of ink, is to soak the screen in a 5 percent solution of sodium hypochlorite (bleach). After soaking for 5 minutes, a pressure washer or a strong water spray may be used to remove all traces of the coating.

ATLASOL DIRECT PHOTOGRAPHIC EMULSION

Screen printing must continue developing its resources so that it can meet the varied industrial and graphic communication needs more fully. The direct printing screen is growing in importance because it is meeting screen printing demands. It has been refined and at the same time simplified in procedure so that it is practical for most jobs. Today's screen printer has the advantage not only of choosing a direct, indirect, or direct-indirect screen for a printing job, but also has a choice of varied products in each of the three classifications.

Atlasol* direct method photographic emulsion is one of the practical direct emulsions for preparing printing screens. It can be coated onto any screen fabric used in the trade; produces a tough screen that will print on any surface including textiles, ceramics, and plastics; will print the varied inks generally used in screen printing, can be processed easily, has latitude in the percentage of sensitizer required for sensitization and latitude exposure time. It does not require a darkroom for processing and exposing. The emulsion is available in blue and red colors. The red emulsion tends to produce better detail in printing, especially when it is coated on white nylon or stainless steel. The major advantages of these emulsions is that they can be applied as sensitized emulsions and processed; or the screen may be coated with the unsensitized emulsion, the coating dried, and the screen sensitized at a later time when needed. This makes it possible to coat as many screens as desired to store them, and then sensitizing the screens as needed.

The emulsion comes unsensitized and may be kept indefinitely in the unsensitized state, if stored under ordinary room conditions, in a cool dark place, in a well-stoppered glass or polythylene container. Although the writer has successfully used a sensitized emulsion which was 18 weeks old, it is suggested that a sensitized emulsion not be used for more than a week. When stored in the sensitized state for a longer time, the emulsion has a tendency to become thinner in viscosity, which may require more applied coats on fabric, especially coarse fabrics. The emulsion should not be allowed to freeze. The emulsion may be sensitized with bichromate sensitizers or with diazo sensitizers.

Generally, the procedure for preparing the printing screen consists of sensitizing the emulsion, coating the screen fabric, drying the coated screen, exposing the screen, and washing out exposed screen with water. The same

---

*Atlas Silk Screen Supply Company, Chicago, Illinois.

127

materials and equipment are needed for processing this direct emulsion as other direct screens. Before preparing the screen, the printer should have the following ready: (1) a screen stretched with screen fabric that is perfectly clean and dry; (2) Atlasol emulsion; (3) a stock solution of ammonium bichromate or potassium bichromate, or a diazo sensitizer supplied by the manufacturer; (4) a coater, soft squeegee, or sharpedged piece of cardboard for applying emulsion to fabric; (5) a plain electric fan; (6) a source of actinic light for exposing screen; (7) a vacuum frame, a photographic contact frame, or any other method that will hold the positive and screen in perfect contact; (8) a source of hot and cold water with a mixing faucet arrangement; (9) a positive containing design or copy to be reproduced; (10) a photographic thermometer; and (11) some newsprint or blotting paper.

Preparation of Sensitized Emulsion

A stock solution of ammonium bichromate, potassium bichromate, or a diazo solution may be used to sensitize the emulsion. This may be done by dissolving 4 ounces by weight of chemically pure or photographic bichromate powder in a quart or 32 ounces of water (113 grams in 946 cubic centimeters). Although clean water that is fit to drink and does not have unusual chemicals in it may be used, it is better to use distilled water. A diazo stock solution may be made by dissolving the diazo powder supplied by the manufacturer in 4 liquid ounces of warm water (118 cubic centimeters) and shaking well to dissolve the powder. The stock solutions will keep indefinitely, if stored in a cool dark place and keep in a well-stoppered brown or opaque glass or polyethylene container.

The sensitized emulsion coating may be made by mixing 1 to 2 parts of the stock bichromate solution in 10 parts of the emulsion. If the diazo stock solution is used, 4 liquid ounces (118cc) is mixed in 1 quart (946cc) of the emulsion. The sensitized emulsion must be stirred thoroughly after addition of sensitizing solution. The two solutions should be stirred in one direction with a glass rod or spoon. The mixed sensitized solution may be kept in a polyethylene container of the squeeze bottle type for easier application of emulsion to fabric.

Although in a direct screen the fabric is coated on both sides or impregnated with the emulsion, it is still suggested that fabrics, especially synthetic fabrics and metal cloths, be cleaned and degreased before coating. Silk and organdy are easily prepared by washing the fabric on the screen with soap and water, thoroughly rinsing off the soap with water, and allowing the fabric to dry. Nylon may be degreased and cleaned by brushing or by dipping a piece of cotton in a 5 to 10 percent solution of cresylic acid and rubbing the solution on both sides of the fabric to clean and degrease the fabric. The acid should be left on for 2 minutes and then rinsed off thoroughly with water. Another method of preparing nylon is to wet the stretched nylon on the screen with water, sprinkle a kitchen cleanser containing very fine pumice on the nylon, and rub the cleanser over both sides of the nylon with a medium-hard brush or sponge. However, the rubbing must not be too rough, as the nylong may be weakened. The nylon should be rinsed with water so that no trace of the cleanser is left. After the nylon is dry, it may be coated with the emulsion. Polyester fabric may also be cleaned off with a microscopic powder or paste in similar manner to nylon; however, the powder must be rinsed off

128

thoroughly with water. Metal cloth should be cleaned and degreased before coating as for any other emulsion.

Coating Screen Fabric

The screen may be coated under yellow light or under low wattage incandescent light (about 15-watt bulb). The emulsion is poured along one edge on the outside of the fabric and is squeegeed carefully with a special coater, (see Figure 68), a soft squeegee, or with the sharp edge of a piece of cardboard. The coating should be squeegeed rather slowly, just once up and down, first on the outside of the screen fabric, and then stroked once immediately on the inside of the screen with the squeegee, so that a uniform perfect coat is applied. The screen s allowed to dry in the darkness or under a small yellow light. When the first coat is completely dry, a second coat or a third coat may be applied on the outside of the screen fabric. Applying the second coat or third coat on the outside tends to produce a screen which will print sharper detail. After the second coat or third coat is dry, the screen is ready to be exposed. The coating can dry naturally. It will dry in about 10 minutes with the aid of a fan. Heat should not be used.

Generally, two coats of the emulsion will suffice for most jobs. If fabric is coarser than about No. 8 silk or its equivalent is being coated and if a thicker coating is needed in order to print a heavier deposit of ink, then a third coat may be applied.

Exposing

While it is practical to expose the coated and dried screen to an arc lamp, the screen may be exposed to black light fluorescent tubes, photo-flood lamps, pulsed xenon lamps, or even the sunlight. The printer can easily establish the time of exposure with a trial exposure. Four minutes exposure to a 35-ampere arc lamp at 3 feet will produce satisfactory screens. Black light at about 3 inches away from the screen will require 5 to 7 minutes, depending on the unit and on the detail being reproduced.

In exposing, the positive is placed, right side up, on a flat surface and the screen is positioned over the positive and in contact with the positive. Regardless of the method employed, there must be perfect contact between positive and screen. The screen and positive may be exposed in a vacuum frame, in a photographic contact frame, or by cementing positive with rubber cement to screen fabric temporarily and exposing through positive.

After the screen is exposed, it is washed out.

Washing-out

The exposed screen is washed out in warm water that is 100 to 120 degrees Fahrenheit (38 to 49 degrees Celsius). Generally, a spray of water is applied over the outside and inside of screen until the image appears clean and sharp. The screen may also be allowed to soak in water to be washed out. The excess water in the design is blotted with newsprint or blotting paper or it may be blown out. The screen may dry naturally or the drying may be hastened with the aid of a fan. Sensitized or unsensitized emulsion may be used to reinforce and coat edges and corners of screen, if necessary, before starting printing.

Post-Sensitizing

Post-Sensitizing involves first coating the screen with the unsensitized emulsion as it comes in the container. The coating is done and dried in similar fashion to that already explained, except that the drying of the unsensitized emulsion does not have to be done in the dark. After the coats have dried completely, the stock sensitizer is wiped quickly on both sides of the screen with a piece of cotton. This is done by dipping the cotton in the sensitizer, squeezing out excess solution, and applying sensitizer quickly, first on the outside of the screen then on the inside. The screen is then allowed to dry with the aid of a fan in the dark or under a yellow light.

Post-sensitizing eliminates the necessity of mixing and making a sensitized emulsion. It also produces a thicker coating, where it is desirable, since the viscosity of the emulsion is not decreased because it is not necessary to add a sensitizing solution to it.

CAUTION!

INFLAMMABLE: Keep from open flames, lighted cigarettes, etc.

POISON (METHANOL)
Not to be taken internally. Avoid prolonged breathing of vapors.

ANTIDOTE: Call a doctor! Give an emetic or wash out stomach. Give milk, white of egg or flour in water. In case of respiratory failure, administer artificial respiration.

Figure 81. Print made from a screen prepared with a sensitized emulsion on 225 mesh amber colored nylon. Detail print was exactly like original copy and showed no serrations.

The exposing and washing out procedures are the same as for the application of the sensitized emulsion.

Generally it is suggested that sensitized screens be exposed immediately after drying. However, to increase resistance to water-soluble inks and to produce a screen that will print thousands of impressions, the sensitized screen may be stored for four days in the dark before exposing. After this period of storage, the screen is exposed and allowed to soak in water for about 30 minutes or until it begins to wash out. After the screen is washed out and dried, it is given a heat treatment with infrared lamps for 2 to 4 minutes at a distance of 4 feet from the lamps or the screen may be exposed to the heat of the sun for about 1 hour. It is maintained that for printing on textiles and the like this treatment produces a very resistant screen.

Reclaiming or Decoating Screen

Commercial reclaiming agents, available from screen printing suppliers and used for reclaiming direct screens, may be employed for reclaiming nylon and wire cloth screens. However, it is imperative that the ink be completely cleaned from the screen before reclaiming. Reclaiming solutions must be thoroughly washed off with water, as any traces which dry and are left on the fabric may prevent perfect adhesion of another coating.

Figure 81 illustrates a detailed one-color label printed with a screen prepared as explained in this chapter.

NU-SOL DIRECT METHOD PRINTING SCREEN

Nu-Sol* developed by Sidney Schulsinger of New York City is a modified polyvinyl plastic type product which has been formulated and packaged for producing photographic printing screens for printing with ceramic inks, dye inks, water-soluble and other screen printing inks where a tough durable screen is needed. It is a direct screen, since the prepared solution or emulsion is applied directly to the screen fabric. The solution may be coated onto silk, synthetic fabrics, and onto metal screen fabrics. It may be coated onto screen fabrics ranging from Number 6 (74 mesh) to Number 25 (200 mesh). The final printing screen may be employed for reproducing line copy and halftone copy. It has the unusual quality for a direct screen of offering a sharp line in printing. The screen varies from other direct screens in that a coating trough is recommended for application of photographic solution and in that ordinary cold water is used to wash-out or develop the screen after exposure. The trough produces an even coating which ordinarily is not possible with brushing or dipping methods. While the manufacturer specifically recommends that coating be done with the trough, the writer has on varied occasions coated the emulsion onto the fabric with a squeegee.

There are three types of formulae or emulsions of this product available: (1) the first type (Number 1 B) is for printing with ceramic inks and for general graphic arts printing; (2) the second type (Number 2) has been developed for printing on textiles; and (3) the third type (Number 3AA) is employed for printing lacquer inks, vinyls, and oil-vehicle inks.

Each of the formulas consist of a packaged stock solution and a sensitizer. The prepared mixture which is applied to the screen fabric is not sensitive when in solution; however, it does become light-sensitive when it dries. Therefore, after the first coat is applied to the screen fabric, it and the rest of the coats should be dried in the dark. It is not necessary to work under safelights or red lights. An ordinary 15-watt bulb or less may be used when coating the solution on the screen fabric.

Basically, the method of coating is the same for the three photographic formulas. The procedure involves (a) mixing solution, (b) applying the solution onto the screen fabric, (c) drying the applied coating, (d) exposing, and (e) washing-out or developing the exposed screen.

---

*Drakenfeld Division, Imperial Color and Chemical Department, Hercules Incorporated, Washington, Pennsylvania.

Required Equipment

Before starting the actual preparation of the screen, it is suggested that the screen printer or novice have the following materials and equipment ready: (1) Nu-Sol stock solution; (2) Nu-Sol sensitizer; (3) a glass vessel or jar in which to prepare the mixture; (4) a glass or plastic spoon or a glass or wooden rod (not metal) for stirring the solutin; (5) a coating trough (see Figures 82, 83, and 84), which may be bought or made; (6) a screen stretched with the correct screen fabric; (7) an arc lamp, black light, or any strong actinic light for exposing the dried and coated screen; (8) an electric fan for hastening drying of applied coats; (9) a sink with a source of water; (10) some newsprint paper, if the screen is to be reinforced with a plastic coat or hardening agent; (11) some soft, lintless cloths, and (12) an exposing frame of the type illustrated in Figure 86.

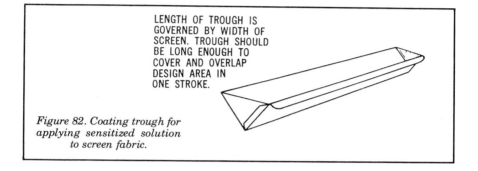

LENGTH OF TROUGH IS GOVERNED BY WIDTH OF SCREEN. TROUGH SHOULD BE LONG ENOUGH TO COVER AND OVERLAP DESIGN AREA IN ONE STROKE.

Figure 82. Coating trough for applying sensitized solution to screen fabric.

Because the procedure for the Nu-Sol formula used for printing ceramic inks (Number 1B) is similar to the other two in its application, the preparation of this screen is explained in detail. Where the other two formulas vary, the variations are presented.

Mixing the Solution

To mix the solution, 1 part of Nu-Sol sensitizer is added to 5 parts of Nu-Sol 1B stock solution. The two are stirred with a glass or plastic spoon or rod (not metal) until the solution is thoroughly mixed. The solution should be mixed until it assumes a uniform color and has no streaks in it. It is then ready to be applied to the screen fabric. If there should be many air bubbles because of improper mixing, the solution may be strained through a piece of screen fabric to remove the excess bubbles.

Coating the Screen Fabric

The screen should be placed in an upright or vertical position so that inside surface of screen faces the printer. The screen must be supported firmly so that it does not move during the coating process.

When the screen is supported, enough of the mixed solution is poured into the coating trough for the coating process. The coating edge of the trough

133

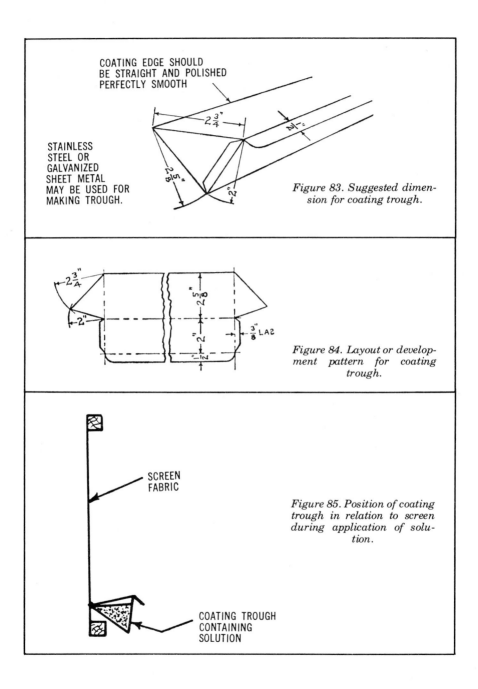

COATING EDGE SHOULD
BE STRAIGHT AND POLISHED
PERFECTLY SMOOTH

$2\frac{3}{4}$"

STAINLESS
STEEL OR
GALVANIZED
SHEET METAL
MAY BE USED FOR
MAKING TROUGH.

Figure 83. Suggested dimension for coating trough.

$2\frac{3}{4}$"

$2\frac{5}{8}$"

$2\frac{1}{2}$"

2"

$\frac{3}{8}$" LAP

Figure 84. Layout or development pattern for coating trough.

SCREEN
FABRIC

Figure 85. Position of coating trough in relation to screen during application of solution.

COATING TROUGH
CONTAINING
SOLUTION

is held against the bottom of the screen at such an angle (see Figure 85) that the solution flows onto the screen fabric. The trough is tilted so that the solution comes in contact with the fabric and the trough is pulled upward along the screen fabric with a rapid stroke in squeegee fashion until the top of the screen is reached. Although firm pressure may be applied, the pressure should not be extreme. When the trough has reached the top of the screen, it is tilted back to draw the remaining solution away from the screen, and the trough is then removed. This applies the first or base coat.

The base coat should be allowed to dry thoroughly in the dark. A fan placed about 1 yard from the screen will hasten drying so that each coat will dry completely in about 5 to 10 minutes depending upon the atmospheric conditions.

After the first coat has dried, the next coat is applied in similar fashion, except that the second coat is applied on the underside or the printing contact surface of the screen. When the second coat dries, a third and a fourth coat may be applied carefully, after each coat is allowed to dry completely. The number of coats to be applied is governed by the thickness of coating desired and by the mesh of the screen fabric employed. The screen is held in an upright position for each coat, using two strokes of the trough for each application — one stroke up then the screen is reversed so that the bottom edge is up and the trough is pulled up again. Experimentation and desired thickness of coat will govern whether one or two strokes of the trough are to be used for each coat. Four coats should suffice for most work. It is suggested that the coating of the various screens be done at one time.

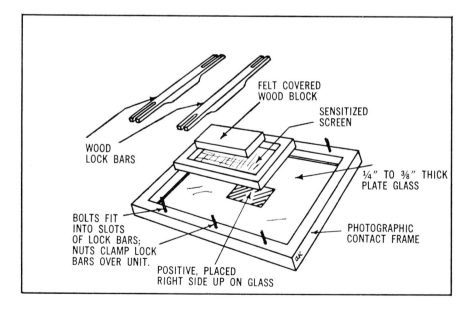

Figure 86. Component parts of exposing frame and sensitized screen in "exploded" position to show relative placement for exposure.

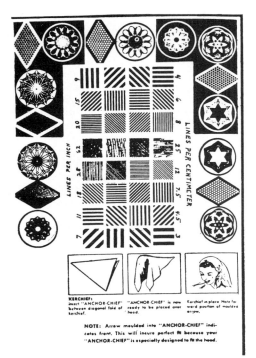

Figure 87. A print made from a screen prepared with four coats of Nu-Sol No. 3AA on No. 16 silk. The screen was exposed for 7 minutes at a distance of 6 feet from an arc lamp producing 110 amperes at the arcs. (Photographic positive courtesy of Elmer F. Kortum, Naz-Dar Company, Chicago, Ill.)

Exposing

After the coats have been applied and dried, the screen is exposed as illustrated in Figure 86. A trial or two will determine the right exposure. It is suggested that a ½" to 1" thick piece of foam rubber be placed between wood block and screen shown in Figure 86 to obtain more perfect contact. When a 25-ampere arc lamp is employed, three minutes may be used to expose a screen that is about three feet from the light. If a stronger light is used as illustrated in Figure 87, the exposure data may change somewhat.

In exposing halftones, the exposure time is decreased about one-fourth or one-third of the regular exposure time. For example, if for line copy the exposure time is three minutes, for exposing halftone copy the exposure time will be approximately two minutes.

Washing Out

The exposed screen is washed out or developed by spraying the screen on both sides with cool water, not ice water, until the image or design is seen clearly. The spraying should be continued until all residue has been washed-out. A high pressure spray may be used. When the screen is completely washed out, it is dried and used for printing.

136

Figure 88. Print made from a screen coated with Nu-Sol No. 1B formula on monofilament nylon, for printing a red, thick alkyd glossy enamel.

Formula for Printing on Textiles

In preparing the screen for printing on textiles (Number 2), the procedure is similar to the above, with certain exceptions. In mixing the coating solution, 1 part sensitizer is added to 4 parts of the stock solution. Also, the screen should be washed-out or developed within a half-hour after exposure to prevent the film from over-oxidizing. If the coating, after being washed-out, is exposed to 180 degrees Fahrenheit heat (82 degrees Celsius) for one hour, it will be impervious to water soluble textile dyes. The screen may also be reinforced with a plastic coat or hardening solution recommended by the manufacturer to produce a coating that is resistant to dyes containing various proportions of acids.

The reinforcing is done by placing the screen, printing surface down, onto newsprint paper or blotting paper. The plastic coat solution is then poured along one edge on the inside, or on top of the screen, and the coat is squeegeed across the screen once and back again. The screen is then turned over and a lintless cloth is dampened thoroughly with a recommended solvent and the solution is wiped out of the open mesh of screen with the cloth. The cloth should not be saturated with the solvent for this step. The solvent is wiped off finally with a dry cloth.

Some screen printers who plan to use the plastic coat for reinforcing the screen, apply the photographic coating with the trough just on the outside surface of the screen, not on the inside. The inside of the screen, being uncoated, makes possible better adhesion of the plastic coating to the inside for reinforcing. The reinforcing solution recommended has affinity for the coating.

While other reinforcing or hardening agents may be used, it is suggested that they first be tested completely, including printing on the planned material, before doing commercial jobs.

137

When the reinforcing coat is definitely dry, the screen may be made ready for printing.

Preparing Screen for Printing Vinyls, Lacquers, and Oil-Vehicle Inks

In applying the third formula (Nu-Sol Number 3AA) the procedure is similar, except that the sensitizer used is a 15 percent ammonium bichromate solution. The sensitizer is dissolved in the stock solution, 1 part sensitizer to 5 parts stock solution. This formula is less light-sensitive; therefore, it is suggested that the exposure time be increased to two or three times that for Number 1B formula.

In washing out this coated screen, the screen should be wetted on both sides and allowed to soak in water for three minutes. Then the screen is washed with water under pressure, but washing out is done only on the outside or underside of the screen.

Figure 88 illustrates a print made from a screen prepared with this formula.

"GA" DIRECT PHOTOGRAPHIC EMULSION

23

The perspective of time ultimately determines what products will last and serve an industry. New practical products generally represent research, time, effort, and a desire to serve an industry. Consequently, the writer has attempted always to objectively experiment with products and to present them to the industry where the product may serve to aid in the growth of the industry.

GA direct photographic emulsion* is an all-purpose direct photographic screen printing emulsion. This, of course, implies that the processing involves coating a sensitized emulsion onto the screen fabric, drying the coated screen, exposing the dried screen in contact with a photographic positive, and washing out the exposed screen. A screen that is prepared correctly with this emulsion resists lacquer type inks, water-soluble inks, oil-vehicle inks, and most inks employed in screen printing. Preparation of a printing screen with this emulsion requires the common equipment found in the average screen printing shop. This emulsion has long storage life and can be coated directly onto any screen fabric including monofilament types such as nylon or metal fabrics. Number 10 through Number 18 silks and other equivalent numbered screen fabrics may be used, although finer or coarser fabrics may also be employed. This emulsion does not have to be applied thick or in several coats to have strength and toughness.

The emulsion is sold unsensitized and is easily sensitized with an ammonium bichromate solution. The sensitized emulsion, therefore, consists of the emulsion and the simple ammonium bichromate solution sensitizer.

Preparation of Sensitizing Solution

The sensitizer is made by dissolving 9 ounces by weight (255 grams) of technical grade ammonium bichromate powder in 32 ounces or 1 quart of water (946cc) by volume. Distilled water or any clean and clear drinking water that is free of sediment may be used. The bichromate powder must be dissolved completely, and the solution stored in a tightly corked amber bottle.

Preparation of Sensitizing Emulsion

After the sensitizing bichromate solution is prepared, it is added to the photographic emulsion. The mixing of the solutions may be done under ordi-

---

*Charles M. Jessup Co., Kenilworth, N. J.

139

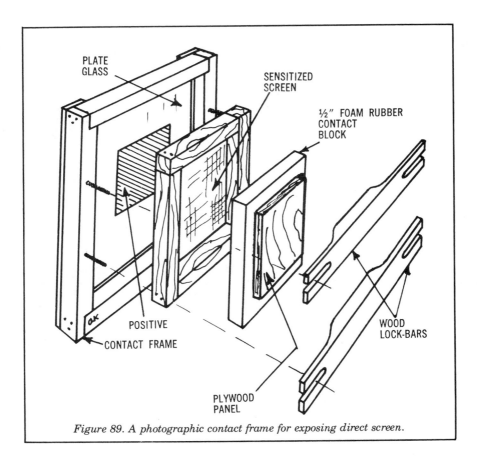

PLATE
GLASS

SENSITIZED
SCREEN

½" FOAM RUBBER
CONTACT
BLOCK

POSITIVE

CONTACT FRAME

WOOD
LOCK-BARS

PLYWOOD
PANEL

Figure 89. A photographic contact frame for exposing direct screen.

nary incandescent light conditions. The sensitized emulsion is made by adding 1 part by volume of the ammonium bichromate sensitizer to 10 parts by
volume of the GA emulsion. The two solutions should be completely mixed
together; the bichromate should be added to the emulsion until the bichromate is uniformly dissolved in the emulsion. The mixture should be strained
through a piece of screen fabric to remove any air bubbles that may be in the
solution, and the mixture is ready to be used.

This sensitized emulsion has a safe shelf life up to 6 months, if the
prepared solution is kept in a dark brown bottle or container in a cool dark
place under normal atmospheric conditions. However, it is best to mix enough
so that the emulsion is used up in about 4 weeks.

Preparing Screen Fabric for Coating

The screen printer must insure that the screen fabric is perfectly clean
before coating the emulsion. Finger marks, grease marks, and the like will
prevent any emulsion from adhering perfectly to the fabric. If silk is being

140

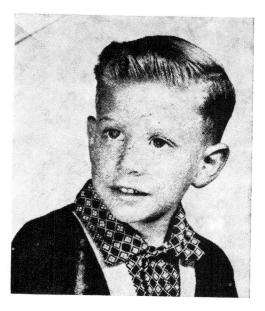

Figure 90. A one-color half-tone print made from a 120-line halftone printing screen.

used, the fabric should be washed well with a good quality soap and water and the soap rinsed off completely with water. The silk or screen fabric should dry before starting the coating.

If nylon or similar fabrics are used, hot water should be sprayed over both sides of the fabric. Then spray a liberal amount of a mild abrasive scouring kitchen cleanser and use a nylon brush to clean the fabric on both sides. Flush the screen with hot water and rub your hand over both sides of the screen to make sure that the scouring powder has been rinsed off.

If a metal screen fabric is employed for the screen, then the metal must be thoroughly washed with hot water to remove grease or oily coating that may cover the fine threads. A metal cleaner of the type used to clean copper pots and available in super markets is practical for cleaning metal fabrics. The printer can never overwash a metal fabric.

As is true with any screen that may be reclaimed, care must be taken in washing reclaimed fabric, if a reclaiming agent or solution has been employed. The agent must be washed off completely and perfectly so that it does not prevent perfect adhesion of coating to screen fabric.

Coating Screen

In coating the emulsion onto the screen fabric, especially fabrics of synthetic types, it is important to apply a thin even coat. It is important that the excess emulsion be leveled off on the screen fabric and along the sides of the screen, since it is in this area that the heavy coated emulsion will soften and wash away in the wash-out process. Pour on the prepared sensitized emulsion at one end of the screen and squeegee upwards, using smooth sharp plastic or metal coaters, wood squeegee, or the sharp edge of a piece of cardboard to

141

apply emulsion. Scrape off excess emulsion, working on both sides of the screen until the coating is smooth and uniform in thickness. After the coating is applied allow screen to dry. The drying may be done in the darkness or under incandescent light that is not stronger than a 15-watt frosted light bulb. Make sure that the drying screen is not directly under the light. However, if possible, it is best to dry the screen in complete darkness.

One coat of the emulsion is sufficient for most printing jobs. If a second coat is desired, it should be applied in similar fashion to the first coat. However, there must be no excess coating left on the fabric. The second coat should be allowed to dry completely. It takes about 15 minutes for one coat to dry with the aid of a plain electric fan. Heat should not be used.

Exposing

Black light tubes, arc lamps, mercury vapor lamps, and fluorescent tubes may be employed to expose the screen; black light and carbon arc lamps are best, however. There must be perfect contact between positive and the screen. The time of exposure to black light will vary from 4 to 6 minutes depending upon the strength of the source, with the unit being 1 to 3 inches away from the screen. Carbon arc lamps about 3 feet away from the screen will require less time. Figure 89 presents a photographic contact frame that may be used for exposing the coated screen. The positive in Figure 89 is placed right side up on the glass and the wood lock bars should be bolted tightly with the nuts.

If the screen printer is in doubt about exposure time, he can make a test or a trial screen with various exposure times, underexposing some areas and overexposing other areas on the same screen. When the test screen is washed out, the best exposure time will be evident.

Washing Out

Either cold or warm water may be used to wash out or develop the exposed screen. First wet both sides of the screen; then use a mild spray to wash out the image. It is suggested that only as many screens should be coated as can be exposed within a 2-hour period, as it becomes more difficult to wash out screen if screen is allowed to dry longer. When screen is washed so that printing or design area is perfectly open in the screen fabric, the screen may be dried naturally or with the aid of a fan. The rest of the screen may then be blocked out with the excess emulsion and the screen made ready for printing.

Reclaiming

Because of its resistance and durability, this type of screen is generally not reclaimed. However, if desired, a nylon, polyester, or stainless steel screen may be reclaimed by flooding the screen with a pure bleach solution. Allow screen to set for about 5 minutes; then rub a cup of acetone into the screen, using a brush for rubbing. The combination of bleach and acetone will soften and remove the emulsion from the fabric. However, acetone is not needed on all screens — only on very stubborn screens.

Figure 90 shows a print made with a screen prepared as explained in this chapter.

RECLAIMING PHOTOGRAPHIC PRINTING SCREENS

As screen printing is producing every type of decorating and printing on varied surfaces and materials, it is evident that all its interdependent processes must be standardized to eliminate problems. The reclaiming of screens is dependent on varied factors and is part of all the related steps in printing screen preparation and printing. In the preparation of screens — whether knife-cut, tusche-glue, direct screens, indirect photographic screens, direct-indirect — the screen printer must plan carefully and deliberately and prepare for reclaiming of screens. The planning in the use of any reclaiming system must give thought to the following factors: Has screen fabric been prepared correctly to receive emulsion or film? Has ink been washed off thoroughly after printing? What type of screen fabric is to be decoated? Is the labor involved in reclaiming more costly than the actual screen? Has a silk or a fabric conditioner been used for easier application of emulsion and for protection of fabric in reclaiming? Is the coating or film applied to the fabric a gelatinous or non-gelatinous one? Will a simple solvent be used or more modern equipment employed for removal of inks and emulsion? If flammable solvents are to be used, will a special area be required?

Generally, most screen printing emulsions and films may be removed from metal cloth, nylon, and polyester fabrics. However, while gelatin emulsions and films may be removed from silk and organdy, these fabrics are more difficult to reclaim when very resistant films and direct emulsions are coated on them. The reclaiming agent or solution which will remove the emulsions may also damage the silk. A direct emulsion is also more difficult to reclaim, since it completely envelops and anchors itself firmly into the mesh. Thus, where a printer is using a new film or emulsion, or reclaiming equipment for the first time with a given fabric, it is suggested that he determine the suitability of a reclaiming agent or equipment by making a trial screen, preferably a small one, and reclaim it under his shop conditions before attempting costly large screens. While a small screen may be included in the total cost of a job and may not be reclaimed, shops which prepare their own screens usually prefer to reuse larger screens. Of course, screen preparation specialists catering to the trade reclaim screens daily.

It must be noted that if it is desired to remove an emulsion that has not been exposed or hardened, the film or emulsion generally may be removed by soaking screen in water or by using a water spray to dissolve the unexposed emulsion.

The best reclaiming procedure, of course, is the simplest — one that uses operational safety and safe materials, that can be reclaimed by unskilled and semi-skilled labor, and one that is most economical. Also, it is suggested that where screens do not have to be saved that they be reclaimed as soon as possible. The longer a screen is allowed to lie around before reclaiming, the more difficult it is to reclaim. If inks and fillers are not given time to set, oxidize, or polymerize completely, the reclaiming may be easier and simpler.

With the exception of the heated tank which uses a chemical reclaiming system, an important prerequisite in decoating any type of screen is first to make sure that all ink used in printing is cleaned off immediately and thoroughly with the safest and appropriate ink solvent after printing. Should particles of ink dry in the fabric, they may prevent the decoating solvent from working on the emulsion and may make impossible the reclaiming of part or all of the fabric.

After cleaning off the ink and removing the emulsion or film, some screen printers clean the fabric with a trisodium phosphate (TSP) solution and then rinse off the TSP completely with water to make the fabric better suited for application of the next film. TSP in powder form is obtainable from screen printing suppliers, paint stores, chemical supply houses, and hardware stores. It will not attack and weaken natural silk.

Reclaiming Gelatin Screens

In removing gelatinous emulsions it is not practical for the modern screen printer to mix difficult reclaiming formulas as was necessitated in the days when photographic screens first made their appearance and reclaim-products were not available. Some of the early formulas were quite complex, of experimental nature, were dangerous to use, and in the long run would not be practical today. For example, one of the formulas which consists of two stock solutions was made from exact proportions of the following ingredients: Lactic acid, glycerine, potassium carbonate, alcohol, ammonium carbonate, caustic potash, borax, and water, and, while it did the cleaning, is a rather complex one to prepare in the average shop.

Most photographic screens are of three general types — gelatinous, non-gelatinous, and a combination of the two. Carbon tissue, pigment paper, gelatin films, and direct gelatin coated screens may be removed by any of the following methods (1) using hot water, (2) using bleaching or other agents, (3) employing enzyme products, or (4) employing commercial reclaiming products recommended by the manufacturer of the specific film or coating. However, there are screens intended for very long runs which are to be stored for very long periods of time and not to be reclaimed.

The hot water method involves placing the screen in a tray containing water that is 110–115 degrees Fahrenheit (43–46 degrees Celsius). This method may be used to reclaim silk, organdy, nylon, polyester, and metal cloth. The water starts the swelling of the gelatin and the gelatin may then be removed by scrubbing carefully with a stiff natural bristle brush. The screen is then sprayed thoroughly with water to assure complete removal of the emulsion. The screen may also be swabbed with a TSP solution on both sides of the fabric to assure a perfectly clean screen ready to receive the next film or emulsion.

144

Reclaiming Photographic Printing Screens

Those emulsions which do not have hardening agents applied to them, which are not older than about two days and on which fillers and inks were cleaned off immediately after printing may also be reclaimed by spraying or soaking in scalding hot water for about 10 to 15 minutes. Although water solutions of lye, caustic potash, and potassium cyanide may be applied to photographic screens with daubers and brushes, their use should be discouraged, since they are unsafe to handle and often poisonous, depending upon the percentage of chemical that is dissolved in the cold or hot water. It is better to apply steam, preferably live steam to the gelatin emulsions and then rinse the screen off with water. If only one side of a film was coated with a hardening agent, more of a cleaning solution should be applied to the film side which was not coated with a hardening agent.

However, while reclaiming and cleaning machines have been developed since about 1955, manual methods and certain formulations are still used very effectively. Some methods include employing commercial bleaching solutions, caustic soda, lactic acid, and washing soda. Where a commercial bleaching agent (sodium hypochlorite) or a caustic soda solution (sodium hydroxide) is employed, they should be used with care. They may damage silk partly or completely, depending on the strength of the solution; however, they can be used on nylon, polyester, and stainless steel.

It is good practice to wear plastic or rubber gloves and goggles when working with any of the solutions, since some products may be slightly corrosive, flammable, or toxic. Also, the screen printer should read directions for the use of new products before attempting decoating of screens.

Where bleach is employed as a reclaiming agent, generally one part of bleach is used in ten parts of water. Where caustic soda is used, a 10 to 20 percent solution is employed. These may be used on direct and on indirect screens, direct-indirect, on chromate and on diazo sensitized screens, and on non-gleatinous screens.

In using either of the above solutions, the screen is first soaked in hot water and the solution is applied by swabbing with a natural bristle brush on both sides of the fabric, allowing solution to remain on fabric for 5 to 10 minutes. It is important that the strength of the solution and the reaction time of the decoating not be exceeded in order to avoid damaging the fabric. Any spots left on the fabric may be wiped off with a cloth that has been soaked in acetone. The screen may then be scrubbed with a TSP solution and rinsed well with water before reusing.

Some other methods of removing gelatin emulsions are by using a lactic acid solution and by employment of washing soda. The lactic acid is applied to both sides of the gelatin screen which has been first wetted with water, the acid application being done with a soft brush or swab. The emulsion may then be washed off thoroughly with a jet of water. Or the screen may be soaked in a tray of hot water in which a cupful of washing soda (sodium carbonate) has been dissolved in a gallon of water. After soaking in the washing soda solution for about 30 minutes, the screen is rinsed off with water.

As has been mentioned, another method that has been used by some screen printers is to add one part of lye to 10 parts of water, stirring the solution with a stick, before immersing the screen in the lye solution. Care must be used in the employment of lye solutions.

The use of *enzyme* reclaiming agents came in after World War II when a safe method was needed to reclaim silk to which gelatin coatings and films were adhered. Enzyme products dissolve or digest gelatin, casein, starch, and protein substances and are safe to use. They may be used on silk fabrics which have been coated with gelatin type emulsions.

Enzyme products are available from screen printing suppliers in powder or solution form with simple directions for their use generally included. However, if the gelatin film has been coated with a hardening agent or an epoxy or vinyl ink to make the image in the screen more resistant to acid or alkali type inks, it will not be possible to dissolve the gelatin with an enzyme. A practical enzyme reclaiming method is to wet both sides of the screen with water over the film or emulsion, sprinkle the powder or solution liberally over the wet areas, and then cover the screen on both sides with a wet rag or with layers of wet newspaper. *Evaporation should be prevented.* The enzyme may be allowed to react for about 10 to 30 minutes or until the dissolving of the gelatin is noticed. The screen may then be rinsed off with hot, warm, or cold water. Stubborn spots may be given a second treatment and scrubbed with a bristle brush. Also, gelatin screens may be left overnight in a tray containing the enzyme solution and then hosed off with water in the morning. Figure 91 illustrates a method of reclaiming small and medium size screens by placing screen in a pan made of aluminum foil, thin polyethylene sheet, or heavy wax paper containing reclaiming solution, and allowing emulsion to be removed. Figure 92 shows one method of reclaiming large parts or smaller areas of a photographic screen by using glass about ¼ of an inch thick, which is smooth on one side and has blunt pyramid shaped extensions on the other surface. This glass is available from glass jobbers and glaziers and may be cut with ordinary glass cutters. Where a specific restricted area has to be cleaned off, it is suggested that the edges next to the glass sandwhich be covered with tape to prevent the reclaiming liquid from seeping over the rest of the screen fabric.

Unless *neutralized*, enzymes may continue their dissolving action when the next gelatin film or emulsion is adhered to the fabric. Neutralizing solu-

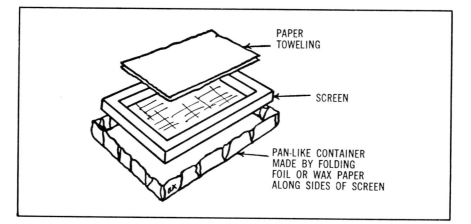

PAPER TOWELING

SCREEN

PAN-LIKE CONTAINER MADE BY FOLDING FOIL OR WAX PAPER ALONG SIDES OF SCREEN

Figure 91. Arrangement of tray, screen, and absorbent paper towels.

146

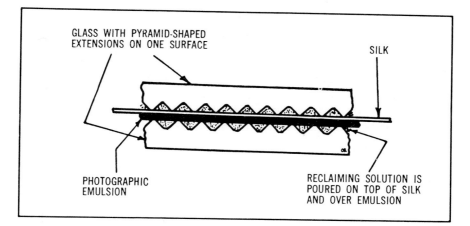

GLASS WITH PYRAMID-SHAPED
EXTENSIONS ON ONE SURFACE

SILK

PHOTOGRAPHIC
EMULSION

RECLAIMING SOLUTION IS
POURED ON TOP OF SILK
AND OVER EMULSION

Figure 92. Detail showing sandwich method of removing photographic emulsion.

tions are employed to deactivate and remove the remaining microscopic enzyme particles so that they will not attack the new gelatin image. To accomplish this a 5 percent glacial acetic acid solution or a household type white vinegar is swabbed on both sides of the entire screen, including the frame. Some screen printers have also used a neutralizing solution which is made by mixing one ounce of muriatic acid (hydrochloric acid) in one gallon of water or a 10 percent solution of TSP. (The acid must always be added to the water; never add water to acid). After application of neutralizing solution, the screen and frame are rinsed thoroughly with water.

Reclaiming Non-gelatinous Emulsions

Where newer type of reclaiming equipment is not available, the reclaiming of non-gelatin emulsions and direct screens consisting of polyvinyl alcohol-polyvinyl acetate formulations has been accomplished by using (1) potassium permanganate solution and potassium metabisulphite solutions, and (2) sodium hypochlorite solution. Sodium hypochlorite solution is supplied in concentrations of 13 to 16 percent active chlorine. For decoating screens a solution of 4 to 5 percent active chlorine has been used. The sodium hypochlorite solution will react quicker on nylon, polyester, and metal cloth than the two aforementioned solutions.

The potassium compounds are available in powder or crystalline form. A cold saturated solution (about a 6 percent solution) is made of each chemical; solutions may be stored for long periods of time. After the solutions are made, it is recommended that they be filtered through screen fabric so that no sharp crystals are left which may cut the mesh.

In using the solutions a liberal amount of potassium permanganate is applied first to both sides of the fabric with a soft nylon brush and solution is allowed to remain on fabric for about 4 minutes. Solution should not remain on the fabric any longer, as it may discolor the mesh. It is then washed off with a water spray.

147

The second solution, potassium metabisulphite, is applied in the same fashion and allowed to remain on the screen for 2 to 3 minutes before washing off thoroughly with water. If a residue should remain on the fabric, it may be removed by rubbing with a cloth that has been soaked in xylene, butyl lactate, or toluene. For very stubborn cases the reclaiming procedure may be repeated. However, after using any of the latter three solvents, it is suggested that the fabric be degreased with a 10 to 20 percent caustic soda solution before applying an emulsion or film to it. The caustic soda solution is applied in similar fashion to the potassium solutions.

Direct type emulsions may also be removed from nylon, polyester, or metal fabric with a 4 percent bleach solution or by soaking screen in a 3 percent hydrogen peroxide solution, rinsing in hot water, and then scrubbing with a TSP solution, to prepare the fabric for future application of films or coatings. Natural silk will be damaged by most reclaiming agents. Therefore, it is suggested that the printer test the reclaiming of silk, should he have any doubts about the decoating results.

Reclaiming Equipment

While reclaiming materials and chemicals have been used for quite a while, the needs for reclaiming printing screens since about 1958 have been solved by the development of equipment by varied screen printing manufacturers. The most common in use are (1) the water pressure screen reclaimer, (2) high pressure automatic screen washers and reclaimers, and (3) special reclaiming equipment consisting of a heated tank containing special chemicals. The varied machines are not difficult to use and, if used correctly, do an efficient job.

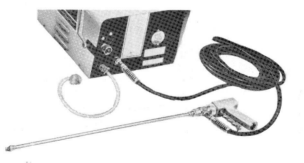

Figure 93. KO Emulsion Remover cleans and reclaims all screen fabrics. Warm water under tremendous pressure is used to spray and blast away photographic screen preparations, direct emulsions, water soluble films, photographic films, and the like. (Courtesy of Advance Process Supply Company, Chicago, Illinois).

The water pressure reclaiming unit consits of a compact cabinet which houses a motor and a pressure pump which connects to a standard hose, as illustrated in Figure 93. Generally this unit may use warm water for blasting off films and coatings and is available in sizes for limited reclaiming, unlimited production, and for large shops which reclaim screens daily for continuous production.

148

Figure 94. A two module screen washer, designed for cleaning, reclaiming, and developing any size printing screen. In use, the screens are placed on a traveling chain and desired spray pressure is set for one or both sides of screen. Unit recirculates solvent and offers a simple system for removal of sludge. (Courtesy of M & M Research Engineering-Printing Aids, Butler Wisconsin).

The second type consists of a large automatic machine (see Figure 94) that can also be built in sections or modules, which safely wash out inks, remove stencils or emulsions, and deliver the screen ready for reuse. It has a conveyor drive on which the screens to be reclaimed or cleaned travel forward or in reverse, with adjustable spray pressure, and will clean one screen after another. The machine will accommodate screens up to about 96 inches wide (244 cm) by any length. The equipment has opposing sets of high velocity nozzles operating at the same time. It has a sludge filter removal drawer, solvent that is recirculating, and solvent can be quickly drained and recharged. The machine has windows for checking the cleaning and reclaiming operations which can go on continuously daily.

The third type of equipment has a dip tank filled with special chemicals which, according to the manufacturers and those who use it, is biodegradable, not flammable, water-soluble, non-polluting, and noncorrosive. (See Figure 95). The dip tank has thermostatically controlled recirculating heat. Steam or electricity may be used for heating and maintaining operating temperature. The use of the heated tank, and the special chemical solutions loosen inks of all types together with direct diazo, direct chromate emulsions, and indirect printing screen films. These are then removed and washed off with a pressure washer which blasts off the ink, films, and residues. The dissolved materials are removed in chunks which can be strained through filter bags or strainers.

149

Figure 95. A special tank designed for reclaiming and removing photosensitive emulsions, water soluble blockouts, and most inks safely and quickly from nylon, polyester, and metal fabric screens. Very large and small screens may be dipped in the tank which contains two electrically heated chemicals. (Courtesy of Naz-Dar Company, Chicago, Illinois).

150

Printers who have previously stored printing screens for repeat runs are reclaiming after printing and are removing both the ink and the emulsion at the same time. This is done because there is elimination of unsafe, costly solvents and rags, does not require a separate process for removing ink, cleans the frame, and degreases the fabric.

The tanks come in varied sizes ranging in outside dimensions from 32 × 37 inches (81 × 95cm) to 96 g 120 inches (244 × 305 cm), have a screen lifting device for raising and lowering screens, and have anti-floating devices for wooden screens. Generally, the chemical employed is safe to use on aluminum and wooden frames and on nylon, polyester, and metal fabrics. The solution is easily mixed and many screens may be reclaimed in the same solution.

In summary, before the screen printer finally decides on the method he will use to reclaim screens, he should investigate thoroughly the varied methods, materials and equipment available. Whether he reclaims one screen or dozens in one day, the screen printer today has a choice of old and new techniques, of materials, of help from equipment suppliers, and equipment for reclaiming screens to fit individual shop needs which will more than pay for itself in time, labor, decrease in fatigue, safety, and efficiency.

ACTINIC LIGHT SOURCES

Making a photographic printing screen or a screen printing plate is an interdependent process in which each step is the result of correct use of procedure, materials, techniques, and equipment. One of the important steps is the exposure of screen emulsion coatings or screen printing films to actinic light in order to harden and change chemically the desired areas or spots on the emulsion. Actinic light is light energy that is capable of changing the properties of photosensitive materials when the materials are exposed to the light source. While the average screen printer attempts to use care in most of the steps relating to the preparation of the printing screen, he sometimes takes the exposing actinic light source for granted. In doing so he overlooks a very important part of the total process.

The actinic light used by the screen printer for exposing screen printing films, coatings, and photographic film is a portion of white light and a form of radiant energy which produces photochemical changes in certain materials. Specifically, actinic light consists of wavelengths of energy in the violet and ultraviolet part of the "electromagnetic spectrum" as explained in Chapter 31 on "Color Separation and Color Effects." The electromagnetic spectrum consists of energy which ranges from the wave frequency of cosmic rays through the frequency of the alternate current waves. The outstanding difference among the various kinds of electromagnetic waves (alternating current waves, radio waves, infrared, visible light, ultraviolet, X-rays, gamma, and cosmic rays) is in the wavelength. Visible light is a part of the electromagnetic spectrum or energy; this visible part is a very small portion of the complete spectrum. In exposing screen printing screens, we are concerned with very short wavelengths which range from ultraviolet to infrared frequencies. The present graphic arts processes use a frequency or wavelength range between 3200 and 7000 Angstroms. (An Angstrom is a unit equal to one ten millionth of a millimeter).

As all light sources do produce a certain amount of illumination on an object, light employed in exposing printing screens and screen printing films should be considered objectively and carefully to fit the photographic needs of the screen printer. For example, the early screen printer managed to obtain results by exposing his gelatinous coated screen to a 150-watt incandescent lamp for about three hours at a distance of two to three feet from the coated screen. He also used sunlight. While the sun may be employed, its rays vary depending on the time of day and on climatic conditions. Its heat may affect carbon tissue, especially wet tissue, and gelatin screen printing films. Also, the availability of the sun is not always constant. Therefore, artificial light sources were developed. The past fifty years have brought suitable types of light for exposing or tanning the light sensitive materials. While the exposing light was not developed specifically for screen printing, the process adopted and adapted light sources from the other graphic arts.

The three basic means of producing light are by (1) incandescence, (2) electric discharge, and (3) fluorescence and phosphorescence. Incandescence involves heating any matter to a temperature at which the matter will give off light; the higher the temperature, the whiter the light. For example, in the carbon flame of the carbon arc, the tip of the carbon reaches a temperature of about 3950 degrees Kelvin. Kelvin temperature, which is equal to the temperature in degrees Celsius plus 273, is also used to measure the "color temperature" of light sources. Color temperature refers to the degree of whiteness of a light source. For example, photoflood lamps which are incandescent light may have a color temperature rating of 3400 degrees K. This temperature is obtained by comparing the color of a light with a standard laboratory radiator heated to the proper temperature to give the same color of light. The higher the color temperature of a source, the richer it is in blue rays; the lower the temperature, the richer the light is in yellow and red.

In the electric discharge principle, light is given off when an electric current or electron flow occurs between electrodes (conductors) through ionized gas or vapor. Gas consists of molecules and molecules contain electrons. When the electrons are sufficiently activated by the voltage and strike other gas particles, the gas particle will absorb some of the energy of the electrons and a portion of this absorbed energy will be radiated as light. The basic structure of the gas determines the color of light produced. However, to some degree, lamp manufacturers can control the radiation by the physical characteristics of the lamp. For example, the fluorescent type and the black light tube are examples of light produced by passing an electric current through a glass tube containing mercury vapor and a coating on the inside of the tube. The coating or chemicals on the inner wall of the tube are known as "phosphors"; the phosphors absorb short wave radiation (ultraviolet light) and emit longer visible rays. The color of the light in the tube depends on the types of gas and phosphor in the tube. The fluorescent tube industry boasts that it produces shades of white light commercially, including one shade that is similar to perfect daylight. Mercury vapor lamps, xenon, sodium vapor, and neon are examples of light produced by electric discharge.

Fluorescent materials simply give off light while being exposed to a source of energy. Phosphorescence is the emission in darkness of previously absorbed light.

The sources of illumination or radiant energy which today's printer employs are: the carbon arc lamp, pulsed xenon lamp, metal halide, mercury vapor lamps, black light and fluorescent tubes, quartz iodine lamps, and photoflood lamps.

Carbon Arc Lamps

Although the light used in the past and still being used is that supplied by the carbon arc, it is being replaced by other light sources such as the pulsed xenon lamp, several types of mercury vapor lamps, metal halide (metal additive) lamp, quartz-iodine (quartz halogen) lamp, fluorescent light units, and incandescent lamps or photofloods. However, the carbon arc is a

153

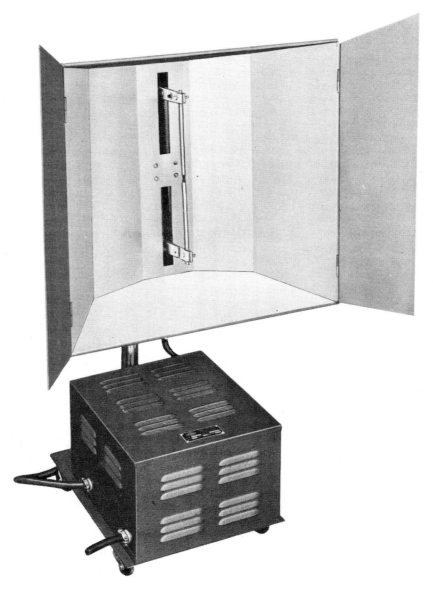

Figure 96. A single carbon arc lamp for exposing areas up to 40 × 50 inches (102 × 127cm) with automatic arc controls. (Courtesy of nuArc Company, Inc., Chicago, Illinois).

154

Figure 97. "Day Star" arc lamp for exposing screen printing films and direct printing screens. (Courtesy of Naz-Dar Company, Chicago, Illinois).

true point light source which is often recommended for exposing screen printed photosensitive coatings. The carbon arc lamp is an example of incandescence and electric discharge. The carbon arc light has high actinic value and may be employed for exposing screens, screen printing films, and other photographic products used generally by the screen printer. The arc has high energy in the violet and ultraviolet region. The light in the carbon lamp is

155

produced by passing an electric current through the carbon which in turn burns matter and obtains a spark when the carbon rod makes contact with the other carbon rod. The contact raises the temperature and produces a flame of burning carbon. When the carbon electrodes are separated, a gaseous conductor is formed which, like the carbon, becomes incandescent and glowing. The total light is obtained from the spark, the white hot carbon tips, and the carbon material. The manufacture of the carbons is done scientifically to aid in producing greater conductivity, uniform light distribution, and uniformity in length of gap between arcs. The carbon lamp, especially that which contains the white-flame or high intensity carbons, is employed where a very bright and concentrated light source is needed. They give an intense, evenly distributed light. There are single-arc lamps and double-arc lamps, the single-arc lamps are employed more for all types of screen printing photographic work. Figures 96 and 97 illustrate commonly used arc lamps.

Generally, the carbon arc lamp consists of two main units: the reflector assembly and the power unit. The reflector assembly has the carbon mechanism and the carbon moving part. There is also a part in the reflector of most carbon arc lamps which makes proper contact and proper spacing between the two carbon tips for producing a constant and even arc. The power unit controls the arc current and voltage so that proper arc and voltage output of lamp consistency is maintained. Arc lamps are designated in amperes. The intensity of the light is controlled to a great extent by the amperage of the lamp; when the amperage is increased, the brightness of the light is increased. Although 60-amperes, 45-amperes, 35-amperes, and 15-amperes arc lamps are used, with the highest ampere lamp being employed for black-and-white copy work and for color-separation work, screen printers use lamps which range from about 8 to 90-amperes, depending upon the light intensity desired. The screen printer must follow directions of the manufacturer in caring for and using an arc lamp. The disadvantage of ash production, a by-product of the burning of carbons, is being overcome by employing an exhaust tube for the ash in the design of the carbon arc lamp.

There are arc lamps which may be wired in 110 volt circuits or in 220 volt circuits. Most of the lamps are equipped with casters or are portable so that they may be moved into various places in a working area. There are varied styles, varied designs, and, of course, varied prices. There are lamps which may be hung from the ceiling and lowered to illuminate a sensitized surface which is in a horizontal position and arc lamps which stand in a vertical position and illustrate plates which are in a vertical plane or position. They are simple to operate but the few directions regarding successful and safe operation must be followed.

Pulsed-Xenon Arc Lamps

The pulsed-xenon arc lamp was introduced in 1958, is one of the newest of actinic light sources, and was developed by the general Electric Company and Berkey Technical. The light of this lamp covers the entire range of visible light. It has a color temperature of about 5600 degrees Kelvin and is being used for high quality black-and-white copy work, halftones, and color-separation. The pulsed-xenon lamps is an arc lamp but it is an electrically operated enclosed arc. Xenon arcs start instantly. The xenon arc light sources are various shapes and sizes of gas filled tubes which produce light because the passage of an electric current through xenon gas causes the gas to glow.

156

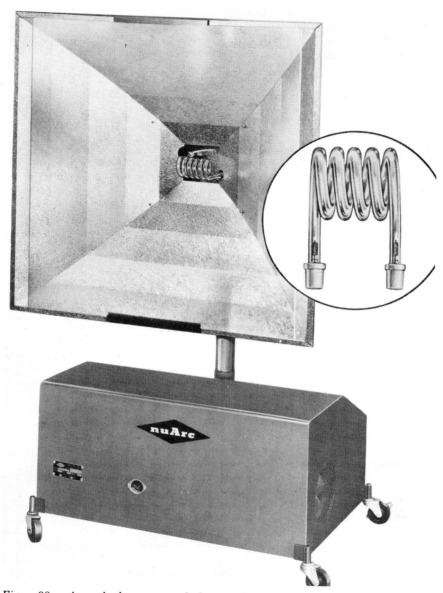

Figure 98. nuArc pulsed xenon arc tube lamp with 8000 watts of point light source and a constant color temperature (6000 degrees Kelvin) for all types of exposing. (Courtesy of nuArc Company, Chicago, Illinois).

Figure 99. A black light fluorescent tube unit with a flat polished plate placed one inch behind the lamps to fill in the spaces between the lamps with light.

158

The color temperature or spectral distribution is controlled by the gas. The tube or lamp consists of a quartz glass envelope with an electrode at each end and has an arc pulsing or flashing 120 times per second between the electrodes. Unlike ordinary glass, quartz will transmit 90 percent or more of ultraviolet light. The xenon lamp has no mechanical parts, and unlike the carbon arc, is clean. Its color temperature is about the same as that of the white flame carbon arc — 5500 to 5700 degrees Kelvin. According to manufacturers, tube color temperature and intensity is constant throughout the life of the tube. Also, the tube may be easily replaced when it burns out. Although the light may be kept nearer the screen when the film or screen printing coat is being exposed, the lamp may be moved farther away from the screen to expose very large areas. The xenon arc lamp is cooler than tungsten bulbs. The tubes are available in 12 and 24 inch lengths and in varied shapes, as illustrated in Figure 98. Exposure time is generally equivalent to carbon arc light. As with other types of light, actual exposure time will depend upon the type of material exposed, frame size, and distance of light to printing screen or vacuum frame. The screen printer must realize that if the screen is moved twice the distance from the light source, the intensity of the light reaching the screen is one-fourth the former strength of light and the original exposure time should be multiplied by four.

Black Light

"Black light" is a popular name for invisible ultraviolet radiant energy (below 4000 Angstroms). The term is descriptive, since the ultraviolet energy from this light cannot be seen by the human eye; however, the effects of the light are obvious. When this radiant energy falls on certain materials it makes them fluoresce or emit visible light. Black light lamps are fluorescent lamps whose phosphors radiate most of their energy below 4000 Angstroms. This light radiates most of its energy in the near ultraviolet (between 3200 and 4000 Angstroms), rather than in the visible light region. It must be noted that the radiant energy from the sun and even the carbon arc lamp produce useful amounts of black light. Generally, black light tubes are available in white-appearing tubes similar to ordinary fluorescent tubes and in dark-appearing tubes or lamps. It is the white appearing tubes which are usually employed for exposing screen printing films and coatings. Although low in power and wattage, the tube works effectively because the tube gives off a cool light and may be brought close to the surface being exposed. They may be used 4 or more inches away from sensitized film and coatings.

The black light tubes differ from the ordinary fluorescent lamp only in the composition of the phosphor coated in the tube. Black light tubes give off ultraviolet rays as soon as they are started and there is relatively little visible light from the white-appearing tubes; there is no visible light from the dark-appearing tubes. The dark tubes make use of a glass envelope which does not transmit any light of longer wave-lengths and then show just a faint violet glow when in operation. Also, the lamps emit a great part of the light energy in wavelengths to which most screen printing films and coatings are sensitive. The tubes are available in different wattages and in varied lengths to cater to the exposing units ranging from small to very large area size. In exposing equipment the long tubes are mounted parallel and close to one another. The 48 and 36-inch long fluorescent or black light tube has been

Figure 100. A fast, fool, even light source consisting of the lamphousing and the power pack, designed for exposing photographic coatings, emulsions, resist materials for printed circuits, photo etching, and chemical milling. (Courtesy of Aristo Grid Lamp Products, Long Island, New York).

used successfully. The length of the tube includes the lampholders at each end of the tube, thus the actual lighted length of the tube may be slightly less. Black light fluorescent tubes or lamps are mounted in the unit with a starter and ballast for each tube. The compact ballast consists of a small transformer and choke coil. The ballast provides proper voltage and proper current for starting and operation and limits the current to safe operation.

Figure 99 illustrates a black light fluorescent unit. Figure 100 shows a practical portable unit for exposing.*

Mercury Vapor Lamp

The mercury vapor lamp is a special type of arc lamp. It is a gas discharge light. These lamps consist of tubes filled with liquid mercury and argon gas. The mercury is activated and vaporized when the electric current is passed between the electrodes which are at each end of the tube. The lamps do require an initial warming-up period for several minutes. Also, after burning, the high mercury vapor pressure of the tube may delay restarting. Several minutes must elapse before the lamp cools down sufficiently to restart. As with most discharge lamps, light distribution and color temperature depend on the type of gas. These lamps are rich in ultraviolet, violet, and blue light. The tube life of mercury lamps is about 1500 hours. Frequent starting and stopping of some lamps may shorten their life. These lamps are generally employed for black-and-white copy. Most mercury lamps produce visible and black light. Figure 101 illustrates a special type mercury vapor lamp designed for all types of exposing. While some mercury lamps are generally

---

*The book — Kosloff, Albert, *Screen Printing Techniques*, Signs of the Times Publishing Co., Cincinnati, Ohio, presents a chapter entitled "A Black Light Fluorescent Exposing Unit" which will help the printer build an exposing unit.

160

Figure 101. Colight Hydrolite, a mercury vapor light source designed to yield a high ultraviolet light output which may be used for the varied types of exposures in screen printing and other graphic arts. (Courtesy of Naz-Dar Company, Chicago, Illinois.

161

used for exposing areas up to about 3 by 3 feet, the one illustrated in Figure 101 may be employed exposing large areas.

Metal Halide Lamps

The metal halide lamp is basically a mercury lamp and differs from the carbon arc, pulsed-xenon, and other mercury lamps in the fact that it has additives or substances known as metal halides. The addition of these substances provides greater light output and shorter exposure time in the desired spectral range. The lamp, which was introduced by Berkey Technical and Sylvania Electric Products in 1967, was designed specifically for graphic arts applications. Metal halide lamps have more actinic energy than the pulsed-xenon, carbon arc, or mercury lamp, when compared on an equal wattage basis.

The addition of metal halides makes it possible to adjust the light energy within the ultraviolet and blue parts of the spectrum. Photosensitive materials may have varied spectral sensitivity within certain ranges and modern lamps do attempt to adjust the light to the range of sensitivity. The metal halide lamps have been successfully used in all types of applications — screen printing films, emulsions, in contact printing, halftones, and the like. It is clean, efficient, and fast because of its high actinic output and relatively high power.

The actinic light part consists of a quartz tube or envelope which contains mercury through which a current passes vaporizing the mercury. (See Figure 102). Depending on the salts used as additives, the lamp can "peak" or give maximum energy at different wavelengths. A lamp may peak at 4000 or 4100 Angstrom units where graphic arts materials are most sensitive. The lamp is also referred to as a "diazo" (diazonium) type, since it is particularly efficient for exposing diazo compound coated materials. There are also metal halide lamps which are designed to be more efficient and peak below 4000 Angstrom units.

Quartz-Iodine Lamps

The quartz-iodine lamp also known as the tungsten-halogen lamp is an incandescent lamp which was developed by the General Electric Company in the 1960's. It is similar to the tungsten or photoflood lamp in that a tungsten filament provides the light. The filament is in a quartz glass case which contains a small quantity of iodine crystals. Quartz is more advantageous than glass and the lamp may be smaller, lighter, brighter, and longer lasting than a photoflood lamp. The iodine crystals become ionized in the presence of an electric current and combine with the tungsten as the tungsten is heated and is being vaporized. The iodine which forms tungsten iodide redeposites the evaporated tungsten back onto the filament and thus increases the effective life of the lamp.

Photoflood Lamps

These lamps are used by the beginning screen printer and on occasion by the advanced printer for exposing screens and film, since they do produce high illumination. These are incandescent lamps and generally are available

162

Figure 102. nuArc Ultra-Plus Printing Lamp with an instant start metal halide tube light source for exposing direct screens, photosensitive coatings, screen printing films, film negatives and positives, and the like; lamp covers a range of 3600 to 4500 Angstroms. (Courtesy of nuArc Co., Inc., Chicago, Illinois).

163

in three wattage sizes: 250, 500, and 1,000 watts. For screen printing exposing the 500-watt and the 1,000 watt photoflood lamps are employed, using one or more lamps in a unit. They do give off enough heat if placed near carbon tissue, especially wet tissue, to cause damage. Therefore, when exposing wet carbon tissue or similar gelatinous wet screen printing film to these lamps, it is suggested that a fan be blowing on the tissue to keep the gelatin from melting. Under standard operation the hour life ratings are about 3, 6, and 10 hours for the 250, 500, 1000 watts respectively. However, the intensity of the light does decrease as the lamp is used.

In summary, it is suggested that when the screen printer is purchasing an exposing source that he compare data of the varied light sources and choose the exposing unit that will best answer the needs of his shop and the services he will offer. He should always make it a habit to test films and coatings for best exposure with his equipment, before doing commercial work.

HALFTONE PRINTING

26

Screen printing is bringing more and more color and effects in today's world and is used daily to print single and multi-color jobs and illustrations. Color work is being printed in varied ways with various photographic printing screens and by employing hand prepared screens. Colors may be printed by depositing solid lines and solid areas by means of hand prepared printing screens especially where the detail is not too fine and where very large areas are to be printed. Color in the form of solid areas and fine detail is printed on surfaces with line copy photographic printing screens. Also, one, two, three, four-color, and full-color work is printed with halftone printing screens on varied surfaces to produce four or more colors in the final print.

The type of copy generally determines whether hand screens, plain photographic printing screens, or photographic halftone printing screens will produce the best job with the least amount of effort. By *copy* is meant the original subject. The original may be art work in black on white such as any pen and ink drawing, or a photograph, colored illustration, a colored photograph, or the copy may consist of a one-colored object or a multi-colored object.

The screen printer reproduces three types of copy — mostly line copy, halftone copy, and a continuous tone copy for posterization. The first type, line copy, consists of originals which have lines or solid areas on them and may be reproduced with hand-prepared screens or photographic screens, depending on the detail in the copy. The second type, halftone copy, consists of originals containing gradations or continuous tones such as found in a photograph. The latter copy is best reproduced by means of photographic halftone printing screens. The third type copy, continuous tone copy for posterization, is peculiar to screen printing. It is treated in Chapter 32 entitled "Photographic Posterization and Screen Printing" and is reproduced by making three or more varied exposures of the same continuous tone or photograph on film. The film is used to make the positives from which the printing screens are made. The screens print light tones, middle tones and shadow parts generally in varied flat tones and varied shades of the same color.

Halftone printing produces values which are between high light and deep shades. When it is necessary to reproduce a photograph, which normally has a wide variety of tones from light to dark, the photograph has to be changed in such a manner so that only solid printing spots or dots are presented to the eye. A printing plate cannot apply less ink to the light parts of a picture than to the dark parts. Therefore, where the gradations of tone have to be reproduced as in a photograph, the subject has to be changed so that solid

165

surfaces are still printed. The halftone method reproduces a picture by breaking up the entire picture into a series of small, various size evenly spaced dots. The larger dots show less white space between the dots than the smaller ones. As illustrated in Figure 103, the large dots close together make up the

Figure 103. A 13" × 17" two-color screen print which makes use of an enlarged halftone as part of the design. The original halftone was enlarged or "blown up" to about 15 lines per inch. (Courtesy of Silk Screen Process, Inc., Cleveland, Ohio.)

166

dark areas or tones; small widely spaced dots make up the light tones. The halftone print depends on an optical illusion. The human eye viewing the dots at a distance translates the mass of fine dots into a lighter tone and the darker closely spaced dots into a dark tone. Also, the dots are placed so that a yellow dot near a red dot will give the illusion of the color of orange. Where a transparent yellow ink is printed over a red dot an orange effect is obtained. This dot structure may be viewed easily by observing a halftone print through a magnifying glass, linen tester, or a tripod magnifier.

Reproduction of a gradation of tone, middle tones, or halftones (halftones) is not the result of one man but the synthesis of the discoveries and results of experiments of much work since about the 1850's of such men in the field of graphic arts as William Henry Fox Talbot, Charles G. Petit, James Clerk Maxwell, William A. Leggo, George Meisenbach, Stephen H. Horgan, Louis and Max Levy, Frederick Ives; men in the screen printing industry such as Harry L. Hiett, and William Reinke and others who dared to experiment and print single and multi-color halftones; and graphic arts suppliers and manufacturers, especially in the screen printing field, who developed the specific inks, screen printing films, and techniques for this type of printing. Truly, the halftone process is the result of the efforts of many individuals in the United States, Europe and Canada.

Although halftone printing from direct silk screens was done in 1914, this type of printing developed in the United States in the late 1920's. Carbon tissue or pigment paper was the screen printing transfer-type film which aided in this development. Today commercial transfer type films, emulsions for direct screens, direct-indirect screens, and carbon tissues may be used for obtaining the final printing screen. Originally, halftone screen printing seemed to imitate lithography because it reproduced small run jobs on large size sheets which were not economical for lithography to print. Today screen printing has its own effective characteristics of brilliancy of color and prints in opaque, semi-transparent, and transparent inks on varied surfaces. Because it is less costly, especially in short runs up to about 4,000 impressions and large size sheets of about 22 × 28 inches to about 40 × 60 inches (56 × 71cm to about 102 × 152cm), halftone screen printing is used to reproduce anything from fine art to large advertising display posters.

Although single color halftone work and color-process work is more involved and deals with films, negatives, positives, cross-line screens, filters, color separation, separation of spectral colors, blending three and four color inks to produce the many colors in the print, varied types of inks, etc., there isn't anything mystifying about the process. The prerequisite for halftone work consists of becoming more proficient in doing and working with line copy photographic printing screens in one and more than one color. The beginning printer should become experienced in printing one color halftones; then in duotone work or two color halftones. Finally, he should proceed to multi-color halftone printing. Screen printing of halftones is an exacting and difficult process even with the new available screen printing films and direct emulsions. Although printing in other graphic communication processes involves printing three colors plus black to print colored illustrations, halftone screen printing may employ three, four, or more colors plus additional colors for effects such as brush marks, for toning colors down, for adding luminescent effects, etc. The main problem in printing halftones is to match the original artwork.

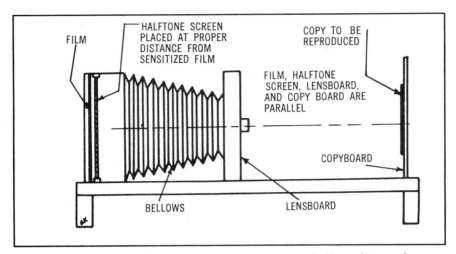

FILM

HALFTONE SCREEN PLACED AT PROPER DISTANCE FROM SENSITIZED FILM

COPY TO BE REPRODUCED

FILM, HALFTONE SCREEN, LENSBOARD, AND COPY BOARD ARE PARALLEL

COPYBOARD

BELLOWS

LENSBOARD

Figure 104. Relation of basic parts of process camera in halftone photography.

Halftone Printing Procedure

Regardless of the method of reproduction, generally, the common way of producing the dots for halftone printing since its introduction in the latter part of the 19th century, has consisted of photographing the original continuous tone copy through a screen known as a halftone screen. The halftone screen, consisting ordinarily of a pattern of opaque lines on a transparent surface, is placed at an exact distance in front of the sensitized film, generally in a process camera. The copy is placed on the copyboard in front of the camera lens at a specified distance (see Figure 104), and an exposure is made by illuminating the copy with a practical source of light. The lamps illuminating the copy are arranged so that they point at the center of the copyboard without producing glare. Although illuminating lights are set up so that they are 45 degrees to the optical axis or center line (see Figure 105), the manufacturers of the given camera and film being used to make the halftone negative generally are able to recommend the best position and best angle of lights in relation to the copyboard. The dark areas of the copy reflect less light through the camera lens and through the halftone screen onto the sensitized film. The lighter areas of the copy reflect more light onto the film.

After the exposure, the halftone negative is developed out and a halftone positive is made from the negative. The correct size halftone positive is used for making the final printing screen by exposing the positive in contact with the screen printing film, direct screen or direct-indirect screen.

A screen used for halftone screen printing is only as good as the negative and positive used to produce it. The positive for halftones must be absolutely opaque with a clean and sharp edge to each dot. The beginner doing halftone work must realize that he may be using two types of film, one type for making the negatives and positives and a second type or screen printing film, which is adhered to the screen fabric of the final printing screen. Any quality brand of standard film for making positives and negatives will work. How-

168

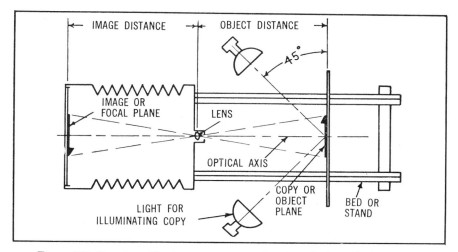

Figure 105. Top view of basic process camera showing relation of lights to copy.

ever, the screen printer should work with one practical brand and the related chemicals recommended for the film until he has mastered the processes. The films may be obtained from screen printing suppliers, photolithography suppliers, or graphic arts suppliers.

Halftone Screens

A halftone screen consists of a transparent glass or film base upon which are very accurate parallel opaque lines, either crossed at right angles to one another or single lines, having transparent openings between the crossed or parallel lines. There are varied makes and classifications of halftone screens. Regardless of the style or make, halftone screens are classified in standard rulings or by the number of opaque lines per inch or lines per centimeter. A screen with a pitch of 50 or 50 lines to the inch would have 50 × 50 lines to the square inch or 2,500 dots to the square inch.* There are varied line ratios, however, a 1-1 line ratio as illustrated in Figure 106 is the standard ruling used by screen printers. The standard screen rulings employed for screen printing are 45, 50, 55, 60, 80, 85, 100, 120, and 133. Although some printers do print finer lines, the average job in screen printing does not use a finer screen than about 100 lines to the inch.

Glass screens are manufactured in two standard shapes: rectangular and circular. Process cameras employed for making halftones have special holders and devices for the screen which may move upward or to the side of the camera out of the way of the image field. Square or rectangular screens range in size from about 6 × 8 inches to 32 × 40 inches; circular screens range in diameter from about 13½ inches to 55 inches. Fine line screens, as a rule, come in smaller sizes.

---

*Since the metric system uses the standard *lines per centimeter*, the number denoting lines per inch is divided by 2.54 to obtain lines per centimeter.

Halftone negatives may be made by employing two-sheet glass screens, single-sheet glass screens, contact screens, and by using a prescreened halftone film which makes a halftone negative automatically in the camera without employing a halftone screen. Such screens as the world famous Levy screens are made by properly spacing and ruling parallel lines in with an opaque lampblack composition. The sides of the glass with pigmented rulings are cemented together so that the rulings are face to face and at right angles to one another.

The second type screen, exemplified by the Buckbee Mears halftone screen which was introduced to the trade in 1948, is etched with crossline rulings on a single sheet of specially selected plate glass. They are used in exposure similarly to the two sheet halftone screens. These screens are available in 50 lines to 150 lines per inch and in rectangular sizes from 8 × 10 inches to 20 × 24 inches.

The two-sheet glass screen and the single sheet glass screen are not in contact with the sensitized film during exposure. Each type specifies its "screen separation" or distance from the sensitized film in order to obtain the best halftone dot in the final printing. Contact screens, which are treated in Chapter 27, are designed to be used in the closest possible contact with the sensitized material during exposure. They are available in varied screen rulings and in varied sizes. Generally, the novice screen printer uses contact halftone screens.

Screens are expensive, are expertly made using precision techniques in their manufacture, and require the same care in handling as any optical instrument. When not used, they are generally kept covered to prevent dust from accumulating on them. Dust will interfere with the production of dots. They are cleaned with materials or cloths recommended by the manufacturer. They should not be handled on the surface but around the reinforced edges and must be kept free of the minutest scratch.

Screen printers also use a prescreened halftone film. This is a specially prepared film which produces a dot pattern automatically without the use of a halftone screen when the specially prepared film is exposed in a camera to a continuous tone subject or to any other subject. After the negative is developed it has a dot which may be enlarged to any size to produce the desired size dot. This film, which is explained more completely in Chapter 28 is obtainable in 133-line rulings.

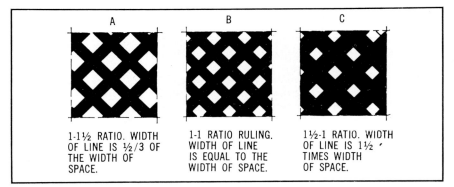

Figure 106. Ratio of width of opaque lines to width of space on halftone screens.

Although screen printers have made home-made screens, they do not work well and it is suggested that the printer planning to go into this type of work purchase a halftone screen or screens which will answer his purpose best. One screen will suffice for the average screen printer, unless he plans to specialize in halftone printing. If he obtains a fine line screen such as 120 lines or 133 lines, he will be able to reproduce fine detail and ordinary detail. For example, he may use a 120 line screen in order to better capture the detail in the original and then "blow up" or enlarge the negative to the desired size. Supposing the screen printer owns a 120 line halftone screen, 8 × 10 inches in size and needs to print a halftone job approximately 4 times this size. He may expose his copy through the 8 × 10 screen and then enlarge the negative to 4 times this size which will be 32 × 40 inches in size and produce dots with 30 lines to the inch. Because of the large size of the printed sheets done by printers, the dots may sometimes be enlarged to about 10 dots to the inch.

Doing Halftone Printing

Problems such as using the correct type of halftone screen in relation to the screen fabric, elimination of "moire," the type of ink to use, and method of printing will be gradually eliminated as the printer works in the halftone field.

As was mentioned, although 133 line dots are printed in some shops with screen printing, the average screen printer does not print above 100 dots to the inch. For inside posters most of the work is done between 65 and 85 lines to the inch; for outside posters the dot size may vary from about 30 to 65 dots to the inch. The screen fabric to which the final screen printing films with the halftone dot is attached limits the size of halftone dot that the screen printer may print. For example, if a Number 12 silk which has approximately 125 threads to the inch is used for the screen it is obvious that there would be difficulty in adhering a halftone screen printing film made from a 120 line screen or one which has 120 dots to the inch. The dots, especially the smaller ones, would not have enough threads to permanently adhere or would be in the openings between the silk threads and would drop off in the printing operation. A good first job for a beginner is one that is printed on a dull finished enamel paper or onto a good quality offset paper about 11 × 14 inches in size, printed in one color, using 45 to 65 lines to the inch, and adhering the screen printing film to a Number 16 silk or an equivalent numbered fabric or finer mesh. For example, if a 45 line halftone is to be printed, the number of the fabric should be about a 200 mesh so that the average halftone dot will adhere to three or four threads. Any good grade direct screen, direct-indirect screen, or screen printing film may be employed. Experimentation with direct screens, has indicated to the writer that a screen in which the photographic emulsion is prepared directly on the screen fabric is practical for halftone printing. The design areas consisting of the dots in such a screen are etched out or washed out directly in the screen, are part of the emulsion coated or impregnated screen, and do not fall off as easily as in transfer type printing screen.

Another problem confronting the beginner and advanced printer is the elimination of "moire" or a pattern in the final print. A moire is an undesirable symmetrical pattern produced when a halftone film is placed incorrectly over screen fabric in a screen or when a set of close parallel lines such as that found in a halftone positive is placed over another screen or halftone positive or negative. To do away with this pattern in single color halftone printing it is best to place the screen fabric over a light, place the correct size positive on the screen fabric and position the positive on the screen fabric. The positive should be rotated until the pattern disappears. With the positive in the correct position over the screen fabric, the fabric is marked with a soft pencil on the outside edges of the positive or in some other fashion, and the screen printing film which is made from the positive is adhered in the same marked area on the screen fabric. Where a direct screen or a direct-indirect screen is being prepared, the screen is placed over positive so that no moire shows. Elimination of moire in multi-color printing is explained in Chapter 31. With the available indirect, direct, and direct-indirect printing screens, silk, nylon, polyester, and metal fabrics may be used for the printing screen.

As far as inks for printing are concerned, there are many types of halftone screen printing inks but basically they fall into two types. The first type intended for one-color halftone printing is similar to regular screen inks. The ink may be an opaque one or transparent. The ink is ground very fine and will go through the finest mesh. Transparent inks, lacquers, and even enamel inks may be used for halftone printing, if the halftone screen is enlarged to about 40 lines per inch or coarser. Any thinly ground ink mixed in small proportions with an inert transparent extender base may be used for coarse halftone printing, especially one-color printing.

The second type of halftone screen printing inks are designed for four-color process work where varied colored dots are superimposed for colored reproduction. Transparent inks are employed where one color must print over another to produce the desired colors. Ink manufacturers and screen printing suppliers recommend the best ink to use for given jobs for the mixing of inks where this is essential.

There are factors which govern the manufacture of ink and the choice of an ink for halftone printing. The type of ink to use is governed by the size of the dot printed. The ink should be of proper consistency, not clog the screen, and not be too thin. The ink must cling to the printing surface, dry quickly on the surface after printing either naturally or by mechanical means. The printed dots should lie absolutely flat without spreading out and destroying one another.

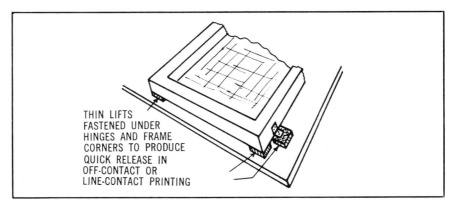

THIN LIFTS FASTENED UNDER HINGES AND FRAME CORNERS TO PRODUCE QUICK RELEASE IN OFF-CONTACT OR LINE-CONTACT PRINTING

Figure 107. A simple method of obtaining off-contact or line-contact printing.

The squeegee used in the application of the ink should be sharp and pulled rather lightly over the screen. Off-contact or line-contact printing should be used. In line-contact or off-contact printing the printing screen does not remain in contact with the stock once the squeegee has moved over the stock, since only the line area of the squeegee is in contact with the silk and print. On the other hand in full-contact printing most of the screen is in contact with the stock or object printed. The intent in off-contact printing is to make the screen snap away from the print as soon as the squeegee has passed over a part of the screen. Because of the adhesiveness of the ink, the production of static electricity when two surfaces are rubbed together, and sometimes the very thin nature of the stock, the stock or material has a tendency to stick to the printing screen. Off-contact printing prevents the screen from sticking to the material after printing, does away with smeared dots and lines, and generally produces sharper prints on very smooth surfaces such as glass, metal, metallized acetate, and in halftone printing. To produce an off-contact effect the screen may be built up with lifts or shims as illustrated in Figure 107. The lifts should be the same thickness under the hinges and under the frame corners. Other methods used to produce off-contact are applying tape to the underside of the frame to raise the screen fabric and design of the printing base and taping a paper cut-out or paper-mask around the printing area on the underside of the screen as shown in Figure 108. It is suggested that the thinnest lifts be used that will aid in quick and perfect release. Screen printing machines or presses are designed for easy adjustment for printing off-contact or full-contact.

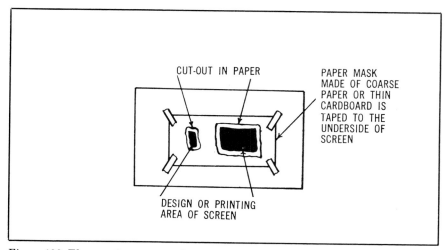

Figure 108. The use of a paper mask or paper cut-out in obtaining off-contact printing or quicker release of thin printed sheets.

The most practical way to keep thin sheets on the base so that it is not necessary to peel them off the screen is to use vacuum bases or vacuum tables under the screen. Vacuum bases have a partial vacuum as an aid to suck or hold the stock down to the base during printing and immediately after printing and are found on many presses and hand printing units.

173

Halftone printing like any screen printing technique must be based on experience and testing. Testing should be done on the stock that is to be printed for the job under exact shop conditions.

HALFTONE CONTACT SCREENS
FOR SCREEN PRINTING

27

Halftone contact screens, like glass halftone crossline screens, are designed for making halftone negatives and positives from continuous tone subjects for photomechanical reproductions in screen printing and other forms of printing. Continuous tone copy, exemplified by photographs, is that type which blends tones one into the other — from black to white. As has been mentioned, halftones are intermediate tones between black and white produced in printing by varying sizes and patterns of dots. Line copy which is composed of solid dark areas has no intermediate or middle tones. Halftone contact screens change intermediate tones of continuous tone copy into solid dots of varying size but of equal darkness or density. Thus, it is the halftone screen which produces the difference between line photography and halftone photography. Another way of saying it is — the halftone contact screen changes continuous tone to line copy because it is not possible for the printing screen or printing plate to apply different shades or tones on a printed surface. Screen printing like other major printing processes produces two uniform tones or shades in printing — the tone or shade of the ink being printed and the shade of the material or paper. Halftone printing makes possible the printing of very small or larger dots with one color ink which makes the print look as if it had been printed in different densities ranging from white to black.

Glass halftone screens must be set at a specific and predetermined distance from the film in a camera. Contact screens are placed in direct contact with the high contrast film to produce the halftone dots on the film. Contact screens are composed of vignetted dots on a flexible plastic sheet support. Generally, the vignetted dots, (unlike the sharp lines and sharp dots on a glass halftone screen), decrease in density from the solid dye (silver, in the case of the grey screen) in the center of the dot to the transparent area away from the center. The amount of light passing through the screen determines the size of dots produced on the film or negative.

Contact screens are available in a variety of screen rulings or lines per inch or dots per inch (or dots per centimeter), and in a variety of sizes. They are available in about 32-lines to about 300-lines per inch and in sizes varying from about 8 × 10 inches to 40 × 40 inches from various manufacturers. They can be used with a process camera or with an enlarger to make halftones from continuous tone negatives and positives. They can also be used with continuous tone separation negatives to make halftone positives for four-color screen printed work. To do this the screen printer may use only one contact screen or he may employ individual contact screens for each of the

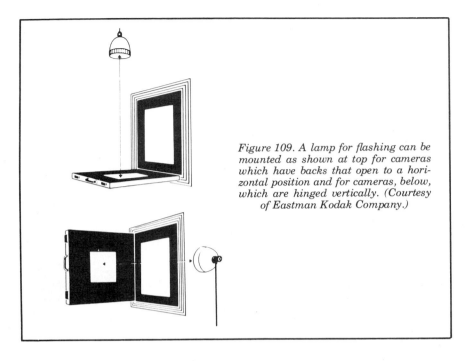

Figure 109. A lamp for flashing can be mounted as shown at top for cameras which have backs that open to a horizontal position and for cameras, below, which are hinged vertically. (Courtesy of Eastman Kodak Company.)

three basic colors and for black. The lines of dots are arranged at different angles on the individual screens for the different colors to prevent moire or undesirable geometric pattern effects in printing.

Since their introduction in 1941 by the Eastman Kodak Company, contact screens have been revolutionizing screen printing and other phases of printing and will give excellent results, if used for the purpose for which they are designed. The screen printer uses the magenta contact screen, the gray or neutral tone contact screen, and special effect screens. Contact screens are available in conventional dot design similar to glass screens, in elliptical dot designs, and in special effects designs.

The magenta contact screen is used for making negatives directly and for producing halftone positives from continuous tone negatives. There are magenta contact screens for making negatives for photomechanical reproduction and magenta contact screens for making halftone positives from continuous tone negatives. These contact screens may be used with arc lamps, quartz iodine lamps, and pulsed xenon lamps.

The gray contact screens are used for making halftone negatives from black and white copy and for making direct color separation negatives from color copy. Generally, the screen printer may use a gray screen first.

The screen printer also uses contact screens to obtain special effects. These special effects screens do not use dots in the formation of the image. The special effects screens, which may be used with either black and white or colored copy, consist of crossline, straight line screens, wavy line, spiral lines, mezzotint, and etching effect screens. The regular contact screens and the

176

special effects screens are available in percentage of tint areas producing required lighter or darker effects in printing. The manufacturer generally recommends that usually a negative screen be used for making a negative and a positive screen for a positive. Because a contact screen consists of a dye or silver image on a film base, the manufacturer's recommendations must be followed and reasonable care must be exercised in its use.

Since much of the screen printing done is usually not finer than about an 85-line, this type of screen may be the first size that he will use. However, the screen printer may desire to start with a finer dot screen to obtain finer detail and then enlarge the final positive to obtain any desired size dots that will not fall off the screen fabric during the making of the printing screen or during the actual printing. It is suggested that he start with a one color halftone job for his first effort.

A line negative may be made directly on film by photographing copy and the line negative will record light areas as dense areas and solid dark areas as clear image areas on the negatives. The screen printer must maintain the closest possible contact between the contact screen and the film. He may use a vacuum holder on a process camera, or an enlarger with a vacuum frame

Figure 110. A halftone negative made with an 85-line gray contact screen in a process camera using an f/16 lens opening. A 40 second main exposure and 24 second flash exposure was used. The negative was developed for 2¾ minutes in a tray. (Courtesy of Eastman Kodak Company).

177

for this purpose. Generally, this is done by placing the copy or design to be reproduced in the camera copy holder, and focusing the camera to the desired image size. After focusing, the high contrast film is placed on the camera back with the contact screen over the film, emulsion side of film in contact with emulsion side of contact screen. Lens openings or f-stops on camera do not generally affect contact screen dot formation. Therefore, the screen printer can use larger lens openings such as f/16 to obtain shorter exposures.

When a camera-enlarger is used (which may be made from a photographic enlarger), the copy is first focused by projecting onto the enlarger base or onto the vacuum frame or table which later will hold the screen and film. The vacuum frame or table holds the screen in contact with the film, emulsion to emulsion. In exposing, the light passes through the contact screen and onto the film forming dots in the film.

The screen is larger than the film so that screen overlaps film on all sides. The type of screen used, the light employed for exposure, the film used, and the processing of the film, all affect the type of halftone that will be produced. The screen printer will have to become acquainted with the contact screens and acquire enough knowledge about their use. Practical results are obtained by standardizing procedures as far as possible: the same contacting, exposing, film processing, and printing techniques must be used each time to obtain the same results. The standardization will depend on the type of equipment that the screen printer is using. Some of the equipment such as a process camera, enlarger, light source, varied chemical solutions, dark room procedures, and the like, will be familiar to the screen printer from his experience in making line copy negatives and positives.

While a light exposure produces a range of tones of the copy and contact screens are designed to reproduce a range of tones, most contact screens will not reproduce desired and needed dots with a single exposure in all tones of the copy. Since a halftone consists of varied size dots producing different tones in printing, it is necessary to bring out these dots so that the highlights and shadows will print well. In the production of halftones with contact screens the screen printer will use a "controlled flash method" of exposure. This method generally consists of two exposures: (1) a main, detail or basic exposure and (2) a second exposure known as a flash or shadow exposure. The latter exposure is made through the contact screen as illustrated in Figure 109. However, a third exposure, known as a "bump" or highlight exposure may be made; this third exposure is made without the contact screen. It is usually made after the main and flash exposure, because the contact screen is difficult to replace in exactly the same position. This highlight exposure made without the screen may be from 2 to 15 percent of the main exposure time and is an exposure to the copy.

The main exposure is made with white light or filtered light where filters are used over the light. The main exposure time will vary with the type of original copy, lights, lens, and processing. (See Figure 110). The main exposure is made for highlight areas and generally does not bring out pinpoint dots for the shadows. It is longer in time than each of the other exposures. The main exposure must first be determined by the screen printer for his particular conditions and equipment. Its purpose is to reproduce the subject — not necessarily in all the steps of the gray scale. There are graphic arts exposure computers or charts, reflection density guides or gray scales as

178

illustrated in Figures 110 and 111 with each of the tones or shades of the scales numbered for determining the exposure or determining the density between the light tones (highlights) of a photograph and the darkest areas (shadows).

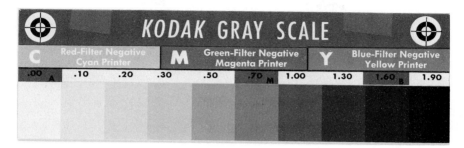

Figure 111. A gray scale or step wedge with density figures and colored patches. The gray scale, which is placed as near to the original as possible, is used to compare tone values or densities of a reproduction with an original, to find correct exposures through different filters, and to find development time for negatives. The colored patches make identification of color separation negatives easier. (Courtesy of Eastman Kodak Company).

The flash exposure is used to extend the halftone scale into the darker tones which would not have a printable shadow dot from the main exposure alone. The flash exposure may be made through the screen with a light such as a safelight having a 7½ watt white frosted lamp with a safelight filter (Wratten series 00) at a distance of about six feet from the screen. The manufacturer of the contact screen generally recommends that the main exposure and the flash exposure be calibrated by means of an exposure computer or chart. These are generally available from the contact screen manufacturer.

The copy reflects varying light intensities to form varying size dots. The shadow areas on the copy reflect little light; highlight areas reflect more. However, between the shadow and highlight areas different tones are formed. Thus, the screen printer must establish the copy range. The copy range is the difference between the light tones or highlight density of the copy and the darkest areas or shadows. Since the darkest and lightest points of some copy are not easy to find, their equivalent densities or tones may be located and controlled or determined by means of a gray scale of the type illustrated in Figure 111. The gray scale or step wedge consists of a series of tones, each of the steps in the scale having a density difference and each step identified or calibrated with a number (log number). The first steps are more closely spaced for greater control. The gray scale is placed on the copy board with the copy when photographing, as illustrated in Figure 110. There are also gray scales with holes punched in each of the numbered tones for easier determining of the tones. The printer then determines the highlight density and the shadow density. Each contact screen has a "basic density range" which is the range of tones that the halftone screen will reproduce with a main white light exposure and without flash exposure.

Besides the available contact screens and the negative film known as a prescreened halftone film (see Chapter 28) today's screen printer has a choice of other equipment to aid him such as a diffusion transfer process machine, duplicating film, and photomechanical transfer paper.* The high speed duplicating film is designed for making duplicates or copies from line and halftone negative or positive originals. These duplicate films are designed to produce negatives from negatives and positives from positives, with normal exposure and processing, using either tray or machine processing. The screen printer may use this film with originals made on transparent or translucent materials, having scribed, inked, penciled, or crayon lines.

Another photographic aid for the screen printer is the use of photomechanical transfer paper. These products which are available as negative papers, receiver paper, reflex paper, and also as transparent receiver film, may be used to make quality screened prints from line copy for paste-up copy work. The photomechanical transfer materials offer a quick and simple system for photomechanical work. The photomechanical transfer negative paper can be handled in subdued light. In use, the negative paper is exposed through a contact screen from an original continuous tone print. The exposed halftone paper negative is placed in contact with a sheet called photomechanical transfer receiver paper and both papers are run through a small unit known as a "diffusion transfer process machine. This unit holds the chemical activator and has two rollers which press the papers together, producing a finished halftone paper positive or a screened print of the copy very quickly.

When the screen printer is making mechanicals or paste-up copy consisting of line and halftone copy for screen printing reproduction, he may employ the above screened prints in pasteups. A screened print is a halftone print made on photographic paper from a negative and pasted on the necessary place on the mechanical. The pasted paper halftone on the copy gives the screen printer a line negative of the whole page which may have other line copy on it. He may then make a positive from the copy and use the positive for producing the printing screen or printing plate. It is best to make these types of paste-ups on matte or non-glossy paper so that no flare is encountered in exposing.

Photography is and will continue to be a process that is common to all the graphic arts reproduction methods. Screen printing, one of the major graphic arts reproduction methods, must be aware and keep up with photographic refinements.

*Eastman Kodak Company, Rochester, New York.

A PRESCREENED HALFTONE FILM

Halftone screen printing has always been a challenge and has required technical knowledge, precision equipment, and specified copy or originals. It is still not an easy task for the average printer. However, because leadership is constantly emerging to answer a need or to solve some problem, halftone negative making is being simplified.

Conventional crossline halftone screens give practical results but require exact processing and equipment that is costly. Where the contact screen is employed, it generally requires a vacuum back for halftone production.

In 1953, a successful new negative film material known as a *prescreened film** was introduced for producing halftones. This film is manufactured so that the halftone or dot formation is already incorporated in the sensitized emulsion of the film. Although the film originally was developed for making halftone negatives for lithography, it is practical for making halftone negatives for screen printing. The film is manufactured so that the sensitivity of the film is varied and produces varied dot patterns, the dot pattern depending upon the strength of the light reflected upon the film from the copy or object being photographed. It does not require special apparatus and has a short exposure time. While it does record detail, it does not require a halftone screen nor a vacuum back for exposure. The film will produce a dot pattern automatically when exposed to a continuous-tone or line copy. It will reproduce still copy, type matter combined with picture matter, or anything that a camera may capture ordinarily. The film, therefore, opens up a new potential for the printer, especially the one who does not have access to costly photographic equipment and does not do much halftone printing. It offers a photographic tool for the screen printer.

The prescreened film may be exposed to arc lights or tungsten lights in an ordinary view camera film holder or any camera that will hold sheet film. Of course, process cameras may be used successfully. A much wider lens aperture may be employed than is used for conventional halftone screen photography. It is important, with any camera, that the copy or image be focused correctly in the camera.

The film is available in 133-line rulings and in two sizes — 8 × 10 inches and 11 × 14 inches. This ruling which is finer than is normally used in screen printing, makes it practical for capturing detail in an original exposure or copy. Fewer lines or dots per inch may then be obtained by conventional

---

Making Halftones With Kodalith Autoscreen Ortho Film 2563. Eastman Kodak Company, Rochester, New York.

enlargement of the exposed and developed halftone. For example, if a 65-line halftone or less is needed, as is common in screen printing, an exposure is made in a camera on the prescreened film for the halftone negative, and the negative after development, is enlarged to obtain the required ruling or size dot for the job. Positives for masking the actual printing screen may be made from the negative either by the contact method or enlargement method onto actual film such as Kodalith or any similar high contrast film. A contact print, however, would be too fine a screen ruling.

Generally, the following are the steps in preparing the prescreened film for screen printing; (1) exposing; (2) processing film; (3) making halftone positive; (4) exposing halftone positive to sensitized printing screen or to screen printing film.

Exposing Film

The lighter side of the film is the emulsion side. The manufacturer of the film recommends that the film be handled and developed by the light of a safelight filter of the Wratten Series 1A (light red safelight).* Ruby bulbs are not safe for handling the film. The safelight lamp should be one that has a 15-watt bulb and be at least a distance of four feet from the film. So as not to impair the dot quality, it is recommended that the film should not be exposed to the safelight longer than 3 minutes.

Camera exposures can be made either by using white-flame arc light, pulsed-xenon, tungsten, or quartz-iodine illumination.

As has been mentioned, the film may be exposed in any sheet-film camera, copy camera or process camera. The film requires two simple exposures: first a *detail exposure* taken in the camera, then a *flash* exposure which must take place in the darkroom and may be exposed in a contact frame. The detail exposure controls the highlight dots. The highlight dots on the negative are those which appear the blackest and the largest. The flash exposure controls the contrast and the size of the shadow dots. The shadow dots on the negative are small dots which are in the lightest or most transparent part.

For the average job under normal shop conditions, at same-size reproduction, the detail exposure may last for about 30 seconds (at f/22) or two 500-watt 3200 K lamps in reflectors or Number 2 photoflood lamps at 3 feet from film. If two 35-ampere white flame arcs are used, then the detail exposure may last for 10 seconds (at f/32) at 4 feet (1.2m) exposure distance. Detail exposures shorter than 1 second should not be used.

Any low level tungsten light may be used for the flash exposure. The flash exposure unit may be arranged as shown in Figure 112. About 25 seconds exposure time is generally required at a distance of 6 feet from the film when a 25-watt bulb and a Kodak safelight filter Wratten Series OA are used. For the novice, experimentation will be necessary; one must expose for highlights and flash for shadow effects.

The illustrated halftone in Figure 113 is the result of a detail exposure made in a 4 × 5 view camera using an f/16 lens opening with a 5 seconds exposure time. Figure 114 which was an ordinary glossy photograph was used as copy. The halftone film was then given a flash exposure to a 7½-watt bulb at a distance of 6 feet from the film for 8 seconds.

Kodak Filters for Scientific and Technical Uses. Eastman Kodak Co., Rochester, New York.

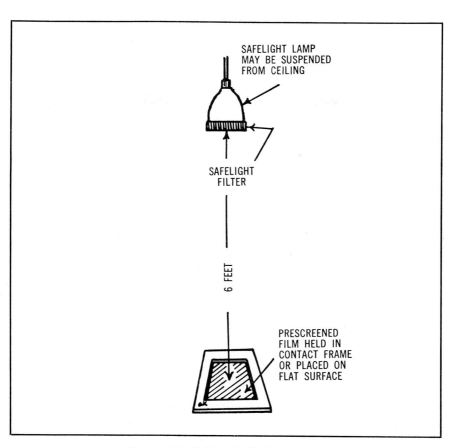

SAFELIGHT LAMP
MAY BE SUSPENDED
FROM CEILING

SAFELIGHT
FILTER

6 FEET

PRESCREENED
FILM HELD IN
CONTACT FRAME
OR PLACED ON
FLAT SURFACE

Figure 112. Making the flash exposure.

For a first attempt at photographing specific copy, it is suggested that two trial exposures be made in the camera and the flash exposure may then be varied to obtain a desired result in dot effect. For best results, shadow dots should be larger and highlight dots more open than is usually the case.

Processing the Film

The film is processed in three solutions: a developer, a stop bath, and a fixing bath. The solutions recommended are: Kodalith developer, Kodak stop-bath SB1a and Kodalith fixer. The solutions are easily mixed from packaged chemicals according to the directions on the container. The three solutions should be arranged in the following order: first, the tray with the developer; then, the stop bath; and finally, the fixing bath.

After the detail and flash exposure have been given, the film may be developed by the inspection or time and temperature method. If the latter method is employed, fresh developer must be used for each exposed negative

183

Figure 113. Screen print made from a positive which was enlarged to twice the size of the prescreened halftone negative. (Illustration actual size.)

to be processed, temperature must be controlled to plus or minus ½ degree Fahrenheit, and the developing tray must be agitated constantly during processing to insure an even flow of the chemicals over the emulsion at all times.

If the inspection method for development is used, the safelight should not be turned on until the film has been in the developer for 1½ minutes. The film should be developed in a transparent tray such as a glass tray; the film should not be taken out of the tray for inspection as this would interfere with the still development.

The developer should be of room temperature (68 degrees Fahrenheit or 20 degrees Celsius). A still development technique is used to develop the film. In still development, the tray with the film is first rocked vigorously for a period and then allowed to remain still or motionless for a period. The developer should be agitated vigorously for a few seconds before immersing film in it; then the tray with the film is agitated for 1½ minutes. The film should

184

Figure 114. A glossy photograph was used as copy for making the prescreened halftone negative. (Illustration actual size.)

then be allowed to lie still in the bottom of the tray for another ¾ minute until it has been in the developer for a total of 2¼ minutes. The film or tray containing the developer should not be moved during the still period, as streaks may be produced on the film.

After the film has been developed, it is rinsed in the stop bath solution for about 10 seconds and the tray agitated at the same time. The temperature of the stop bath should be about the same as that of the developer (65 to 70 degrees Fahrenheit or 18 to 21 degrees Celsius). The purpose of the stop bath is to check or stop development, prevent spots or streaks on the developed film, and prolong life of the fixing bath. A stop bath may also be made by dissolving 16 liquid ounces of 28% acetic acid in one gallon of water (U.S. measure), or 125 cubic centimeters of acetic acid to one liter of water (Metric system).

After 10 seconds in the stop bath the film is taken out and immersed in the fixing bath and left in the fixing bath for about twice the length of time it takes the film to clear. The temperature of the fixing bath is the same as that of the stop bath. The purpose of the fixing bath is to prevent further action of light on the film. The film must be agitated frequently during the fixing process.

After having been processed in the three solutions, the film is washed in an adequate supply of running water for about 10 minutes and then the film is allowed to dry in a dust-free place.

Making Halftone Positive

Halftone positives may be obtained either by the contact printing method or by enlargement projection method. If the halftone positive is to be the same size as the negative, then the negative is placed in direct contact with film in a photographic contact frame and exposed. However, if, as is usually the case in screen printing, a larger dot or ruling is necessary for printing and for better attaching of dot to the screen fabric, then the developed and processed halftone negative will have to be enlarged in a photographic enlarger or in a process camera to any desired size. The halftone negative may be enlarged onto Kodalith Ortho Film, or onto a similar high contrast film for making halftone positives. In enlarging, the focus must be adjusted so that the image is equally sharp over the entire desired area. The positive is processed by the still development technique in similar fashion to the pre-screened film and in the same type of solutions.

Making Printing Screen

After the halftone positive is made, it is placed on the underside of the prepared and cleaned screen fabric of the screen in order to plan for elimination of a "moire" pattern. As has been mentioned before, a moire pattern is an undesired symmetrical pattern which may be produced in the final printing when the halftone screen effect and the lines of the screen fabric or silk are brought in contact. To eliminate this, place marks with a pencil on the silk matching the corners of the halftone positive when the halftone is in the desired part of the silk or when there is no moire pattern.

An indirect, direct-indirect, or direct screen may be exposed to the halftone positive and printing screen is prepared in the usual and careful manner.

186

HANDMADE INTAGLIO POSITIVE

Screen printing produces a need for many techniques and materials, varied related information, and for many hand and machine processes. Although most positives and negatives for the preparation of photographic printing screens are made photographically with cameras, positives are also made by hand by means of brushing or inking the design with special opaque inks onto thin transparent or translucent plastic sheets. These hand prepared positives are practical for reproducing processed jobs which do not have fine detail. For jobs requiring the printing of fine detail the detail in hand prepared positives is limited by the instruments and tools employed to make the positives and by the skill of the processor.

To overcome the latter problems the writer has developed and introduced a positive which he named the *handmade intanglio positive*, since the lines making up the design in this positive are incised or sunk below the surface. Basically, this positive is made in the same fashion as that explained in the book (Kosloff, A., *Celluloid Etching*) on making a drypoint etching plate or a celluloid etching plate. The fine detail in this positive is produced by scribing or scratching the design in tracing fashion with a sharp needle instrument onto a transparent plastic surface. The very fine sharp lines are then filled in with any opaque screen printing ink.

This positive is easy to prepare, has very opaque lines and detail, and is ideal for reproducing etching effects. Since a needle point is used to make the lines, fine detail and shading effects may be reproduced. One can trace this positive from line copy, from photographs, or from parts of larger designs. It offers the printer another type of positive in an emergency. The positive does not require any photographic equipment for its preparation and once made is very durable. The positive can be exposed in direct contact with direct screens and in direct contact with sensitized dry or wet carbon tissue or in contact with any other photographic screen printing material.

To make this positive the printer will need the following: (1) a piece of transparent acrylate plastic sheet (either Plexiglas or Lucite) about 1/16 inch in thickness or less or a piece of any other transparent plastic rigid sheet slightly larger in area than the design to be reproduced; (2) a sharp needle instrument of the type illustrated in Figure 115 which may be made by the beginner; an etching needle which may be obtained in any art shop, or any large sewing needle may be inserted in a penholder to serve as the etching needle; (3) opaque screen printing ink; (4) clear vinylite lacquer, or clear lacquer of the spraying type, a good grade of clear varnish, or a commercial

187

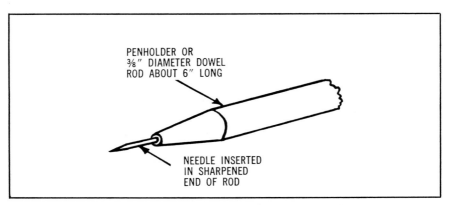

Figure 115. Suggested tool for preparing handmade intaglio positive.

transparent spray of the type used as a protective coating over art work: (5) some soft clean lintless cloths; (6) a high melting point type paste wax; and (7) a design to be reproduced.

Generally, the procedure for the positive involves tracing the design in scribing or scratching fashion onto the thin plastic sheet; rubbing ink into the scribed lines which make up the design; pouring or coating a transparent protective coating over the scribed and inked surface; and polishing protective coating with a paste wax.

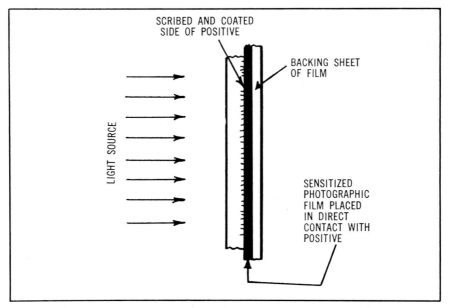

Figure 116. Exposing positive in direct contact with sensitized film.

188

Procedure

To make this positive tape the design onto any smooth surface board and then tape the transparent plastic sheet over the design so plastic extends beyond the limits of the design about an inch on all sides. It is suggested that a simple design be reproduced for the first attempt. Then holding the etching needle or scribing needle as one holds a pencil, in tracing fashion, begin to scribe or scratch the design into the surface of the plastic sheet, scribing slowly. Where it is necessary to produce shading effects or shaded areas criss-cross or cross-hatch lines with the needle. With a little practice the scribing or tracing with the needle becomes almost as simple as tracing with a pencil. Where lines are straight a ruler may be used as a guide for the scribing tool. Continue scribing in a tracing fashion until the whole design is completed.

Although it is not essential, to test one's work for completion a little ink may be rubbed into the scratched lines. The ink will make the design more visible.

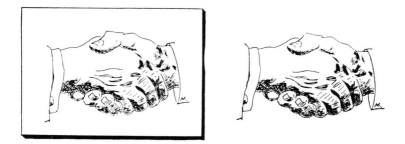

Figure 117. (Left) The handmade intaglio positive on a thin transparent plastic sheet.
Figure 118. (Right) Screen print made from polyvinyl alcohol printing plate which was prepared from handmade intaglio positive.

When the design has been completely traced with the needle, rub opaque screen printing ink with a piece of cloth into the scribed lines. Although any screen printing opaque type ink may be employed for this purpose, it is suggested that a black or red quick drying oil-vehicle type of ink be employed. A flat poster ink, regular printer's ink, or etching ink may also be used. After the ink has been rubbed well into the lines so that the design parts on the plastic sheet are completely covered, carefully wipe away with a soft cloth the excess ink outside the design areas, leaving the plastic surface outside the design areas perfectly clean and transparent. In wiping the surface make sure that you do not remove the ink from the scribed lines. If desired, the processor may rub a second coat of ink into the lines and wipe the surface clean again. This rubbing and cleaning away of the excess ink also removes the minute burrs which may have formed by the scribing or tracing of the needle point.

After the ink dries, the complete scribed surface side of the plastic may be given a protective transparent coating so that it will be possible to expose this side in direct contact with any sensitized photographic screen printing

189

film or carbon tissue, (either wet or dry) or in contact with a direct or direct-indirect screen. This protective coating which may consist of clear spraying lacquer, vinylite lacquer, collodion, varnish, or a commercial transparent spraying coating, may be applied by spraying on, by brushing, by dipping the positive in the solvent, or by pouring the coating over the scribed surface and allowing the excess to drain off. In brushing, the coating is brushed on just once in the same spot. Where a good quality synthetic oil-vehicle type of screen printing ink is filled into the scribed lines, it is not necessary to cover the scribed surface with a protective coating. The purpose of the coating is to protect the scribed lines and to offer a smoother surface for the wax polishing which is the next step.

Although it is not always necessary, when the positive is exposed to some types of screen printing films, waxing and polishing the positive will allow the positive to drop off by itself from the film, especially where the wet-carbon tissue method is used to prepare the photographic screen printing plate. Generally any type of paste wax may be used. A high melting point type of paste wax will produce a better polish over the coating. The wax is obtainable from screen printing suppliers or from hardware stores. The wax is applied with a cloth and the excess wax is polished off with another soft cloth before placing the scribed, coated, and polished surface in direct contact with the photographic film to be exposed.

In exposing, the unit is arranged so that light goes through the back of the positive first, as illustrated in Figure 116. To expose, place photographic sensitized screen printing film or carbon tissue in contact frame and then place positive, scribed and coated surface down, and in direct contact with film. Place glass of photographic contact frame or vacuum frame over positive and lock unit. Because positive has very opaque lines and positive is in direct contact with film, no light seepage will occur. Where a contact frame or vacuum frame is not available, the cement method of exposure explained on page 124 may be used.

Figure 117 presents a handmade intaglio positive prepared as explained above. Figure 118 shows a print made from a direct polyvinyl alcohol printing screen which was produced from the positive.

190

DIRECT PHOTOGRAPHIC POSITIVES FOR SCREEN PRINTING
(Autopositive Film)

Ordinarily, photographic screen printing plates or printing screens are made from photographic positives which consist of the required design on a transparent or thin translucent plastic sheet or glass. The positive is generally made from a negative which was produced by photographing the copy or original. The positive may be made by exposing film in direct contact with the negative or by projecting the negative onto film.

The *Eastman Kodak Autopositive film or direct contact positive is a product employed to produce a direct film transparent positive which eliminates the intermediate step for making negatives or positives. It is accurate and differentiates between the fine and black-and-white detail in line copy, if the directions of the manufacturer are followed and care is used in processing. The film may be processed with ordinary photographic solutions that are generally available from photographic and graphic arts suppliers. The film can be handled and processed in daylight and is exposed in an ordinary photographic frame in direct contact with the copy that is to be reproduced. The film may be used for making duplicate negatives and positives.

Because the film has to be exposed in direct contact with the copy, it will reproduce positives that are the same size as the original or copy. Where copy must be reduced or enlarged, the enlarging or reduction must be done before making the direct positive.

The principle of the autopositive film is that the film has been already "exposed" in its manufacture. In producing a desired positive from the film the original exposure is taken out by placing a transparent yellow sheet or yellow gelatin sheet over the film when the film is exposed in direct contact with the original copy to an arc light or to a photoflood lamp. The theory is to burn out the original exposure in areas where the white copy reflects light back to the film. The black portions in copy will reflect too little light to burn out the original exposure. If the film were developed out of its original container it would develop out absolutely black. To test for maximum opacity or blackness or to test a developer it is suggested that a sample of the unexposed autopositive film be developed in the dark. To test for different degrees of opacity, it is necessary to vary the time of exposure or the distance of the film from the exposing light.

The film has a matte or dull-finished surface on both sides. It is colored brown on one side and gray on the other. The gray side is the emulsion side.

---

*Eastman Kodak Company, Rochester, New York.

The film is obtainable in a wide range of sheet sizes and in rolls up to 44 inches in width by 100 feet in length. Wider film rolls may be had on special order. Either side of the film can be written or drawn on with india ink, opaque ink, or pencil after the film has been developed and processed. The film should be handled by the edges, since finger marks and oil marks may produce unwanted spots on film.

Good copy or good original design is essential for this process. The copy employed should be black and white, printed, drawn, or reproduced on perfectly white paper, preferably enameled or calendered paper. Perfectly white paper is desirable, since the light in exposing goes through the yellow sheet, the autopositive film, strikes the copy, and is reflected back by the white in the copy. The black in the copy has a tendency to absorb the light, therefore, it does not reflect light back and the parts of the film that are over the black areas on the copy remain black. If typewritten material is to be reproduced, the typewriter ribbon used must be perfectly black and each character should be struck at least twice.

The actual processing of the film is simple, although directions given here for the film are detailed intentionally. Most of the photographic chemicals for processing are powders and are easily mixed with ordinary water. Water that is fit to drink may be used to make the mixture. If ordinary clear water is not available, then clean rain water or distilled water may be used. All that is necessary are three trays for holding the solutions, each tray being large enough to hold the film. When processing the film, the three trays containing the solutions are arranged in the following order: first, the tray with the developer; then the tray containing the rinse or stop-bath; and last the tray with the fixing solution. The last tray should be nearest to the sink, since the film can then be washed in the sink. Basically, the process of making the direct positive consists of the following steps: (1) preparation for exposing; (2) exposing; (3) developing; (4) rinsing; (5) fixing; and (6) washing.

Preparation for Exposing

To prepare the film for exposing place the original design or copy face side up. Over the copy place the autopositive film, emulsion side or gray colored side down, and in direct contact with the copy. Place yellow sheet over film. The whole sandwich consisting of the copy, film, and yellow sheet, with the film in the center, is placed under the contact frame glass (see Figure 119), the yellow sheet being in contact with the glass. The writer has found that a more practical way of exposing the unit is to place the copy under the film with film directly under the contact frame glass and then lay the yellow sheet on top on the outside of the frame glass, covering the film area. The important thing is that the yellow sheet be placed between the light source and the film. There must be perfect contact between film and copy. Of course, a vacuum contact frame, if available, may be used for exposure.

In the event that the original copy should consist of all or part of a printed page, such as from a magazine or book, and there is printing on the reverse side of the sheet, the original from which the positive is to be made must be placed with the back side in contact with a black surface such as a sheet of opaque black paper, black cardboard, or similar material. Placement of the original on a black surface is essential in this case, to prevent the

192

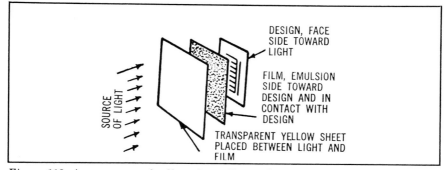

DESIGN, FACE
SIDE TOWARD
LIGHT

FILM, EMULSION
SIDE TOWARD
DESIGN AND IN
CONTACT WITH
DESIGN

SOURCE OF LIGHT

TRANSPARENT YELLOW SHEET
PLACED BETWEEN LIGHT AND
FILM

Figure 119. Arrangement of yellow sheet, film, and copy of original design for exposure.

printed matter on both sides of the paper original from registering on the autopositive film. Light passing through the paper will be absorbed by the printing on the back side of such an original which is to be copied on the film, as well as by the printing on the face side of the sheet.

Exposing

The film may be exposed to a carbon arc lamp or to a plain Number 2 photoflood lamp, being careful that the lamp or carbon arc do not have hot spots in them and that the light strikes with the same intensity on all areas of the contact frame. In exposing, the film is kept about 4 feet from the source of light. When exposing to a carbon arc expose film for about 1 to 1½ minutes. When exposing to a Number 2 photoflood lamp expose film for about 2 minutes. A little experimentation will easily determine the time of exposure and the distance of exposure. A tint of gray or fog over the background of the copy or design indicates insufficient exposure and that longer exposure is necessary.

Developing

While developing the film or producing a visible image on the film may be done with normal photographic solutions, it is best to develop the film in developers recommended by the manufacturer. Developers are mixed according to directions on the package and developers are available in prepared form in several package sizes. The temperature of the developing solution should be kept at 68 degrees Fahrenheit (20 degrees Celsius). The exposed film is immersed in the developing solution and the tray containing the developing solution is agitated continuously for the development time recommended by the manufacturer. Stock solutions for the developer may be kept for a recommended length of time. In using any of the developers, the solution should be discarded when it turns yellow or brown.

Agitate solution slightly during development to prevent uneven development and production of streaks. Enough development solution should be poured into tray to cover film completely. Keep film under solution at all times until image or design shows up very clearly. The time of development may vary from about 2 to 2½ minutes, depending on the developer used. A developer such as Kodalith* may be better for the beginner, since it devlops out the image slowly and the printer can take his time and produce a better image. When the image on the film is black, the film is immersed in rinsing solution or stop-bath.

Rinsing

The purpose of a rinse or stop-bath is to stop development immediately and prevent streaks and stains on film. Fresh water may be used or an acid bath may be made for the stop-bath. A simple acid bath consisting of 1 part of 28 percent acetic acid and 7 parts of water (making a total of 8 parts) makes a practical stop-bath. The 28 percent acetic acid solution may be bought in any photographic shop. The film should be left in the stop-bath for about 10 to 20 seconds at a temperature of about 65 to 70 degrees Fahrenheit (18 to 21 degrees Celsius) before placing film in fixing solution. The 28 percent acetic acid solution will keep indefinitely, if the bottle or container is well stoppered. Other stop-baths recommended by the manufacturer may be used for rinsing the film.

Fixing

After rinsing, the film is immersed in a fixing solution for 2 to 4 minutes. The purpose of the fixing solution is to make the film inactive as far as light and handling is concerned and to remove any sensitive substance that has not been acted upon by the light or developer. The fixing solution is mixed with water according to directions. The writer has obtained good results with Kodak Acid Fixer.* The fixing solution may be used over and over, provided it is kept in a well stoppered bottle. Other fixing solutions recommended by the manufacturer of film may be employed.

Washing

After the film is fixed it should be well washed to remove all traces of chemicals. It may be washed by placing the film in a tray of cold water or it can be left in the sink in which there is a spray of running cold water. The film should be left in the water for at least 10 minutes.

Film may be hung to dry naturally or it may be placed in front of a fan to hasten drying. After the film has been properly processed and after it has served its purpose, it can be stored in an envelope for future use.**

---

*Eastman Kodak Company.
**The following book covers other photographic techniques that may be of help to the printer: Fossett, Robert O., *Screen Printing Photographic Techniques*, Signs of the Times Publishing Co., Cincinnati, Ohio.

194

COLOR SEPARATION AND COLOR EFFECTS

More and more screen printing of colors and blending of two, three, or more colors is being done photographically. Basically, screen printing color separation printing is an interdependent photographic and printing process which requires experience in this type of photography and in blending and superimposing correct colors in printing. The screen printer uses both hand methods of color separation and photomechanical separation. In hand color separation printing he prepares each printing screen by hand, that is, without the use of photographic halftones, to print each desired color. Ordinarily, the hand prepared screens are made from knife-cut film, knife-cut paper, or tusche-glue screens. These hand printing screens are used by the screen printer to print and register the colors in order to reproduce the desired color copy. However, photographically, the color separation is more precise, is more complex, and is capable of reproduction of fine detail in color. The photographic process deals with spectral or colored light; the actual printing process deals with blending of pigment or screen printing ink colors.

Color separation or "process" color printing involves separating out the original colored copy into three colors by photographing the original through three different color filters onto three black-and-white halftone negatives. The negatives are used to make the desired size halftone positives from which the printing screen is produced. Actually, a "color separation" is a photographic negative in which a desired color has been recorded in black-and-white by using a color filter which absorbs the other colors of the original and allows the desired color to be transmitted or pass through the filter.

When the screens are produced, the printing of the colored illustration with the printing screens is done either by hand or by machine by superimposing the three ink colors of cyan (blue-green), magenta (bluish-red), and yellow, with black ink added to improve the dark tones of the illustration. Plus the black ink the printer may add other colors for special effects.

Since light energy is employed in photographic work to reproduce the shape and tones of objects and illustrations, the beginner must have at least a basic understanding of it. Also, since pigments or inks are used to print the two, three, four and other colored effects in order to obtain a final color print, it is essential that the beginner know the relationship of the two.

Light

Pure white light or sunlight contains all colors. It is a form of radiant energy which originally comes from the sun. Although there are several theories of light, the wave theory provides enough explanation for color printing. This theory is based on the work of James Clerk Maxwell and Heinrich Hertz and others and stresses that light consists of waves. Light is one of several types of wave motion or groups of waves known as Electromagnetic Waves. As illustrated in Figure 120, each group has its own wavelength. The visible waves of light range from about 400 millimicrons (4000 Angstrom units) to about 800 millimicrons (8000 Angstrom units) in length and the waves carry energy in all directions and travel approximately at a speed of 186,000 miles per second (approximately 299,790 kilometers per second). As can be seen in Figure 120, ultraviolet rays are below 400 millimicrons and infrared waves are above 800 millimicrons. The waves ordinarily travel in straight lines and the farther the light travels the weaker it becomes. Light can be reflected or thrown back into the medium or substance from which it came. Light can be absorbed. It can be refracted or bent when it passes from one medium or substance into another. Light can be transmitted through transparent substances. The color of the transparent object depends upon the color of light which the object transmits or the color of light which passes. For example, red glass absorbs all colors but red, which it transmits. The color of an opaque object is the color it reflects. For example, a red opaque object absorbs most of the other colors but reflects red to the eye.

Because light travels in a straight line it can form images by being reflected from a smooth surface as in a mirror, by being projected as through a pinhole camera, and by refraction or being bent as through a lens in a camera.

Light can also be dispersed. Sir Isaac Newton (1642–1727) an English mathematician and physicist showed that white light can be dispersed or separated into its colors to illustrate that light is composed of every color. When white light passes through a spectroscope (an instrument for studying the band of color) or a glass triangular prism so that light is dispersed, all of its colors appear as illustrated in Figure 121.

Color

Color is a property of light which produces a psychological sensation upon the normal human eye. It causes objects to have different appearances

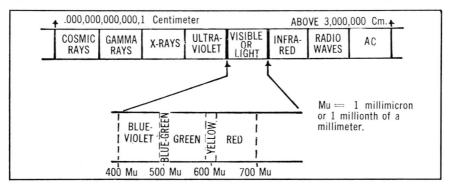

Figure 120. Electromagnetic spectrum with enlarged illustration showing relation between wave lengths and colors.

196

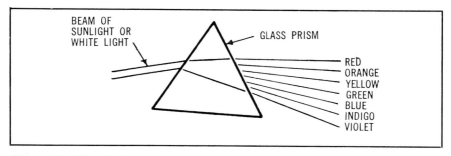

Figure 121. White light is refracted or bent and dispersed or separated into the seven elementary colors or spectral colors by means of a triangular glass prism.

to the eye. The printer who intends to do color work must have the ability to recognize and to distinguish between varied colors. Although white light consists of all colors, for practical printing purposes it consists of red, green, and blue (bluish violet). These three light colors are referred to as primary colors, since correct mixtures of red, blue, and green light will match all colors. Combining the three light colors as illustrated in Figure 122, will form white. Also the primary light colors can be combined in varied proportions to produce secondary colors or to duplicate any of the colors of the spectrum.

Mixing colored pigments produces different results than mixing colored light. It also absorbs or subtracts from the white light the colors present in the object. When pigments are mixed each pigment subtracts or absorbs certain colors from white light; the final color depends upon the light waves that are not absorbed. For example, when blue and yellow light are added white light is produced. When blue pigment and yellow pigment are mixed or added not white but the pigment color green is produced. The reason for this is that each pigment subtracts or absorbs certain colors. For example, yellow pigment absorbs blue and violet and reflects yellow; blue subtracts or absorbs red and yellow; green is the color that is not subtracted or absorbed by yellow or blue. Therefore, yellow and blue pigment produce green. As illustrated in Figure 122, the three primary pigment colors are the complements of the three primary light colors. Color complements or complementary colors are any two colors that unite to form white light. The opposite colors in Figure 122 show the complementary colors; red is complementary to blue-green (yellow); blue is complementary to yellow, etc. The primary pigment colors are yellow, red, and blue.

The artist and the ink mixer work with pigment colors or red, blue and yellow. The color photographer also works with three primary colors but most of the time they are red, green, and blue.

Color Filters

In color separation work the filter used holds back some colors and allows one color to pass through or to be transmitted. The colors of the filters generally employed for screen printing are red, green and blue. The three filters employed for color separation work divide the color spectrum into three main

197

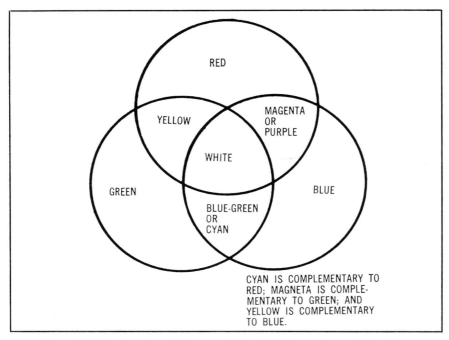

RED

YELLOW

MAGENTA
OR
PURPLE

WHITE

GREEN

BLUE

BLUE-GREEN
OR
CYAN

CYAN IS COMPLEMENTARY TO
RED; MAGNETA IS COMPLE-
MENTARY TO GREEN; AND
YELLOW IS COMPLEMENTARY
TO BLUE.

Figure 122. Overlapping adding, or mixing of the three primary light colors.

parts. Each filter allows only the light of its own color to pass through and absorbs other colors. The color which passes through is called complementary to that which is absorbed or, vice versa, the color which is absorbed is called complementary to that which is transmitted. Either one color is needed to be added to the other to complete or make white light. Since white light consists of green, blue and red light, a green filter will absorb blue and red light and allow green to be transmitted; a red filter will absorb green and blue and allow red to pass through; and a blue filter will absorb green and red and allow blue to pass through. (See Figure 123). Where *black* is to be printed as a color a yellow filter is employed. Thus, it becomes possible to separate all the visible colors in a color copy into three primary spectral or light colors.

Filters used in screen printing work are named and numbered, the number corresponding to a certain color. The specific color of a filter must always be exact and standard. Filters may consist of colored gelatin, sheet gelatin cemented between glass or dyed glass. The filter is used in front of the lens, between the copy and the lens, to filter, absorb, transmit, or separate the primary colors in three-color photography. The Wratten type filters illustrated in Figure 124, are commonly used separation filters. The gelatin filter, which is lacquer coated, to protect the gelatin, is a practical filter.

Since a color filter absorbs a certain part of light, an additional exposure must be given. Another name for this additional exposure is *filter factor*. The ratio by which the exposure must be increased or the number by which the exposure is multiplied is actually the filter factor. Generally, filter factor data are supplied by the manufacturer of the filter.

198

Assuming that a red filter is employed, it will allow all of the parts of the original copy which are red to photograph as black on the photographic negative. The positive being the opposite of the negative will have the black appearing as white. The positive is minus the red color and is actually portraying the green and blue parts of the picture. Green and blue are the complementary colors of red. In the same fashion the positive made as a result of the green filter exposure will show green areas as clear and will portray the red and blue parts of the picture. The blue filter negative photographs the blue areas and the positive will show the red and green parts of the picture.

If each of the printing screens made from the positive is printed correctly in the color which is the complement of the color that was recorded on the positive, the final print will be a full-color reproduction of the original copy. For example, as is illustrated in Figure 125, to print the positive that is minus the red color, a *cyan* process ink would be used which is a blue-green ink combination and represents the light of the original picture. Assuming that the positive is minus red, it must contain the green and blue. In similar fashion the magenta color (red and blue) ink is printed representing the positive having red and blue but minus green. Yellow ink would be used to print the positive which is the result of the blue filter and is minus blue.

The Color Separation Halftone

One of the most important steps in color separation work is the making of the negative. Shops specializing in color separation generally make the negatives and positives. The beginning printer who does not have access to a camera may have the negative and positive made by a larger shop, by a screen printing photographic establishment, or by a photoengraving or photolithography establishment.

The negative made from a colored subject is generally made on panchromatic film or film recommended by a reliable industrial graphic arts suppliers. Panchromatic film is film that is sensitive to red, blue, and green light or to white light. Since this film is sensitive to red light, the ordinary red safelight employed in darkrooms is unsafe to use with this film. The film should be loaded and developed in total darkness. Screen printers also employ blue-sensitive and orthochromatic film. Blue-sensitive film is only sensitive to blue; while orthochromatic film is sensitive to green and blue light only.

The halftone may be made directly or indirectly. In the direct method the halftone is made directly behind a halftone screen from the copy; in the

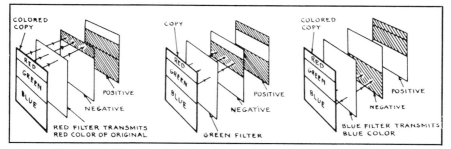

Figure 123. Photographic effect of the red, green, and blue color filters.

NUMBER	COLOR OF FILTER	COLOR TRANSMITTED	COLOR ABSORBED
25	RED	RED	BLUE and GREEN
58	GREEN	GREEN	BLUE and RED
47	BLUE	BLUE	GREEN and RED
12	YELLOW	YELLOW	BLUE
32	*MAGENTA	MAGENTA	GREEN
44	**CYAN	CYAN	RED

*RED-BLUE   **BLUE-GREEN

Figure 124. Data of commonly used Wratten Series color filters.

indirect method the halftone positive is made from a continuous tone negative. Regardless of the method of making the halftone, the screen printer or beginner is concerned with obtaining as large and opaque a dot as possible so that the dots will adhere to the screen fabric.

COLOR OF FILTER	PIGMENT COLOR PRINTED	ANGLE OF HALFTONE SCREEN OR COPY		
		4 COLORS	3 COLORS	2 COLORS OR DUOTONE
RED	*CYAN	75° OR 105°	45°	FOR STRONGEST COLOR OR KEYPLATE HALFTONE SCREEN OR COPY IS PLACED ON 45° ANGLE. SECOND COLOR IS ROTATED 30° AWAY FROM FIRST ANGLE.
GREEN	**MAGENTA	15° OR 75°	75°	
BLUE	YELLOW	90°	15° OR 105°	
YELLOW	BLACK	45°		

*BLUE PROCESS INK   **RED PROCESS INK

Figure 125. Color filters used in screen printing color separation, ink color printed in color process work, and angle of halftone screen or angle of copy for elimination of moire.

In making the color separations a control patch consisting of a gray scale, register marks, and a patch of the tricolor process inks are attached near or to the original before photographing. The gray-scale is a graduated strip showing tones ranging from black to white and is a means of determining accurate exposure. (See also Chapter 27.) If the same tone or gray of the scale has been recorded in each of the negatives, the various negatives have been correctly exposed and processed. Register marks in the form of simple crosses or other marks are placed or drawn on the opposite margins of the copy or original before photographing. The marks aid in registration in printing by assuring that each mark exactly overprints the other marks and are reproduced in each negative and in making the printing screens. The marks may be removed before the actual printing. The control patch may be bought, attached to the copy semi-permanently, and reused.

Making the Positives

It is suggested that for the first few times the beginner make or have a positive made on photographic paper in black and white. This photograph or

200

the photographic paper will be an aid and will show up the dots better, especially if the print is enlarged, and will serve as a guide to the screen printer as to how the actual positive or final print will look. Also, any dots that are not black enough may be touched up by hand.

The same type of film that is used for making the negative may be employed for making the positive. The dots in the positive must be very opaque. To produce the printing screen the positive may be exposed in contact with a direct screen, an indirect, or direct-indirect screen. If an indirect or a screen printing film is used, then it is advisable that the film be processed on the same day so that film is not affected by atmospheric conditions.

There are other methods that may be used by the beginner to obtain halftone negatives and halftone positives. The screen printer may use the individual color letter press or lithography halftone printing plates to obtain halftone negatives and positives. Since the printing plates have halftone dots on them already, the plates representing the yellow, red, blue, and black colors are each printed in black on white paper. These black prints or proofs representing each color are then placed on the camera copyboard and enlarged to the required size. The halftone positives made from the prints are used to make the printing screens. Figure 126 represents a four-color separation screen printing job which employed printing plates for the preparation of the halftone negatives.

Elimination of Moire

The term "moire" refers to an undesirable pattern obtained when two or more halftone printing screens are improperly made and printed. It may be practical for the printer first to experience printing one-color and two-color (duotone) halftones, before printing with more colors. The elimination of moire is more of a challenge when printing two, three, or more colors than when printing single-color halftones. If the printer will superimpose or rotate two halftone screened tints, one over the other, he can easily observe the pattern. The undesirable pattern will be minimized or eliminated when one halftone tint is rotated over the other at a specific spot or angle. The common method of eliminating moire is to rotate the halftone screen in the camera or rotate the copy on the copyboard to a certain angle.

Although there are variations, experience and experimentation has produced varied angles at which each of the separation exposures is to be photographed. The angles illustrated in Figure 125 have been found to be practical for screen printing. For example, a 30 degree angle separation between colors is satisfactory for three-color work. The screen angle is the angle between the vertical or horizontal and any one of the rows of parallel lines or dots. The normal angle for one-color screen printing is 45 degrees, since rulings ordinarily are at this angle and the screen pattern is least obvious to the eye at this angle for one-color printing. In other words, a set of dots or lines on the halftone screen make a 45 degree with a horizontal or vertical line on the copy. For one-color halftone printing some printers attach the screen fabric at an angle (about 45 degrees) to the screen frame and adhere the screen printing film or expose the positive in contact with the fabric so that the halftone dots are parallel to the frame.

The printer will make the halftone printing screens from the halftone positives. Either a direct screen, indirect, or direct-indirect printing screen may be prepared. The fabric mesh on the screen should be fine enough so that

201

the average dot will adhere to at least three fabric threads. In making the actual printing screen the printer is also concerned with elimination of moire. For example, when finally attaching the screen printing film to the screen fabric (or exposing the halftone positive in contact with the coated screen fabric), the general method of eliminating moire is to determine the best angle or spot at which to place the film or positive image in relation to the threads on the screen fabric. As with one-color halftone printing, this may be done by laying the positive on the screen fabric over a light source and rotating the positive until the best image is obtained. Soft pencil marks may be made on the screen fabric in this position. The screen printing film (or the halftone positive for direct screen exposure) is then placed in the same position and adhered to the underside of the screen.

Inks

When more than one color is being printed by the halftone method transparent inks must be employed. These inks must be mixed to proper consistency and compounded so that they dry quickly. The halftone ink used should be of the type that is produced expressly for screen printing. The inks are available from screen printing suppliers and ink manufacturers. The printing may be done by hand or by machine. In machine printing the printed ink is generally dried on combination conveyor-dryer machines of the type discussed in Chapter 34. The inks dry in about ½ to 2 minutes. This implies that the printed card or object is placed on a conveyor and when it reaches the end of the conveyor it is dry and is either picked up manually or is stacked automatically into a pile.

Those colors of ink should be used which best bring out the colored original in as few color impressions as possible. Although generally the order of printing is yellow, red, blue, and black, where black is necessary, the sequence of color printing may vary. In full-color printing as illustrated in Figure 126, the three primary pigment colors and black are used with special effects added to produce the original. In some cases the key plate or print may be printed second to aid in register of colors. The key plate or print is the one which is the strongest or furnishes the main character of the copy. The sequence of colors depends on the original subject to be reproduced and upon the trapping or overlaying of the inks or colors. When one color is printed over another the result is similar to what happens when two different color inks are mixed. The registering or laying down of the colored inks must match the copy. The blending of the transparent colors in printing will produce dozens of colors.

Where it is difficult to register the color yellow, a reddish-blue glass or blue glass or plastic may be used to examine the yellow. Under this glass the yellow will appear black and will be seen easier.

Duotone

A duotone (duograph, duotype, or a duplex print) is a two-color print. Very pleasant color combinations are possible in screen printing by means of the duotone method. It is possible to produce an appearance of more than two colors by printing one color of ink over another. It is a more economical method of adding color to prints than printing with three or more colors.

202

Figure 126. An 11" × 14" screen printed 85-line halftone full-color job printed on a screen printing press and dried mechanically. (Courtesy of Oil Color Litho Company, Chicago, Ill.)

Duotone printing is the intermediate stage in the mastering of the technique of three- or four-color separation and single color halftone printing. This type of printing is not limited to halftone work but can be done by hand and photographically from line copy, shaded copy such as Ben Day, or from halftone copy, either from black-and-white or from a colored subject.

Duotones imply the making of two photographic negatives of the subject, one negative for each color to be printed. One of the negatives serves for the key plate. The other negative represents the tint or lighter color which is often printed first. The key plate or key print is printed over the tint.

203

For line copy the undesired color on each of the two negatives may be blocked-out or covered with an opaque by hand. For halftone two-color printing, the halftone negatives are ordinarily made with filter colors that are complementary. The two negatives may be made from the same black and white copy. As illustrated in Figure 125, two halftone images are made from the same copy by employing two different angles for the halftone screen or copy whether the copy is colored or of one color. The halftone for the strongest color or key plate generally is placed on a 45 degree angle. The second color is placed 30 degrees from the first angle. The second color is placed 30 degrees from the first angle. This is necessary to make sure of the elimination of a moire or pattern in printing. To aid in registration it is advisable to have register marks on the copy being photographed.

Positives for the printing screen are made in the usual manner from the negative.

Much of two-color illustration is done in complementary colored inks. However, other pleasing color combinations besides the complementary colors are: blue-green and deep red; orange and blue-green; black and red or another color; a dark and light tint of the same color or shades of the same hue; a range of grays from white to black; etc.

Fake-Color Printing

Fake-color work offers the screen printer a technique of printing a transparent color over opaque or transparent colors to produce a darker tone over each of the colors printed. It is a method of darkening the other printed colors. For example, if a poster is printed with three different colors and then overprinted with a correctly compounded transparent color or a "fake-color," it becomes possible to obtain seven colors with this one printing. The fake color over portions of each color produces a darker tone to those parts.

Fake-color work for screen printing is practical, especially where the artwork has two shades of each color. The printing screens for this type of printing are generally prepared by hand, although they may also be prepared photographically. Each printing screen prints at one time the light and dark areas of each color. Then a printing screen is prepared for the fake-color which will darken the varied required areas of the different colors.

A screen printing crystal clear base to which a little black has been added may be used for the transparent ink to produce the desired fake-color. Transparent inks for this type of printing may be obtained from screen printing supply establishments or ink suppliers.

Other Printed Color Effects

The screen printer uses other color separation methods. Two very commonly used methods are the *overlay* and *masking* techniques. These are hand and photographic methods and are generally used for line copy or where detail can be reproduced practically with such instruments as knives, inking instruments, and brushes. Both of the above methods are common ways of obtaining negatives and positives for screen printing.

The overlay method is employed with black-and-white copy or colored copy. It involves placing an *overlay* consisting of a transparent or translucent acetate, vinyl or vellum paper and painting or inking with an opaque ink on

Figure 127. An enlarging projector which casts images of opaque subjects or copy on surfaces for accurate tracing to enlarged scales for use on such jobs as designing outdoor posters, enlarging artwork, and the like. Original 6" × 6" copy at 144 inches from screen or projected surface will produce an enlarged image of 88" × 88" (223.5cm × 223.5cm). (Courtesy of F. D. Kees Mfg. Co., Beatrice, Nebraska).

the sheet over those areas where a specific color is to be reproduced in printing. A transparent sheet or overlay must be prepared for each color that is to be printed. Register marks should be made on the original and on each overlay to aid in registering colors and in registering the printing screens. Each overlay separates the colors and may serve as the negative or positive. The overlay may be enlarged or reduced photographically if necessary.

A practical method employed by screen printers for producing enlarged artwork is by using a projector (see Figure 127), projecting the copy onto a large surface and tracing the copy in the required size. The artwork may be finished on the projected surface in the desired colors. The printer may use the artwork for preparing hand printing screens for producing large area printing. Also, the projected finished colored artwork may be reduced photographically, should it be necessary to print smaller size sheets.

Masking or blocking out light is done with red or deep yellow transparent thin sheets or opaque sheets. The prepared mask is placed over the copy or drawing and masks out or prevents exposing light from reaching certain areas of the design. Masking with knife-cut film is a common method employed for color control or for blocking out an area that is to be photographed. This type of film is similar to the film used for the preparation of knife-cut screen printing plates. The masking film consists of a transparent lacquer type coating or film which is laminated semi-permanently to a thin translucent or transparent plastic backing sheet. The color of the film is generally a transparent red because red can be photographed as black.

To prepare a positive or negative the knife-cut film is taped over the copy, film side up, and the desired parts of the film are cut away with a stencil knife. The cutting is done only through the film and not through the backing sheet, knife cuts extending past corners to make peeling of film easier. When the cutting is completed, the film coating may be easily peeled away from those parts of the design which are to be exposed. The film remaining on the backing sheet makes up the positive or negative, whichever may be required. Since the exposing light will pass only through the transparent backing sheet but not through the film, the knife-cut positive may be placed in contact with the sensitized screen or screen printing film and exposed.

There are also transparent sheets of plastic similar to the above which have a transparent color added, generally red, to one side of the sheet. The plastic sheet is prepared for masking in similar fashion to knife-cut masking film, except that the color is scraped off with a sharp instrument in the desired areas. The prepared scraped sheet may then be used as a positive or a negative.

PHOTOGRAPHIC POSTERIZATION AND SCREEN PRINTING

32

Technological revolution is being created and is affecting our age in every respect. The rapid pace of technological advancement is a dominant factor in developing and changing our society. Our job in society and in industry is to employ and blend these advancements for the best growth of society and of industry. Photographic posterization which has been made possible because of photographic developments, refinement, and experimenting on the part of screen printers, is one phase of graphic arts which offers color impact for better and more practical visual communication.

Posterization originated in the screen printing industry; the screen printed solid masses of opaque colors made posterization practical for screen printing. Originally, this was accomplished with hand-prepared printing screens. Later, posterization in screen printing began to achieve a series of color tones or of grays that approximated a continuous tone original. A continuous tone original or continuous tone copy consists of a whole range of tones from light to dark as exemplified in a photograph or in collotype printing. A photograph, for example, may contain various values of grays from pure white to deep black. While posters may be and still are being done by hand, posterization today can be more realistically produced by employing photographic processes. It is a means of obtaining dramatic effects with several tones with the aid of a camera, or by employing a photographic negative, or by using a photographic print on photographic paper as copy. In this process a continuous tone or photographic copy, having obvious sharpness and detail, is changed to a line type illustration having solid areas of printing. It produces dramatic photographic-like illustrations without using halftone screens, although the screen printer may use it with halftone printing, if such is the original planning of his copy.*

The principle of photographic posterization is simple and the process, once standardized and mastered, can be used practically and excellently to advantage for fine art and commercial work. This method of reproduction which generally offers a limited number of flat tones, is an effective way of producing screen printed artwork. In posterization, a poster-like print interpretation, usually printed with opaque colors, is obtained that has several tones of the same color (monochrome) or of different colors.

---

*Kodak Bulletin for the Graphic Arts No. 6, Eastman Kodak Company, Rochester, New York.

207

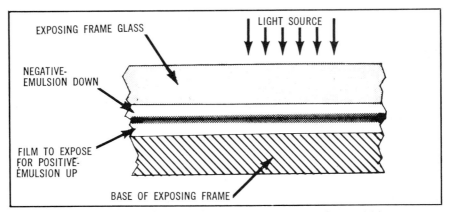

Figure 128. Exposing film in contact with negative to obtain positive.

In its simplest form, posterization starts with the production of photographic negatives made on identical high contrast litho line type films from a continuous tone original. Each negative represents a part of a group of tones of the original. The exposures of the different negatives are varied progressively in time in order to record different amounts of the continuous tone original or photograph on the film. Generally posterized reproductions are classified according to the number of tones they possess. For example, a three-tone posterized print may consist of black, white, and a gray tone. The exposures of the three negatives are made so that each exposure is increased by an even amount of time; for example, the first exposure may be 8 seconds, the second exposure 16 seconds, and the third exposure may be 24 seconds. The first negative should show highlights on it only in black; the second negative will show highlights and middle tones in black, and the third negative will show highlights, middle tones, and shadows. While the highlight step may be one-fourth that of the time of a regular line copy shot, the printer should experiment with his equipment to determine the time of exposure.

The negatives are all developed the same length of time, at the same temperature, in the same developer, and generally processed the same. The only variation is in the time each negative is exposed, making sure that each negative will actually have different amounts of the photograph on it in black. Then positives are made from the negatives and printing screens are made from the positives, generally by direct contact of positive to screen printing film or to coated sensitized screen. To make the positive, the negative is placed in contact with film, emulsion side of negative in contact with emulsion side of film as illustrated in Figure 128, and exposure is made through the back of negative. The positives are all exposed for the same length of time and development and processing conditions are the same for the positives. The film positive with the highlights will be black over most of the film and the screen made from this positive will print the lightest color. The second positive is used to produce the screen which will print the middle tones. The third positive, which is mostly clear film, is used to make the printing screen for printing the dark color.

Figure 129. The original black and white photograph in continuous grays and black from which the following posterized color illustration and the negatives and positives were made is shown. This, and the following illustrations in this chapter are by courtesy of William L. Butler, Elmira, N.Y. Mr. Butler supplied the original negatives and positives from which he made the printing screens, as well as the keyed reproduction of the color illustration at right.

Figure 130. Numbers on the reproduction of the 6-color posterized screen print indicate the warm sunny colors. Areas of gray in the reproduction marked as No. 1 indicate a light yellowish buff. No. 2 indicates a light, warm tan and No. 3 a darker tan of the same character. No. 4 represents a light, warm, chocolate brown. No. 5, as marked, indicates black. The sixth stencil for the gray areas was hand cut.

When the printing screens are produced and printing is completed, each of the several ink impressions will represent a certain amount of the original tone subject in any desired color. In actual screen printing, the print may be reproduced with the light tone being printed first, then the middle tones are printed over the light color, and the final printing of the darkest color on top of the middle and light tones. Printing must be planned and done so that one printing does not cover a previous printed color completely.

Generally, in screen printing photographic posterization, larger number of tones are not employed, since the objective in posterization is to obtain a suggested printed image with attractive color opaque inks which can be

Figure 131. Negative No. 1 appears at left, positive No. 1, "flopped" as it appeared on the under surface of the printing screen is shown at right.

printed, one over the other, usually printing the lightest color first. If too many tones are printed, the final print may look too much like the photograph or halftone and the poster effect may be lost. However, posterization may be rendered in 9 or more shades. Also, the screen printer may obtain the effect of an extra color, if the color of the paper or surface on which the printing is done is counted.

Using a Camera for Posterization

Copy such as photographs, paintings, halftones, or wash drawings may be used for camera reproduction. While other cameras may be used, process cameras ordinarily used in screen printing shops are employed for the photographic work. In actual work where a camera is employed, the copy is placed on the copyboard of the camera with a gray scale or step wedge at one edge of the copy and register marks are attached in the borders of the copy. Gray scales are commercially available on paper and on transparent film from the graphic arts supply firms and offer a method of measuring the density or darkness of tones in the copy. The gray scale is divided into an arbitrary, uniform, measurable, and convenient number of steps on a strip of photographic paper from white to black. Some scales have 10 and some have 12 steps with step No. "1" being white; each step becomes progressively darker until the last step (black) is reached. When the negative is developed, its

210

Figure 132. Negative No. 2, positive No. 2, (Light tan printer) are shown here, the positive as it would appear on the lower side of screen. Compare areas with Fig. 163.

density tone may be compared to the density step of the gray scale. Each progressively darker step on the scale represents a longer exposure than the preceding lighter step.

Register marks are special marks or designs on cards which are attached or may be drawn in the outside margin of the copy. These are used to register or match up the separations on the negatives, positives, and colors in printing with printing screens. Register marks are necessary to assure that the tones or colors are printed in register with each other. After screen printing, the printer may trim off the register marks which are in the border or outside the design areas.

With practice, the screen printer will be able to match the gray of the gray scale with that of the copy. The important thing is that the printer take time to test and to standardize his steps in processing and increase his control over each photographic step.

In actual screen printing, the print is reproduced with the light tones being printed first, then the middle tones are printed over the light color and the final printing of the shadows on top of the middle and light tones. Various shades of grays, blues, greens, browns, and combinations of tones may be used in screen printing. Sometimes a different color may be added to the monochromatic colors to strengthen the impact of a detail in the copy as illustrated in Figure 129.

211

Using a Photograph or Negative as Continuous Tone Copy

Where a camera may not be available, a continuous tone photograph or a negative of the copy to be reproduced may be used. These may be made by professional photographers outside of the shop. The photograph, if it is the correct size and density, is oiled by saturating with any bland oil such as castor or baby oil to make it transparent or translucent so that it may be exposed in contact with high contrast litho film in order to obtain the required three or four separation negatives. In making the negatives, the photograph is placed so that the face or right side of picture is in contact with emulsion side of film and exposure is made through the photograph. The

Figure 133. Now note difference in black and white areas, comparing this No. 3 negative and positive with those in figures 143 and 144.

exposure time will be longer when a photograph is used. However, this may be an advantage, since it gives a longer time control over exposures and thus desired tone contrast may be easier to obtain. When the desired negatives are processed, the positives are obtained by contact printing the negatives with photographic films, and the positives are employed to make the printing screens.

A practical method of obtaining positives is to employ the correct size negative of the continuous tone picture that is to be reproduced and to make separation positives from the *one* negative. The negative and the film to be

212

Figure 134. Comparing the sets of negatives and positives at this stage clearly reveals the larger black areas in the negative above which are gained by increased exposure. Transparent areas in positive correspond to opaque areas in negative.

produced as positives are placed in a contact or vacuum frame as illustrated in Figure 128. The exposure is made through the negative, varying the exposure time of the positives so that each film is exposed at a different time, increasing the exposure so that positives of varying density or tone are obtained. The development time and the rest of the processing is the same for the positives. When the positives are processed completely, they may be used in the preparation of the printing screens.

Figure 129 is a reproduction of black and white photograph from which the reproduction of the posterized color print, Figure 130 was ultimately screen printed. Figures 131 through 135 show step by step exposures of negatives and corresponding positives for each color printed, including black.

The development of photographic posterization in the screen printing industry is another example of how modern screen printing is creating new processes for modern visual communication.

Figure 135. Black covers the least area in the print. Negative No. 5, above, the one from which the black printer positive and screen are made shows density over the major portion of its surface, the positive showing corresponding transparent areas. Only the opaque areas as shown in the positive will form the printing image for the black.

214

PROCESS CAMERAS FOR
SCREEN PRINTING

33

The full impact of factors such as mechanization, of the graphic arts and other industries, accuracy in the screen printing introspection of processing techniques in the screen printing industry, and the need for information in order to produce good standardization, produces requests for new equipment. The photographic camera which has made possible the reproduction of pictures, objects, and color in the other phases of the graphic arts is making daily contributions to the screen printing industry. Screen printing shops are being equippped or are equipped with process cameras in order to give better integrated service to its clientele and to better control the complete processing of the printing screens employed in the screen printing industry. The camera equipment chosen by printers is chosen after deliberation based on prospective requirements in the industry and after consideration of the flexibility of the camera for the varied work needed in the versatile screen printing field.

Historically the term *process camera* did not originate with screen printing but emanates from the photo engraving field where it has been and is being employed for copying line, halftone, and photographic color reproduction. Although some cameras have been designed specifically for screen printing work, the process camera used in the screen printing field is similar to the process cameras employed in the other printing fields.

In photographic work the process camera uses photography or writing or drawing with light on a sensitized or photographic emulsion to produce the transparent positives, negatives, halftones, and color separations which are later employed to make the photographic screen printing plates.

Although a camera could be made from a light-tight box or from a light-tight room (the word *camera* comes from Latin and means "room"), cameras employed today are precision built machines with micrometer-like adjustments which will produce negatives, positives, and separate out colors in colored copy or originals; cameras will enlarge and decrease the size of copy, originals, and objects; they will reproduce both line and halftone copy; and generally will do anything that may be required photographically by the printer. The camera may be purchased or may be built to specifications by a manufacturer to suit particular shop needs. They are not difficult to operate and generally the manufacturer will even train the printer in its daily use and provide illustrated instruction books which are written in simple nontechnical language, explaining all about the camera and even the care of the darkroom if the camera is of the darkroom type.

215

Figure 136. A lamp carrier with three quartz iodine (800-watt lights) lamps in reflectors, each reflector individually adjustable. (Courtesy of nuArc Company, Inc., Chicago, Illinois).

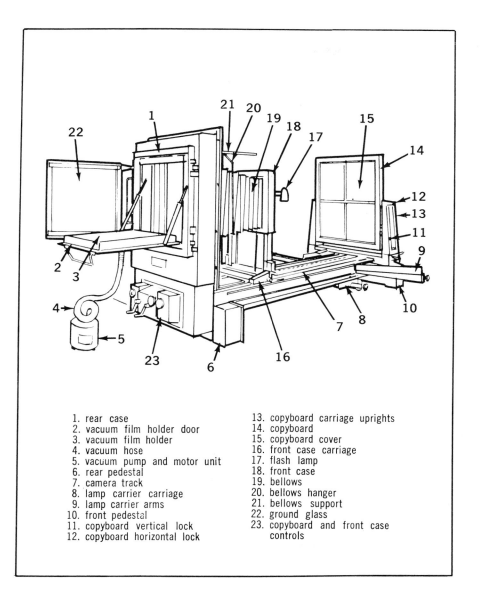

1. rear case
2. vacuum film holder door
3. vacuum film holder
4. vacuum hose
5. vacuum pump and motor unit
6. rear pedestal
7. camera track
8. lamp carrier carriage
9. lamp carrier arms
10. front pedestal
11. copyboard vertical lock
12. copyboard horizontal lock
13. copyboard carriage uprights
14. copyboard
15. copyboard cover
16. front case carriage
17. flash lamp
18. front case
19. bellows
20. bellows hanger
21. bellows support
22. ground glass
23. copyboard and front case controls

Figure 137. A horizontal process darkroom type camera showing main parts. (Illustration courtesy of book In Focus, Robertson Photo-Mechanix, Inc., Des Plaines, Illinois).

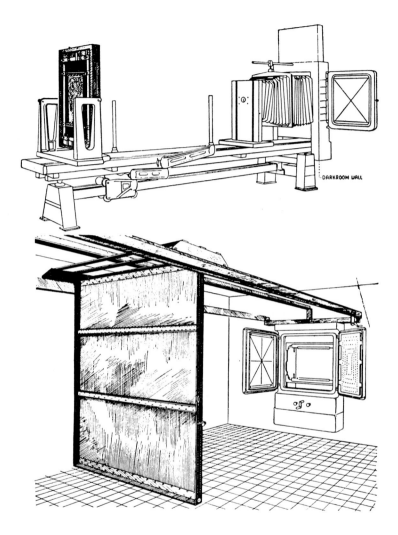

Figure 138. Two views illustrating a large darkroom process camera. The top illustration shows the basic camera outside the darkroom wall; the lower illustration presents an addition to the basic camera in the darkroom. The addition consists of a very large stay-flat type of film holder. The darkroom serves as bellows when the large film holder is adjusted to perfect focus. (Courtesy of R. W. Borrowdale Company, Inc., Chicago, Ill.)

218

The modern cameras are designed and engineered so that they are vibration-free; constructed generally of resistant metal, especially where the parts are subject to wear and stress; they enable the operator to secure exact size image in very little time and with minimum effort; may be operated on standard electrical circuits; and use compact floor space. Most of the cameras have push-button type timing devices for obtaining exact exposure time; may be equipped with any type of lamps for illuminating the copyboards, (see Figure 137); and the distance between lamps and copyboards on cameras may be automatically adjusted. Many cameras have exact register devices for resetting the lensboard and copyboard assemblies in relation to one another. There are mechanical computing devices for focusing lenses and for determining exposure time when changing the distance of light or of angle of the illuminating lamps from the copyboard.

Generally, process cameras are classified either as vertical or horizontal, or as darkroom or gallery process cameras. Vertical cameras (see Figures 141, 143 and 145) have copyboards near the base with the lensboard and film holder above the copyboard. Horizontal cameras (see Figures 137, 139, 142) have the copyboard, lensboard, and film holder mounted horizontally. There are advantages and disadvantages in both types and the screen printer must deliberate and decide which will be most practical for his work.

Figure 139. Robertson Comet Overhead Camera, a large darkroom process camera with quartz lights and automatic controls. Camera takes film size up to 32" × 32" and reproduces film negatives, positives, halftone work and makes enlargements and reductions. (Courtesy of Robertson Photo-Mechanix, Inc., Des Plaines, Illinois).

As far as the classification of darkroom and gallery process cameras is concerned — A darkroom camera is one in which the rear part of the camera protrudes or extends into a darkroom and is operated in the darkroom. Either the entire or at least the film holding end of the darkroom camera is located in the darkroom. (See Figures 138 or 144). This enables the operator to load and unload the camera in the darkroom and to generally control operations from the darkroom.

219

The gallery camera may be placed in any area of the shop and is generally not dependent on a darkroom for its operation. Where gallery cameras are placed outside the darkroom, the film is loaded in light-tight holders within a darkroom or a dark area before exposure and then carried to the camera. After exposure, the light-tight holder is moved back to the darkroom for processing.

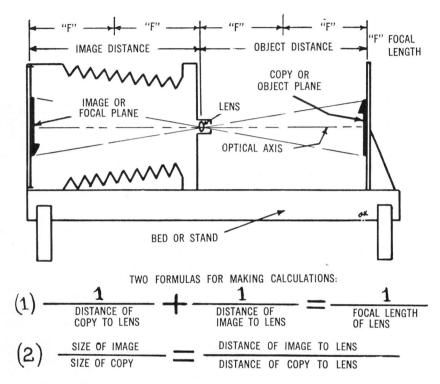

Figure 140. Basic terms and data used when referring to process cameras.

The cameras may be obtained in price ranges from several hundred dollars to thousands of dollars. Some printers have started the practice of photographic work using 4 × 5, or 8 × 10 view cameras because a view camera offers control of perspective, depth of field, a practical lens for producing required size of image, a ground glass or "view" glass upon which copy or subject may be viewed, and varied adjustments may be made before actually photographing subject. The printer may have his choice of cameras which give a range of reproduction from 35 millimeters in size to film size that is about 54 × 80 inches in size (137 × 203 centimeters). Some cameras are available that will fit in a very compact space. Although most cameras as sold consist of basic units and the camera offers enough service to start the printer

220

doing practical work, other units and accessories may be added to the camera as the need for a specialized type of work arises.

Basically, the equipment consists of the camera proper, a stand or bed for supporting the camera and other parts, and a board or copyboard unit upon which the original or copy to be reproduced or photographed is placed or attached. The copyboard, or, as it is technically referred to, the *object plane* or object surface, is parallel to the *focal plane* or image plane or surface upon which the object or image is focused or projected. (See Figure 140). The lens on the lensboard is in the front part of the camera in front of the bellows, if the camera has bellows, and is also parallel to the copyboard and to the image surface or the ground glass surface at the rear of the camera upon which the image is focused. As the name signifies, the ground glass is a sheet of glass with a ground surface upon which focussing is done. It is mounted in

Figure 141. The Simple Simon vertical camera showing quartz iodine lamps illuminating maximum size copy (13" × 19"). The camera enlarges and reduces copy and offers a choice of 13 settings. It occupies a space 48" high, 52e wide, and is 28" from front to back. (Courtesy of Buckingham Graphics, Inc., Evanston, Illinois).

221

a frame at the exact distance that the sensitive film will be when the film or plate is exposed.

The stand or bed-frame, the design of which is governed by the lens and the other parts of the equipment, is rigidly constructed and is obtainable in varied sizes and styles. The bed may hug the floor and may be supplied with casters, as in the case of a gallery camera, so that the camera may be moved to any desired area in the shop. There are available beds which are spring suspended; the bed design may have three-point ball suspension in order to eliminate vibration while photographing. Some equipment is supplied with a monorail or one rail upon which the camera and copyboard are hung or suspended; some cameras and beds are designed so that camera and copyboard are counterbalanced on one rail for easy adjustment when camera and copyboard are being operated in a vertical position. The whole unit may be vertically mounted in order to save room (See illustrations).

Figure 142. Borrowdale Photomechanical System Camera, a precision camera designed for printed circuits, photochemical etching, and other work; the camera accepts reflection copy up to 44 × 44 inches and transparent copy up to 40 × 40 inches. Camera makes 4:1 enlargements and up to 20:1 reductions; it has a 16 × 20 inches metal vacuum film holder and insures even lighting at the image plane. (Courtesy of R. W. Borrowdale Co., Chicago, Illinois).

The copyboard or unit upon which the original to be reproduced or photographed is placed, offers just as much versatility as the beds. There are copyboards which are reversible, that is, the camera may employ the copyboard for holding a transparency or transparent copy. Generally, copyboards may be tilted to a horizontal position for easy loading and then put back into a vertical position. The copyboard may vary from the simple, perfectly flat wooden panel or large drawing board to which the copy may be tacked or taped to the type of copyboard which has very precise vacuum arrangements which suck the drawing or positive to it by means of atmospheric pressure. There are flat open panel type copyboards, open face vacuum copyboards, and closed type vacuum type copyboards. There are also the handmade variety type of copyboards which the printers employ to hold the copy which may consist of two plate glasses between which the original is held perfectly flat.

Figure 143. The Kenro Model V-242, electronically controlled vertical process camera for the production of line negatives and positives, halftone negatives and positives, art and copy preparation. Camera operates on 220/230 volts at 50-60 cycles and has a 22" × 26" copyboard, allows for 20" × 24" film, has a vacuum head, density modulator, lens shutter, filter holder, automatic exposure controls, auxiliary lenses, and a foot switch. (Courtesy of Kenro Corp., Cedar Knolls, New Jersey).

Arrangements for Halftone Screens

By producing halftones and other effects, the process camera has made possible one, two, three, four, and full-color work in screen printing. The printer has almost any choice of cameras from which to choose for reproducing varying shades, middle tone or halftones from line or continuous-tone copy.

The printer may choose a camera which eliminates time consuming methods of changing from line copy work to halftone work, which automatically sets the halftone screen distance from the sensitized plate, which eliminates excess handling of screens and prevents formation of dust and finger marks on screen, elimination of which is very important in halftone photography. On most cameras, the halftone screen removal mechanisms are optional equipment. However, where the inserting and removing of a halftone screen without disturbing the position of the sensitized film is of definite importance, the screen elevating mechanism in which the screen is raised out or the sliding mechanism in which the halftone screen is moved to the left or right becomes a necessity.

Figure 144. nuArc Supersonic Darkroom Process Camera allows for 20" × 24" film size, has a copyboard 30" × 40" with transparency opening of 21" × 25", has a contact screen capacity of 21" × 25", enlarges copy three times orignal size and reduces copy to one-fifth its size; camera has 6 quartz iodine lights, each 800 watts. (Courtesy of nuArc Company, Inc., Chicago, Illinois).

The cameras manufactured will hold either rectangular halftone screens, or circular halftone screens. Some cameras employ a hand method of taking out the halftone screen; others employ mechanical means. Cameras are made so that they use also contact halftone screens, that is where the screen is placed in direct contact with the positive or negative to be reproduced. (See Chapter 27). Other cameras employ "screen separation techniques," that is, the halftone screen is separated an exact small distance from the sensitized positive in order to produce the desired dotted halftone effects in the final positive and screen printing plates.

Lenses

Although volumes have been written about lenses, understanding some simple facts about the lens will aid the screen printer in obtaining more practical use of the camera. The lens, the very important part of the process

224

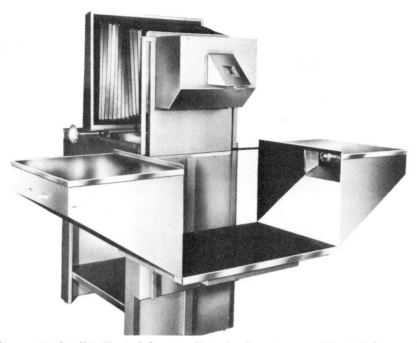

Figure 145. Goodkin Vertical Camera allows for film size up to 20" × 24", has a pris-matic head accessory making possible correct reading of paste-ups and proofs, has four quartz lamps which are attached to copyboard providing even illumination. Camera is equipped with a 24" × 36" vacuum copyboard permitting a range of jobs including reductions and enlargements. (Courtesy of M. P. Goodkin Co., Irvington, New Jersey).

camera, is an optical precision glass or instrument which distributes or bends light in such a way that the lens produces an image of an object on such a surface as a ground glass or on a sensitized film. The lenses used on process cameras are anastigmat or without the error of astigmatism. This means that the lens brings horizontal and vertical lines to a sharp focus at the same time on a flat surface. The *focus* of the lens is the point at which the lens forms a sharp image of the original to be reproduced. The focus of the lens is gener-ally equal in size to the diagonal of the largest negative or positive to be made. Two other terms used when referring to process cameras and lenses are *focal length* and *f-number.*

The focal length of a lens may be considered another name for the size of the lens. This length of a particular lens does not change, since it is fixed by the way the lens is manufactured or ground. The focal length of the lens is approximately ¼ the distance from the copyboard to the ground glass (or negative holder) when an original or copy is focussed so that the copy is the same size as the image. (See Figure 140). Technically, the focal length of a lens is the distance from the center of the lens to the film plane when the lens is focussed on an object at infinity (an unlimited distance). In other words, it

225

Figure 146. Deardorff Precision View Camera, 8 × 10. Camera is available in other sizes and produces negatives for color and for black-and-white photography. It has a bellows extension of 30" and will accommodate lenses with focal lengths from 4 to 30 inches. The front of the camera raises and lowers and the back of the camera may be swung verti-cally and laterally on each side of center. (Courtesy of L. F. Deardorff and Sons, Inc., Chicago, Illinois).

is the distance from the lens to the film plane where the image of distant object (practically about 600 or more feet away) is formed. Because the camera is used for reducing and enlarging by the screen printer, the distance between lens and copy and lens and image will vary. The closer the copy is to the lens the greater the distance must be between the lens and the ground glass or the film. When the distance between the lens and the ground glass is twice the focal length, the image is the same size as the copy or object. (See Figure 140). Distances for varied reductions and enlargements may be worked out by using simple formulas supplied by the manufacturer in the camera handbook or the formulas may be obtained from any physics or photographic data book which deals with lenses. The focal length of the lens really determines the length of the camera bed and the minimum and maximum positions of the lensboard in relation to the copyboard. Some cameras may use any focal length lens or more than one lens. The lenses generally may be interchanged quickly.

Where the printer makes a home-made camera, the lens used on the camera should be reasonably speedy, produce a flat even image without distortion, and work with the same speed on all parts of the image. It is advisable that the printer use a lens that is somewhat larger than the camera on which it is used, since a smaller lens or even one that has the capacity of the camera may not reach the extreme corners on the largest sensitized image.

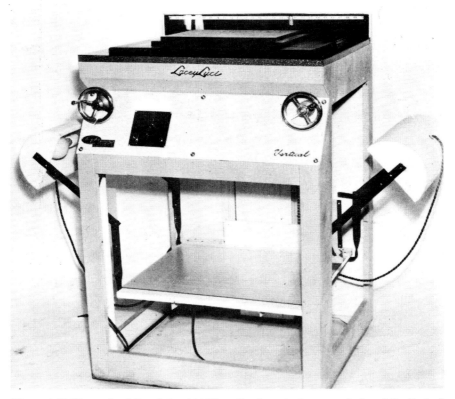

Figure 147. "Lacey-Luci Royal Art Aid Visualizer" vertical camera designed for limited floor space, will reproduce screen printing line and halftone negatives and positives; has adjustable lights, aids in correction of art layout work, and will produce 500% enlargements and reductions. (Courtesy of Lacey-Luci Products, Inc., Manasquan, New Jersey).

227

The lens, of course, is in the front part of the camera and is supported by the lensboard or is part of it. The lensboard has in many cameras both horizontal and vertical adjustments and may be adjusted from the rear of the camera for convenience. Modern lenses have a means of controlling the amount of light that passes through them. This is regulated on most cameras by what is known as the iris diaphragm and also by means of a slot in the lens barrel. Slides having various sizes and shapes of holes in them may be inserted in the slot of the lens barrel. Commercially, the slides are known as stops. A *stop* is an opening or the diaphragm aperture of a lens which allows light to pass. It is used to increase the sharpness of an image, to equalize the illumination in focussing, and to obtain other effects. The openings or stops are now commonly known and are standardized with *f-numbers* or factor-numbers which is a measure of the speed of the lens. The f-number marked on most lenses shows the relation between the diameter of the lens aperture or opening and the focal length of the lens. In order words, the f-number of a certain aperture or stop is equal to the focal length of the lens divided by the diameter of the particular opening. The f-number expresses the speed of the lens. For example, if the diameter of the opening of a lens is 2 inches and the focal length of the lens is 32 inches, the speed of the lens would be signified as f-16. Also, if the lens is marked with f/16 it means that the opening or hole in the stop or diaphragm has a diameter which is one-sixteenth (1/16) of the focal length of the lens. The higher the number marked on the rim of the lens mount or stop the smaller the hole and the longer the exposure must be. This implies that if an exposure is known for one f-number and that it is necessary to close the lens down to the next stop or f-number, twice the exposure must be given. For example, if the known correct exposure for f/8 is 10 seconds and it is desired to stop down to f/11 then the new exposure must be 20 seconds. Figure 148 presents two systems of signifying factors numbers. The U.S. (Uniform Scale) system shows the exposure ratios for the stops. For example, it takes 32 times as long to make an exposure at f/22 as it does at f/4; it takes 32 times as long to make an exposure at f/32 as it does at f/5.6; etc. The U.S. system is no longer used but old lens still have these markings on them.

f-Numbers	f/4	f/5.6	f/8	f/11	f/16	f/22	f/32	f/45	f/64
U.S. Numbers	1	2	4	8	16	32	64	128	256

Figure 148. f-numbers showing sizes of stops in the international f-system and the Uniform Scale (U.S.) system of numbering stops.

An f/4.5 lens is considered a fast lens. However, a slower one such as f/8 or f/11 is satisfactory for copy work in screen printing.

Each camera manufacturer stresses the lens in the camera, as this item is the basis of the optical system, the camera being the support for the optical system. The screen printer should become well acquainted with the properties of the lens or lenses that he plans to use.

In summary, the process camera offers the screen printer the answer to his problems photographically. However, the printer's purchase of such equipment is dependent upon his being able to increase production, give better efficiency, and use the equipment to full capacity.

The representative process cameras illustrated in Figures 137 through Figures 147 are presented to illustrate the extent and variation of the manufacturing of this equipment. The specifications or descriptions given for each camera with the illustration are not complete but are varied in description to give the reader a more comprehensive background of the parts, properties, and accessories of the cameras.

QUICK DRYING INKS AND DRYING MACHINES FOR PHOTOGRAPHIC SCREEN PRINTING

Screen printing photographic developments and the mechanization of screen printing is bringing to a climax the need for quicker, more controlled, more uniform, and more constant drying time. The above has been brought about by a desire to eliminate as much of the hand racking as possible. Hand racking is ordinarily necessitated by the use of many types of racks and shelves on which the printed objects are placed when the slower drying inks are employed. Because of the peculiarity of screen printing and the overlapping of the industry into other industries and processes, the problem of drying and drying machines has presented and presents challenges which are based on many related and unrelated factors. The industry has grown up without developing any neophobia or fear of the new. The experimental factor in most shops has been a constant consideration and the average screen printer, unlike the ordinary printer, will generally attempt a job that has new elements in it. The industry has reached a state, because of its interdependency, where there is not such a thing as a screen printing secret. Each shop, each interested individual, each manufacturer, duplicates the same project in a fashion peculiar to the individual or agency. The screen printers have become aware of one another's problems and this awareness tends to bring out the problems that are common. The drying problem has been attacked from two main avenues of approach: the development of quicker drying inks and the mechanization of the drying process itself.

Quick Drying Inks

The development of quick drying inks is a problem that has been solved to some extent. Although establishments which do and have done hand printing were always anxious for the perfect quick drying ink, machine printing and mechanized drying have accentuated the need. The problem is one to which the screen printing ink manufacturers, suppliers, and the Screen Printing Association have given much attention and upon which they have done much research.

Where mechanized conveyors and drying facilities are employed, the drying problem has not been as great. Where hand racking is essential, without some form of accelerated drying, printing by machine involves more racking area, extra help, slow up of production, more worker's fatigue, a decrease in volume of printing, and, of course, a higher cost for printing.

230

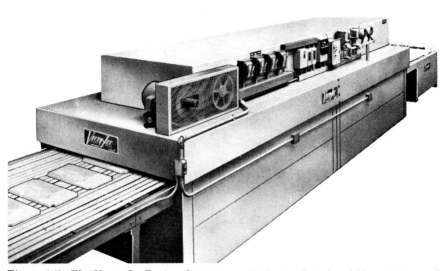

Figure 149. The Vecto Jet Drying System, a unit designed to dry different sizes and thicknesses of varied materials which are printed with evaporative colors, clear coatings, halftones and solids. Volumes of fresh air are impinged across large printed sheets, absorbing volatiles at the same time, and exhausting the saturated air to the outside of the plant. (Courtesy of American Screen Process Equipment Company, Chicago, Illinois).

In order for research in the industry to serve a definite and practical purpose, it is necessary to obtain a standardized meaning for the relative term *quick drying inks*. Data seem to indicate that as far as a mean or average is concerned, quick drying inks refer to inks which dry either normally or by some accelerated means in a range from 15 seconds to 15 minutes as compared to slower drying inks which dry in about ½ hour to 24 hours.

It is not apologetic to state that there are inherent problems in producing the quick drying inks which are available now both for machine and hand screen printing. These problems concern factors such as the printing process itself, the drying procedure, the surface upon which the printing must be done, the formulation of the ink, the necessity for the cost of the new ink's being comparable to square foot coverage of the materials that have been used before, and a combination of all the above factors. One problem governs the other.

The reasons for the slower development of quick drying inks were that the universal impetus of mechanized printing and drying was not felt until about the end of World War II. Besides, for screen printing to be effective, it must be printed with a much thicker coat to be practical in most instances. The thickness of the ink deposit in screen printing is about 10 to 20 times that of the ink deposit applied by other printing methods. Of course, this thicker coat is also one of the big advantages of screen printing as exemplified in every-day work, in printing fluorescent and phosphorescent inks, in printing decals, in obtaining weatherability, in printing on textiles, on ceramics, in printing electronics circuits, etc. The print should look screen

231

printed whether the ink is a slow or a quick drying one, since the consuming public must, for practical reasons, constantly be aware of the individuality and the difference between screen printing and other printing methods. In printing, inks which dry quickly must do so on the stock or object being printed, yet not dry or clog the printing screen or dry on the hand operated squeegee. When dry, the inks should not be brittle, should not develop oil or solvent rings, and should not *post heat* or heat up when printed material is piled after printing. After a second coat or another color is applied on the stock or over a first color the second color must dry just as quickly. As far as

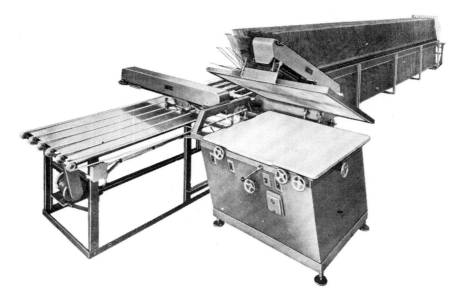

Figure 150. Illustrations show a 30-foot wicket dryer being driven directly by an M and M Model press. The press will print on any material up to %" in thickness and up to 35" by 45" in area. Unit provides one man production speeds to 1000 impressions per hour. Printed material slides into wicket, material travels in vertical position the length of dryer, and air dried sheets are removed at end of wicket. (Courtesy of M & M Research Engineering Co., Butler, Wisconsin).

the process itself is concerned, an ink may work well in hand printing; yet, because of the uniform quicker operation of the squeegee the ink will cling to the machine operated squeegee so that gravity will not pull the ink down quickly enough. On the other hand, an ink may clog in hand printing and may not do so in machine printing. When an ingredient is added to or taken away from a given ink, the changing of the ingredients may take away a desirable property.

The surface printed on has an effect on and may be affected by extreme drying. Paper and cardboard, which is the stock much used in printing with quick drying inks, can be dried in much shorter time by an elevated drying temperature. Where multi-colored printing is concerned, however, the same

232

Figure 151. "American Rack-King" metal drying racks with models of racks varying in shelf size from 26" × 36" to 45" × 68" and 1⅛" space between shelves. Openings in each wire shelf allow for drying of small and large items. (Courtesy of American Screen Process Equipment Company, Chicago Illinois).

233

Figure 152. Cincinnati Super-Jet III dryer, designed to fit any automatic screen printing press, has insulated inner liner which restricts heat transfer to shop air, has automatic controls for drying varied thicknesses and sizes of screen printed stock, and is designed to remove the solvents at fast speeds and at low temperatures. (Courtesy of Cincinnati Printing and Drying Systems, Inc., Cincinnati, Ohio).

extreme accelerated drying of the stock will produce shrinkage, which, in turn, causes the difficult problem of obtaining perfect registration of colors. Other surfaces which do not have "tooth" or to which the ink will not stick, have to be prepared for this properly or they will require a longer time for drying. Some inks which dry mostly by evaporation and can be dried quickly, produce other problems such as bad odors and the storing up of fumes which make possible fire hazards. To counteract this, more ventilation, air conditioning, and space is required. Again, if the ink dries too quickly, it may cause printing operation troubles. The ink in drying has to fix itself to varied materials so that it cannot be rubbed off in normal wear.

The problem in the drying procedure involves using the correct temperature and the correct type of heat so that, in drying, the object itself will not be distorted, scorched or damaged. Designers of drying machines are aware of the fact that there must be enough time allowed for the drying process and a way of leaving the dried and stacked material alone until it can be picked up either automatically or by hand.

The formulation of the ink involves experimentation and changes based on research on the part of the manufacturer and in actual printing. It may involve using a substitute in place of certain raw materials; it involves making an ink which can be used under ordinary printing conditions for most surfaces and materials printed. It means formulating an ink that will dry normally and by accelerated methods using all the drying processes — evaporation, absorption, oxidation, and polymerization. An instantaneous drying ink, if such an ink could be made, would leave no room for doctoring the ink for varied needs, and in all probability would have to be used to too exact specifications.

In spite of all these problems, screen printing quick drying inks are meeting prerequisites and increased production requirements. The cooperation of the ink manufacturer, screen printer, and consumer has overcome

234

Figure 153. A Fostoria-Fannon Infrared oven, 100 feet long for drying point-of-sale screen printed material up to 144" wide. Drying time is one minute or less depending on the material being printed. (Courtesy of Fostoria-Fannon, Inc., Fostoria, Ohio; and San Miguel Brewery, Philippine Islands).

many problems. Quick drying and slower drying inks are being printed and dried with the aid of drying machines, ovens, and varied types of conveyors which are heated by various methods. Special compact dryers are being built for the screen printing industry to handle varied printed jobs and in many cases they were developed by the printers themselves. There are inks which print with relative opacity and which may be dried by varied forced methods from 15 to 60 seconds at about 300 degrees Fahrenheit (149 degrees Celsius), depending on conditions of the job, and inks which will air-dry normally in 10 to 15 minutes. Where a higher drying temperature may be too high and possibly distort certain stock, it is possible to decrease the temperature in the dryer to as low as is necessary. Wicket-conveyor dryers which may or may not use heat are being employed. The reduction in temperature, while it increases the drying cycle time, at the same time is able to take care of rubber base inks, oleoresinous inks, lacquer type inks, and daylight fluorescent inks. While the slower drying inks may not dry in a given drying cycle

235

Figure 154. Screen Printed plastic bottles are cured or dried in a 14-foot Fostoria-Fannon infrared oven. Depending on the type of plastic container and on the ink used, the curing temperature may vary from 100 to 150 degrees Fahrenheit and the time may vary from 10 minutes upward. The oven may also be used for curing screened designs on glass containers. (Courtesy of Fostoria-Fannon, Inc., Fostoria, Ohio; and Familex Products, Ltd., Montreal, Quebec).

236

time, the fact that the printed ink and stock passed through the dryer or conveyor cuts down greatly on the complete drying time of the slower drying inks. They can be air-dried then, in much shorter time. In using any of the ink, the beginner and experienced screen printer must follow recommended manufacturer's procedures. As is evidenced by the present, the future screen printer will bring to the world a pictorial, word, and light message using the versatile screen printing inks, fluorescent, phosphorescent inks, and light or spectral color effects.

Drying Machines

As far as drying machines are concerned, then, consideration must be given to the variations of the inks employed, to the variations in the actual drying, and to the fact that there must be elimination of dimensional changes in stock or objects due to quick drying in machines, especially in multi-color work. Then there is the practical range or minimum or maximum drying time or cycle in which a machine may work in a specific shop. The drying of the printed matter is dependent upon press speeds and other printing operations. In some cases quick drying is not practical and often impossible.

There are also the mechanical considerations for the operator and designer to consider. Regardless of the drying method or dryer employed, any dryer used must be simple to operate, safe as far as fire and explosion hazards are concerned, sturdy and long lasting. It should be capable of being normally attached to electrical, gas or other power outlets, it should not distort the printed objects or material in the drying process, it should have some flexibility so that the machine may be employed for drying varied types of inks and materials, and it should not destroy the brilliance of the color. The latter is often a problem with making or firing ceramic inks, especially for the novice.

The machine employed should have uniform temperature throughout a given heat zone in its design and also must have a means of drawing in fresh air and getting rid of stale air; and, of course, should accelerate drying and be economical enough for the average shop likely to use it. The drying machine must not completely alter the standard operations in a shop; rather, it should supplement and cut down on the disadvantages of drying without increasing the cost of the final printing. The drying equipment which may involve automatic or semi-automatic conveying and handling methods must be concentrated in the smallest practical area.

Although it is a matter for the designer or manufacturer, one must consider the methods of heat drying or air drying that machines generally employ. Drying machines generally use heat and air motion to hasten drying. The heat or air employed for drying is transferred through the machine by means of radiation, convection, chemical vapor method, and employment of a dual system (radiation and convection). The source of heat where heat is used, may be electrical power, gas, oil, or steam. Where air is employed to aid and hasten drying, the air may be supplied by fans usually driven by electrical power.

Radiation involves producing penetrating rays from a source, the commonest source being infrared lamps with or without reflectors. These lamps are primarily designed to furnish heat instead of light. The infrared waves, a form or part of the family of electro-magnetic waves and given off by the infrared lamps or glass plates, strike an object or an ink. The ink absorbs the rays or radiant energy and changes the radiant energy into heat energy. The rays travel in straight lines until they strike a non-reflecting object or material which transforms them into heat.

Convection involves the transfer of heat through fluids such as air currents, water, steam, and other liquids. Fresh air or recirculated air is heated and then forced into the heating system either by pumping methods or by natural means, due to the rising of hot or warm air and falling of cooler air which creates a convection current. Ordinarily for screen printing an indirect source of heat is employed and is placed externally or outside of the system being heated. Although burners may be placed in an oven or kiln or direct heat may be used for fusing screen printed electronic circuits and ceramic inks, convection currents still play a big part in the fusing of such printed matter.

The following are principles by which inks, paints, and finishes dry or are changed from a liquid to a solid: (1) by absorption, penetration, or setting; (2) evaporation; (3) by oxidation; (4) polymerization; (5) by subjecting a coated film to a vapor; (6) by means of microwave drying; (7) by employing an ultraviolet energy curing system; and (8) a combination of the latter methods.

In the absorption method, a thin film is absorbed by the paper or stock, leaving a thin coat on the surface. In the evaporation method, the solvents in the ink pass into the air and leave the dry coating or film on the surface. In the oxidation method, the oils in the inks combine with the oxygen in the air, and, because of this chemical action, form a solid. Synthetic finishes and inks dry by means of a chemical action in a process known as polymerization. Polymerization came in with plastics and plastic finishes and involves a reaction in which single molecules are linked to form large molecules without changing the chemical composition.

The chemical vapor drying process,* a method of drying screen printed matter, does not employ heat for drying, but chemically hardens protective and decorative coatings of inks, paints, finishes, and varnishes by allowing the coating of film to be exposed to a chemical vapor such as sulphur dichloride. Sulphur dichloride is a liquid at room temperature. A vapor is a substance in a gaseous state. The liquid is changed to a vapor in a specially built drying machine. The machine consists of a conveyor traveling inside a chamber, a carburetor leading into the top of the chamber, and an exhaust end with a caustic scrubber for ridding the machine and area of vapors. The screen printed material is placed on the conveyor. As vapor is introduced into the chamber which encloses the conveyor, the vapor dries the film in about 2 to 22 seconds, depending on conditions and on the type of ink used.

The microwave drying or heating principle is a special form of dielectric heating (a dielectric substance is one which is a nonconductor of electricity). Most non-metallic materials are dielectrics. Microwaves are very short electromagnetic waves and heating or drying with these waves results where there is a transfer of energy from an electromagnetic field to a polar dielectric such as a screen printing ink. This absorption of the energy produces quick

---

*The process is known as the Chem-Dry Process and was developed by the Armour Research Foundation of the Illinois Institute of Technology, Chicago, Illinois, in a project sponsored by the Meyercord Company, Chicago, Illinois. (Patent No. 2,528,850, Clark E. Thorp and Layton C. Kenney, Chicago, Illinois, assignors, by mesne assignments, to the Meyercord Company, Chicago, Illinois.)

238

drying. It is maintained that the ink heats and becomes dry before the printed surface becomes hot.

Ultraviolet curing or drying* was motivated by oil and gas shortages and by the attempt to solve solvent pollution problems. The principle of ultraviolet (UV) curing or drying has been known since about 1944; in 1967 it became a production process. Ultraviolet curing has been used in drying screen printed coats of electronic circuits, curing printed coats on wood, adhesives, in metal decorating, on web and litho presses, and in screen printing. It is a revolutionary drying system in which a coating, ink, or an adhesive in semi-liquid state is converted almost instantly by exposing the coat to ultraviolet energy. The quick drying of the ink is due to the fact that the coating contains no solvents as compared with conventional inks which may contain hydrocarbons. UV inks are specifically and chemically formulated to contain photosensitizable or photoinitiator substances, inhibitors, and pigments or dyes. When the photosensitive substance in the ink is exposed to controlled ultraviolet energy, an instant dry film is obtained which is cured or dried in 2 to 3 seconds. However, UV drying cannot be used on all screen printed inks or materials, since the ink is a specially chemical prepared one and must be cured in a unit or oven built especially for this system of printing and curing.

While the latter principles — chemical vapors, microwave drying, and ultraviolet curing — are of special interest, most machine dryers make use of the other principles of drying.

In spite of the involved, related, and complex problem, the screen printer today has his choice of many ovens, conveyors, wicket-conveyors, drying machines, and kilns using convection radiation or a combination of both methods of transferring heat, employing direct or indirect heat as is illustrated in Figure 149 through Figure 154. The efforts by establishments with respect to drying of textiles, paper, and cardboard of all types have produced somewhat better results, because the screen printer, ink manufacturer, and drying machine designer have worked cooperatively in solving the common problems.

There are machines on the market which will answer almost any drying problem that may confront the screen printer. There are small compact machines and very large machines or ovens. There are dryers based on the infrared and on the convection principle. Since most materials change chemically and physically in the drying process, both have advantages and disadvantages. Therefore, it is assumed that before a machine is installed or contracted for, the printer will find out objectively which machine is best suited for his purpose.

Infrared machines may be installed and operated in any position, since they are flameless. Like convection ovens, they may be built to any specifications; they may be designed so that they radiate on both sides of a surface such as printed cloth. Any material whose drying is hastened by heat may be dried with infrared. The cost of infrared is dependent, of course, on the cost of the power of the locality of the shop. There are 48 inch wide belt conveyors constructed under banks of infrared lamps distributed in most practical positions on a panel or panels which will easily take care of 44-inch sheets and

---

*Kosloff, Albert. "Ultraviolet Curing or Drying," Academy of Screen Printing Technology, Screen Printing Association International, November, 1975, 4 pages.

also smaller objects. The banks of lights may be mounted on portable units which can be adjusted to varied positions over the conveyor. There are narrow conveyors about 18 feet in length which will dry in 1 to 18 minutes printed matter placed on the conveyor. There are other conveyors which will dry inks on plastic, plastic aprons, caps, tablecloths, T-shirts, etc., in about 30 to 80 seconds. There are also infrared duplex units which employ glass plates to do the heating. These units are built similarly to two bowling alleys; one-half of the unit may be used at one time for smaller sheets or objects; for larger sheets both conveying units are employed.

There are convection ovens which are capable of controlling a range of temperatures from a minimum to a practical maximum temperature giving flexibility to the varied jobs that are printed in the small or large shops. Thus, raising the temperature for some printed matter may mean decreasing the drying cycle; for other printed material the dryer or oven allows for lowering the temperature and increasing the length of the drying time. There are ovens designed with heat operational zoning where each part or zone of the oven has its own range of heat designed to serve a specific purpose in the drying cycle.

The purpose of the zone is to offer better control of baking cycle, better heat distribution, ventilation, air circulation, and cooling. In the zone type of oven the conveyor carries the printed stock or objects into the oven and passes through the varied zones to dry the matter. The first one or two zones are generally short, have a lower temperature, are used to bring the incoming load to baking temperature and also exhaust the volatiles.

The intermediate zones hold the temperature to the desired baking, heating, or drying specifications. The last oven zone or zones, contains no heating element and is used for recuperative cooling. The heat from the last zone may be transferred to the fresh air supply at zone one or where the printed load enters the oven. The automatic temperature and other controls may be designed to suit individual shops and specific jobs.

Those ovens or dryers which do not employ zones take care of the drying cycle by allowing for lowering of temperature and increasing the drying time, depending on the ink's being printed and on other factors. Actually, a minute or two slower drying does not make much difference once the printed and dried objects are being delivered at the stacking end. In many cases such as that of the wicket-conveyor dryer the necessity of using a slow drying ink is not a disadvantage, since the drying time or cycle for the machine is designed to feed dried printed matter at a uniform rate at the delivery end. After the first sheet arrives at the delivery end, the rest of the sheets will follow, one after another, depending upon how quickly the conveying mechanism moves and upon how quickly the printed matter is placed on the conveying mechanism.

There are also dryers which will meet the needs of both machine and hand operated speeds where drying can be accomplished without heat or at low heat in order to take care of register troubles.

Regardless of the type of machine and method of heating, most of the conveying mechanisms stress the advantage of using vibrationless operation, where necessary, in order not to endanger surface finish of the object or sheet. The drying machines employ baskets, trays, solid flat belts, mesh belts, vibrators, overhead trolley, conveyors with wickets as illustrated in Figure 150 to pass along printed matter into the heat or drying area. In each case the

240

conveyor takes the printed matter into the oven or chamber, or it may expose it under or over infrared units, or bring it into an area where the objects dry being exposed to air in motion. The air in motion may be convection currents or may be currents supplied by jets in a jet dryer. Jet dryers consist of enclosed systems which collect and exhaust evaporated solvents, employing air, temperature, and time in the drying cycle. Jets blow clean air constantly over the printed matter through holes in plates which are at a minimum distance from the print. The air is impinged at a great velocity and achieves a scrubbing action. The temperature can be set as required and the time can also be controlled and depends on conveyor speed. The drying time in jet dryers is usually a matter of seconds.

Conveyors on dryers are designed so that they are timed to the speed of the drying cycle necessary for practical production. The conveyor may be stopped at any time, either manually or automatically. Regardless of the type of heat transfer or dryer, conveyors are designed so that controls are interlocked with the conveying mechanism and so that the heat source is turned off automatically when dryer or oven is stopped and cannot be turned on when machine is not in operation.

The machines illustrated in the preceding pages are representative of the drying equipment available to the screen printer. These are not all the different drying and conveyor equipment nor do they consist of the only equipment being offered by a specific manufacturer. Details presented under each illustration are for basic characteristics, and more information may be obtained from manufacturers and suppliers.

MACHINE PRINTING

Historically, most screen printing machines were developed to answer a particular need in a specific shop situation by or under the guidance of an enterprising and ingenious screen printer. As the industry grew, especially since World War II, various machines were developed. This development of various machines is based on the fact that the variety of work produced by screen printing excludes the consideration that any one specific machine or any one type of equipment will cover all problems. For example, the shop or the mill specializing in textile screen printing may require different types of machines and equipment than the shop doing poster work or ceramic screen printing. See Figures 158 and 168. Also, some machines were designed primarily to duplicate a hand operated screen unit and there are varied types of manually operated screen units. Mechanization has grown and is growing because it stresses the positive results.

There are however, certain types of machines that are becoming common and standard in the industry. There are screen printing presses which are being employed to print on very flexible stock, on rigid and thick stock and objects, on irregularly shaped materials, on cylindrical and cone shaped objects, and on spherical shaped objects using the varied types of available screen printing inks. While no one screen printing press can print on all types of surfaces, shapes, dimensions, and materials, it is possible today to obtain the type of equipment best suited for a specific shop situation.

The average manufacturer catering to the industry has machines available in varied sizes and will build machines in special sizes to order where required. There are the simple, efficient "squeegee pushing" machines to the more complex machines, each serving its purpose. The machines print on any material that can be printed by screen printing. There are presses that will print areas from the size of a postage stamp to posters the size of about 4 feet by 14 feet.

There are screen printing machines which print many colors and multiple subjects in one impression with one printing screen. By employing a two-impression technique on these presses, the screen printer can use one impression for printing all the colors he desires and then employ an overprint or second impression for outline or background.

The pressure of the squeegee on the printing area can be controlled and regulated throughout the length of the stroke by making simple adjustments. Varied lengths of squeegee may be used on the same machine to print on varied size screens. The printing is more uniform and sharper because uniform control and pressure is applied mechanically. The squeegee may print in

Figure 155. Masterscreen press designed for precision printing of electronic circuit boards, decalcomanias, name plates, etc.; will print on objects 13½" × 19½" × 2" at production speeds varying from 100 to 1200 impressions per hour. (Courtesy of Jos. E. Podgor Co., Inc., Pennsauken, New Jersey).

one stroke, in one direction only or in both directions, that is, on the forward and on the return stroke. The squeegee may print on every stroke. Squeegees on the press spread an even layer of ink over the entire surface. Based on square foot coverage of ink, presses generally use less ink. Where a heavy penetration or deposit of ink is necessary, this may be accomplished by regulating the squeegee or by using a double stroke of the squeegee or both.

The machines available have varied speed ranges in printing, Screen printing presses print from about 300 to 3000 impressions per hour, depending upon the machine, on the type and size of stock or object being printed,

243

and on whether the racking is done by hand or mechanically. Although very high speeds, because of the nature of the printing and the type of material that is printed, is not so important a factor, there is a definite increase of production and efficiency and a great saving of manpower. The machines have proved practical for long runs and for short runs, especially where a short run is being printed on large sheets or material. Drying arrangements, dryer-conveyors, and drying machines can be furnished in lengths and in drying time cycles to meet specific needs and may be synchronized to press operation.

Figure 156. The Precision Vacuumatic is an hydraulically operated screen printing press designed for printing on varied thickness of 35" × 45" paper, board metal, plastics, board-mounted fabric, etc. at 900 impressions per hour. Any type screen frame may be attached to the press master frame. The squeegee is easy to control for length of stroke, speed, and ink coverage. (Courtesy of Precision Screen Machines, Inc., Hawthorne, New Jersey).

Machine printing eliminates the fatigue factor always present in printing by hand, especially when working manually with the larger and the very large two-man hand operated squeegees. The worker dislays more interest in machine printing. Operators may be easily trained by starting the learning operation in running the press dry, then by actually printing on the slower speeds, and finally running the press in varied speeds for different jobs under specific shop conditions.

On most machines the squeegee and the printing screen may be easily and simply inserted and removed in a minimum time. Any printing screen may be used in the presses. The time to change from one stock to another, just as in hand operation, is negligible. The operator may sit or stand when operating most presses and safety is stressed in the design of the press. Safety buttons or safety devices halt press movements almost instantly. Both males and females, young or old, may run the presses. The time required for makeready is at least the same or less than for hand printing. Registering of

244

Figure 157. Roto Screen Press, a web fed screen printing press designed by George Reinke, uses a rigid cylindrical stainless steel printing screen which makes possible the obtaining of 100% printing on a moving web. The ink is forced from the inside of the screen and the squeegee makes contact with the inside of the cylindrical screen. The press uses four printing heads for four color work with dryers underneath the printing head for setting the inks. The speed of the web is about 200 feet per minute. (Courtesy of George Reinke, Roto Screen Press, Inc., Skokie, Illinois).

245

Figure 158. Vastex Textile Printer prints up to four colors on finished garments with screen printing textile inks; printer has a rotary table for holding four screens allowing multi-color wet on wet printing. (Courtesy of Vastex Machine Co., Roselle, New Jersey).

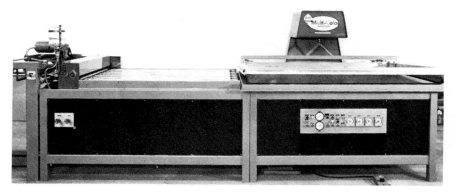

Figure 159. The General PM Multicolor Press has a vacuum screen printing principle which allows press to print any number of colors with one impression, including half-tones up to 65 lines on sheets up to 45" × 64" in size for indoor or outdoor use. Press has fully automatic control panel and foot operated pedal for emergency stop. (Courtesy of General Research, Inc., Sparta, Michigan; and Poster Products, Chicago, Illinois).

246

Figure 160. Cincinnati One-man Vacuum Printer for one-man squeegee operation with automatic lifting and lowering of screen. Unit has vacuum area of 43" × 63" for easy printing of material 44" × 64" with a maximum printing stroke of 80" for squeegee. (Courtesy of Cincinnati Printing and Drying Systems, Inc., Cincinnati, Ohio).

printed stock or objects is simply accomplished by means of knobs, handles, and disappearing guides. In some instances the registration of the printing screen to the stock being printed may be done while the press is running. Washing and cleaning after the day's work is done in a simple manner.

The machines are sturdy and are built to last. Most manufacturers stress simple servicing during press operation. The handbook for the individual machine explains general servicing needed and required care for efficient operation.

Figures 155 through 168 present some of the machines available for screen printing. Although some of the material under each illustration could be duplicated for each machine, the purpose of the description under the individual illustrated machine is to stress some of the individual machine accomplishments.

As far as optional equipment is concerned: some machines have automatic feeding attachments and allow the prints to drop off automatically onto a racking device. The average press is equipped with a vacuum base or vacuum table to insure register and to insure stock being held firmly to the table during printing. Most presses print off-contact or line-contact and the printing screen may also print in full-contact with the stock.

In summary, one factor is common in mechanical printing production, just as it is in the whole screen printing industry, changes and improvements are constantly being made to answer developmental needs of industry and of mankind.

247

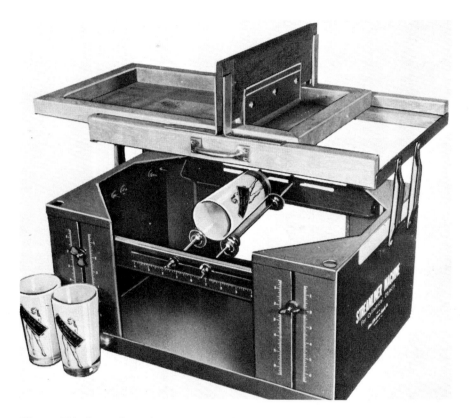

Figure 161. Streamliner Screening Machine for screen printing on cylindrical objects from pen size up to 8" in diameter and 12" long. Squeegee remains stationary and screen moves from side to side during printing operation. (Courtesy of Atlas Silk Screen Supply Co., Chicago, Illinois).

248

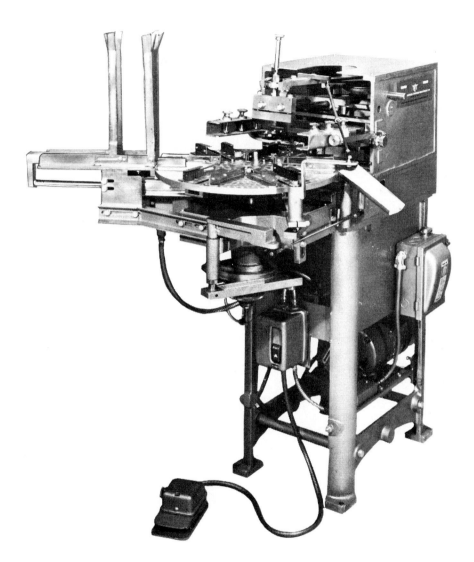

Figure 162. American-Dubuit Turntable screen printer designed for high production precise printing on such items as container caps, cosmetic cases, ceramic substrates, miniature circuits, and dials up to 3" thick. Turntable is tooled up for 6 or 3 station printing and printer allows for automatic feeding and take-off up to 4000 impressions per hour. (Courtesy of American Screen Process Equipment Company, Chicago, Illinois).

249

Figure 163. The Swedo Automatic Flat Bed Press, a unit consisting of an automatic feeding system attached to an automatic press with a built in take-off system. Unit will print on material up to ¼" in thickness, a print area up to 47" × 63", at speeds of 1500 to 2300 impressions per hour. (Courtesy of Cincinnati Printing and Drying Systems, Inc., Cincinnati, Ohio).

Figure 164. General Series 6 Screen Printing Press with feeder, designed for large single sheet or stream feeding of 24 sheet poster type prints. Press prints on rigid, semi-rigid, and flexible material and has vacuum revolving cylinder which holds sheets in accurate registration up to sheet sizes 52" × 85". Standard wood frames may be used on press. (Courtesy of General Research, Inc., Sparta, Michigan).

250

Figure 165. A fully automatic screen printing unit consisting of an American-Hartfeldt press with a sheet feeder, a jet drying and cooling system and an automatic descending-pile stacker and jogger. Press and feeder are available in sizes from 14" × 30" to 52" × 80" with drying, cooling, and conveyor units made to any required length. (Courtesy of American Screen Process Equipment Co., Chicago, Illinois).

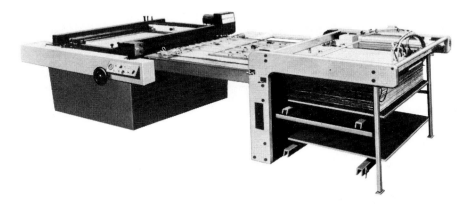

Figure 166. The Sericol Sprinter, a high speed flat bed automatic screen printing machine, having automatic controls with manual or automatic feed, a squeegee stroke that is automatically adjusted with sharp accurate impression, and will print sheets .2" thick up to 48" × 66" in area at 1800 impressions per hour. (Courtesy of General Research, Inc., Sparta, Michigan; and Sericol Group Ltd., London, England).

251

Figure 167. "Thick Film" Screen Printer designed for off-contact and contact electronic circuit printing of 1500 parts per hour. Machine ejects parts to three different conveyor belt locations and infra-red dryers are generally added to conveyor sections. (Courtesy of Affiliated Manufacturers, Inc., Whitehouse, New Jersey).

Figure 168. Buser Rotary screen printing machine for printing fine detail on textile bolt material and on transfer paper with specially engraved rotary 150-mesh screens. Machine is synchronized to feed, print, dry, and automatically deliver material at exit end. (Courtesy of Bowler Industries, Inc., Greenville, South Carolina).

253

EQUIVALENT VALUES OF SOME MEASUREMENT UNITS IN THE CUSTOMARY (U.S.) MEASUREMENT SYSTEM AND IN THE METRIC SYSTEM

Customary or U.S. System

(1) .3937 inch
(2) 1 inch
(3) 1 inch
(4) 39.37 inches

(5) .0328 foot
(6) 1 foot
(7) .10936 yard
(8) 1 yard

(9) 1 yard
(10) 1 point (printer's measurement, .0133889 inch)
(11) 1 nonpareil (printer's measurement, 1/12 inch)
(12) 28.3441 points

(13) 1 pica (printer's measurement, 1/6 inch)
(14) 1 ounce (avoirdupois)
(15) 1 pound (avoirdupois)
(16) 2.2 pounds

(17) 1 ounce (U.S. liquid)
(18) 1 pint (16 ounces, U.S. liquid)
(19) 1 quart (57.75 cubic inches, U.S. liquid)

*Metric System**

(1) 1 centimeter
(2) 2.54 centimeters
(3) 25.400 millimeters
(4) 1 meter

(5) 1 centimeter
(6) 30.48 centimeters
(7) 1 centimeter
(8) 91.4402 centimeters

(9) .9144 meter
(10) .03528 centimeter

(11) .21166 centimeter

(12) 1 centimeter

(13) .42333 centimeter

(14) 28.3495 grams
(15) 453.5924 grams
(16) 1 kilogram or 1000 grams

(17) 29.5735 cubic centimeters
(18) .473168 liter or 473.168 cubic centimeters
(19) .946358 liter or 946.358 cubic centimeters

(20) To change Fahrenheit temperature readings *to Celsius* readings use the following formula: (Degrees F − 32) × 5/9 = degrees Celsius.
(21) To change Celsius temperature readings *to Fahrenheit* readings use the following formula: (Degrees C × 9/5) + 32 = degrees Fahrenheit.
(22) To change degrees Celsius *to Kelvin* degrees use the following formula: Degrees C + 273.1 = Kelvin temperature.
NOTE: Another name for the Celsius scale is *Centigrade scale*.

HALFTONE SCREEN RULINGS:

Customary Rulings Per Inch	Metric Rulings Per Centimeter
50	20
60	26
75	30
100	40
120	48
133	54
150	60
175	70
200	80

*The metric system is based on the *meter* (metre) as the unit of length, *gram* as unit of weight, and *second* as unit of time. The prefixes in the metric system are: DECI (one-tenth, .1); CENTI one-hundredth, .01); MILLI (one-thousandth, .001); and KILO (one thousand, 1000).

INDEX

257

Surface printed and drying, 232
Sunlight as an exposing light, 36, 152
Suspension mixture, 47, 57
Synthetic screen fabric preparation, 79
Swan, Joseph Wilson, 48, 58
Swormstedt, Sr., David R., 4

T

Talbot, William Henry Fox, 167
Temporary support for carbon tissue, 49, 53, 59, 65–73
Time of exposure, 114–115
Time and temperature development method, 183–184
Transfer of drying heat, 237
Transfer type printing screen (see Indirect printing screen)
Test for correct exposure, 109
Trisodium phosphate for reclaiming screen fabrics, 75, 79, 144
True solution, 47, 57
Tungsten-halogen lamp, 162

U

Ulano direct-film printing screen, 69–73, 83, 87
Ulano, Joseph, 4, 83
Ulano presensitized screen printing films, 74–78
Ulano Super-Poly-X screen printing film, 87–93

Unsensitized screen printing films, 83–86, 87–93
Ultraviolet curing or drying, 239

V

Vacuum bag for exposing, 32
Vacuum base or table, 173
Vacuum frames, 30–31
Versatility of screen printing, 1
Vertical process camera, 219
View camera, 220, 226
Visible light, 152

W

Washing out, 109, 115, 120–121, 85, 91, 124, 126,136; carbon tissue, 56, 62, 69, 76; direct screen, 46, 100, 105–106, 142; direct-indirect screen, 66, 81; presensitized film, 81; screen printing film, 77
Water-chromate plastic method of sensitizing, 92–93
Water pressure screen reclaimer, 148
Waters, Sidney James, 48, 58
Waxing temporary support, 53
Wet carbon tissue method, 49, 51–58, 62–71
Wicket-conveyor dryer, 235
Whirler for applying emulsion, 98
Willet, Frances, 4

Z

Zahn, Bert, 4